Under An
African Sun

The author at the ruins of Old Zimbabwe in 1961.

Under An African Sun

Memoirs of a Colonial Officer in Northern Rhodesia

Frank Bennett

The Radcliffe Press

LONDON • NEW YORK

Published in 2006 by The Radcliffe Press
6 Salem Road, London W2 4BU

In the United States and in Canada
distributed by Palgrave Macmillan, a division of St Martin's Press
175 Fifth Avenue, New York NY 10010

ISBN 1 84511 083 8
EAN 978 1 84511 083 3

A full CIP record for this book is available from the Britain Library
A full CIP record for this book is available from the Library of Congress

Library of Congress Catalog card: available

Production co-ordination by M&M Publishing Services, Ware, Herts. SG12 9JL
Typeset by FiSH Books, London
Printed and bound in Great Britain by TJ International Ltd, Padstow, Cornwall

*To all the junior officers of the
British Colonial Civil Service,
who ran the Empire through many turbulent centuries,
and to my wife Susan Bennett without whose
gracious help and encouragement this book
would never have been written*

Contents

Acknowledgements

First I would like to thank my wife Susan and my daughter Donna Sue Jones, for the endless hours they spent typing, proofing and editing my manuscript. Their help was invaluable. Grateful thanks are also due to David Fontenot who helped my daughter in the arduous task of converting my manuscript from one mysterious computer format to another. Also to Sneed Adams and his wife Anne, of Katy, Texas, who prepared my photos for publication, supervised the creation of my web page, and also masterfully edited the book. Last, but not least, warm appreciation is also due to Roni Porfert, of Norfolk, Virginia, who painstakingly edited the first draft of my manuscript and to Kate Sherratt and Mike Moran who guided this book to realisation on behalf of my publisher.

Without all of you this book would still be but a dream and fireside tales.

Chapter 1

Taking The Plunge

1. The First Steps

It was raining. Come to think of it, it was always raining. Well, not always. Sometimes it had just stopped raining; sometimes it was just about to start raining. I should have been a duck, I reflected gloomily, if I was expected to live in this kind of climate.

Morosely, I continued to develop this line of thought, while sitting in Wilding's Barber Shop late one afternoon in the early spring of 1958, waiting to get my hair cut. Idly I picked up the evening paper lying on the bench beside me, little realizing that this casual gesture would change my life forever. As usual I read the sports pages first, and then my eyes were drawn to a small eight-line advertisement in the situations vacant section. Apparently, the Crown Agents were looking for people to join the British Colonial Civil Service. It gave an address to which resumés could be sent, by those wishing to apply.

Just then the barber called 'Next, please.' So I dropped the paper back on the bench, and went to get my hair cut. After paying the barber, I started to leave the shop. It was now raining harder. 'I might as well join the bloody Colonial Service,' I groused to myself as I gloomily faced the prospect of an endless future of endless rain.

Suddenly, a figurative bolt of lightning hit me. Why not, why not indeed? For surely there must be somewhere in the Empire where the sun still shone. Or so I determined to find out, as I slowly turned back into the shop, and asked the barber if he minded if I tore an advertisement out of his paper. 'Go ahead,' he replied without much interest, as I picked up that paper again, tore out the section I needed, put it in my pocket and went home.

That night, I wrote out a brief resumé and addressed an envelope to the Crown Agents, London. After borrowing a stamp from my father, I got out my bike and rode down to the main post office and mailed my request to become a servant of the crown. I then rode home and forgot about my bout of temporary insanity. But it was too late. The wheels had been set in motion and, as I was eventually to find out, these wheels would ultimately deposit me in an isolated part of central Africa, in a country I had never heard of.

2. My Early Years

But let's back up and start at the beginning. The beginning for me was on May 18, 1935, when I was born in the local hospital in Chorley, Lancashire, England. Chorley is a small industrial town in the north of England, and is the midway point between London and Edinburgh. It is nestled at the foot of the western slope of the Pennine Hills, which run like a backbone down the centre of England. To the north lies the stark grandeur of the English Lake District. To the south lies the great industrial city of Manchester. To the west lie the Irish Sea, the holiday resorts of Blackpool and Southport and the industrial port of Liverpool, which may be better known as the home of the Beatles. Finally, to the east, over the bleak moors of Brontë fame, lie the Yorkshire Ridings and the North Sea.

My mother, Lily Bennett, was the working-class daughter of a cotton mill spinner, and worked as a weaver in one of the local cotton mills. Her three sisters were also weavers, since that was what most working women did in the Lancashire mill towns until the 1950s, when foreign imports led to the decline and collapse of the local weaving industry.

My father, Frank Bennett, after whom I was christened, was a railway clerk for the London Midland and Scottish Railways and the son of a road construction supervisor. I was an only child, being born three years after my elder sister, Dorothy, had died at the tender age of two, of rheumatic fever.

The world into which I was born was poised to go up in flames, and if it is true that who you are is largely determined by your experiences in the first few formative years of your life, then I am a product of the Second World War. My earliest memories are of German bombers passing overhead on their way to bomb Manchester and Liverpool. My world was ruled by rationing. We didn't go short but, I didn't see my first banana until I was 11. Not surprisingly, bananas are still my favourite fruit.

Fathers did not really exist in this world. My own father was in the army for six of my first 10 years. All of my playmates had mothers. None had fathers. Of course, this wasn't all bad; it sure cut down on the number of spankings we got. We didn't complain a lot, or ask for things we didn't have. Somehow we knew that there were more serious concerns going on.

For example, when I was about five years old, I clearly remember a large map of Europe and North Africa which my mother had pinned to the living room wall, next to the family radio. My mother stuck little flags in the map – one in each country to show who ruled that country. Each day we would listen to the B.B.C. news and my mother would make adjustments to the map, as the news dictated. The news in those days was always bad. From time to time my mother quietly removed a flag and replaced it with the swastika flag of Hitler's Germany. She didn't say anything, but somehow even at the age of five I knew that this was not a good sign.

One day when I looked at the map, I realized that all of the flags, but two, were now Nazi swastikas. There was a British flag in London, England, and another in Cairo, Egypt. It was not a pretty map. At that moment, I realized that we could lose the war, and I still remember the cold chill of fear that gripped my body and mind. Shortly after this, things got a little better. Montgomery defeated Rommel at El Alemain and Britain celebrated this first victory of the war over the seemingly invincible German army.

Things continued to improve in a dramatic way. A whole new world, pun intended, came to Chorley – The Yanks arrived! By the thousands. They built a base three miles from town and called it Washington Hall. What else? The streets were full of them, and so were the pubs and the parks. Naturally, each English girl had to have at least one American boyfriend. They had such nice uniforms. Mother said that now we would win the war and I, for one, certainly enjoyed this new experience. Especially after I learned to say, 'Got any gum, chum?' Luckily, most G.I.s must have filled their pockets before they left the base, because they almost always gave us a stick or two. Indeed, my fondest memories of the later years of the war revolve around American soldiers, and two instances in particular stand out in my memory.

Every Saturday morning, at 10 a.m., the Odeon cinema had a special film show for children. It cost five pence and I, together with all my playmates, always went. Often, when we arrived at the ticket office to buy our tickets, we would be greeted by a smiling manager, standing there with two or three sheepish looking G.I.s. 'No need to pay today lads,' the manager would say. 'The Yanks have bought your tickets.'

This happened to me not once or twice but many, many times, and I am still deeply grateful to those young soldiers, not for the free ticket, because we were not poor people, but for the kindness that motivated their actions.

However, if one event stands out from those wartime days above all the others, it had to be my 'Daddy for a day' experiences. These miracles, for that is how I viewed them, were the brainchild of some genius at Washington Hall, who came up with the idea of entertaining the local children, on the base, about once every six months. In order to be eligible for this event, your father had to be away from home, serving in the armed forces. Mine was, and so I was able to go to Washington Hall two or three times.

On the appointed day, a U.S. Army bus would come to school about 10 o'clock in the morning, and take us out to the base. When we arrived, each child was assigned a 'Daddy' and, proudly clutching the soldier's hand, we trotted off to share the wonders they had in store for us.

What wonders they were! First, we would go to the mess and eat all the ice cream we wanted. Now remember, I had never seen ice cream until I first visited Washington Hall. Not only was there ice cream, but they had different colours, and different flavors. Then we went to the movies – Mickey Mouse, Donald Duck and all the other Walt Disney characters. Again, it was all new to me and most unbelievable – some were even in Technicolor. Finally, just as it went dark, they took us outdoors and gave us a fireworks display. Imagine the wonder of that, to a seven or eight-year-old child, who had never before seen fireworks.

The best, however, was saved for last. As each child boarded the bus to return home, his 'Daddy' handed him a big box of candy. This was the only candy I ever had. I used to keep those boxes of candy by my bed and eat one piece a day. If I was very lucky, the candy would run out just about the same time as the next 'Daddy for a day' trip was due.

I really don't think anyone could ever have known how much those trips meant to us and to our mothers. I still get a lump in my throat when I remember those young men, some of whom doubtless died on the beaches of Normandy, and what they did for us. Thanks.

From the ages of 5 to 11, I attended a state-run elementary school, Highfield Council School. At 11, I took a state-controlled intelligence examination, and was lucky enough to be selected for a special kind of high school, entrance to which was reserved for gifted children.

This was Chorley Grammar School. I graduated at the age of 18, and went to work at the local Trustee Savings Bank. I stayed there until I was 20, when I first began to display symptoms of the peculiarities that have plagued my life ever since. To settle down or grow up, I regarded as early stages of *rigor mortis* and I still do.

Often, I used to ask my parents, 'If the world is a book, why are so many people content to read only one page of it?' Usually, I got an unsatisfactory answer and had to turn for comfort to my favourite quotation: about the man who seems to be marching out of step, but really isn't, because he hears a different drummer. I'm sure I heard a different drummer.

At the age of 20, I left my job at the bank and spent six months riding my bicycle around Europe. I lived on 10 shillings (50p) a day. Of course, in 1956 a pound was worth a lot more. Although it still wasn't enough to travel with the jet set. When I returned home, I tried to settle down; I went to work as an accountant for Thomas Witter and Company, a local manufacturer of floor coverings.

In 1958, when I was 22 years old, I had been with Witter's for about two years, and thoroughly enjoyed my work. I had tried hard to be normal, or, more accurately, to think like everyone else. But I still heard that different drummer, who may have inspired my dislike for rain and the whim that prompted me to send a resumé to the Crown Agents.

3. Packing My Bags

Within two weeks of that fateful haircut, I received a bulky envelope from the Crown Agents. It was an application for me to complete – a most inquisitive one. They demanded to know more about me, and my ancestors, than either my parents or I knew. They also wanted a list of references they could contact. It took about a week to complete the application and return it to London. Then there was silence.

Finally, about six weeks later, one of my references came to see me, somewhat irate. Apparently, he had just received his third questionnaire from the Crown Agents. 'Just what kind of a job is this?' he demanded. 'Because I don't intend to spend the rest of my life answering their damn fool questions.'

Somehow I managed to mollify him by pointing out that his help could be really important to me, and so, would he please just keep on filling out the forms. Luckily he agreed. Well, I thought, so far so good. I'm still under consideration. A few weeks later, I was summoned to London for interviews. That was obviously a good sign, so full of hope and wearing my best suit, I set off for the big city.

I don't remember too much about my interview with the Crown Agents, so it must have been uneventful. I suppose they asked all the usual questions, and I gave all the usual answers. I do remember being told that if hired, I would probably go to Africa, but I wasn't hired, not yet. However, they did send me over to Harley Street for a pre-employment medical examination. This impressed me, because Harley Street is the most prestigious address for a doctor in the whole of England. The rich and famous always have a doctor with a Harley Street address.

Brusquely, while he was performing all the routine tests, the doctor suddenly asked, 'Where are you going?' 'Africa,' I replied. 'Why?' He snapped. 'Because I think I'll like it,' I weakly offered. 'Have you ever been to Africa?' he probed. 'No,' I admitted. 'Then how do you know you'll like it,' he shot back. I didn't answer. Presuming I had failed the logic quotient in my physical.

After a long silence, he relented a little. 'You'll love it,' he said casually. 'Have you ever been to Africa?' I too innocently asked. 'No,' he admitted. 'Then, how do you know I'll like it?' I shot back. He finished the exam in silence. I left Harley Street somewhat crestfallen. I reflected that if the Crown Agents recruited primarily on charm and tact, then I probably would not get this job.

Several more weeks passed with no news. I gave up. Then, one morning, I received a one page form letter in a window envelope. I opened it in great fear and excitement. It said not to worry, the process was continuing and they had not forgotten me. Another month passed without news and then I got a second form letter. This time I opened it with less excitement and received the same message: have patience, these things take time.

True, but this was ridiculous, and I even began to wonder how on earth we'd found time to build the empire in the first place, if it took this long to staff it. Once again the weeks rolled by and I reluctantly abandoned the idea of ever joining the Colonial Civil Service. Realistically, my future was now quite clear, and I might as well begin taking quacking lessons, because the intermittent showers were growing less intermittent, and the occasional sunny periods were virtually non-existent.

Then, one day in late fall, I received another form letter in a window envelope. This letter informed me that on December 11th, 1958, I would sail from Southampton, England aboard the Union Castle liner, Capetown Castle. I would arrive in Capetown, South Africa on December 25th, 1958. That was all, no job offer, no details about where I was going, nothing. They didn't even wish me a Merry Christmas. I showed the letter to my parents. My mother cried. My Dad looked grim.

On reflection, I have always thought that this form letter said a great deal about the British Colonial Civil Service. It was a very proud and elitist organization. It recruited only at the entry-level ranks, and all promotion was from within the service. Very few people ever resigned from its ranks and very few ever refused the offer to join.

In most ways, it was like joining the army as an officer. There was a relatively high degree of discipline. You went where they sent you, you did what they told you. You could not refuse an assignment. However, I must add that the pay and conditions were the best I ever encountered. I remember, for example, one evening a few years later, when four of us were having a quiet beer and I suddenly posed the question, 'Are you underpaid, fairly paid, or overpaid?' All four of us answered without hesitation, 'Overpaid.'

That's not something often encountered, and obviously I exclude professional athletes from this discussion. In my view, every professional football, baseball and basketball player in the U.S.A. is overpaid. Perhaps, I don't understand some of the finer points of the game. I certainly don't understand the multi-million dollar contract.

In the next few days things went from famine to feast. I was deluged with mail from the Crown Agents. Before, I had resented the paucity of correspondence. Now I could barely cope with its volume. First, at long last, came a three-year contract to sign and return. I was to be sent to Lusaka, Northern Rhodesia as an 'executive assistant, executive officer II/I,' and I was to join the pay scale at 870 pounds per year. Unfortunately, it isn't easy to relate the value of a pound, or a dollar, in 1958 to their values some 30 years later. So many things have changed that almost any comparison is artificial.

Thus, some of the significance of reading Dickens is, I believe, lost for us when he refers to pence and sixpence, such trivial sums today. Eight hundred and seventy pounds per year is probably less than most people now earn per month. But in those days, fish and chips cost about 11 pence and you could ride the bus for one penny. Suffice it to say that my new salary was more than I ever thought I would make in my entire life. I currently made 425 pounds per year. I was about to double my salary.

One of the first things I had to do was resign my position as an accountant with my current employer, Thomas Witter and Sons. They, according to popular rumour, had a very enlightened personnel policy. If you wanted a decent raise, you had to resign. Then, if they liked you, they would offer you more than your new job was paying – very simple. Of course, the drawback was that you first had to find a higher-paying job. Then if they didn't like you, they wished you well and you were gone.

Naturally, I didn't really believe this rumour, but I had to confess that in my two years working there, I hadn't had a decent pay rise. Consequently, as I submitted a formal letter of resignation, the thought of the possible responses piqued my curiosity. The following day my boss, the vice president, sent for me and asked where I was going to work. I told him that I was joining the Colonial Civil Service, and he obligingly uttered the magic words, 'How much have they offered you?'

The rumour was true and he liked me! 'Eight hundred and seventy pounds per year,' I quietly replied. He stared at me in astonishment and said, 'That's more than I make.' I wondered if he liked me that much. He didn't. Instead, he stood up, shook my hand, and wished me well.

Many years later, on one of my infrequent returns to Chorley, I sentimentally went back to see the place where I had worked. It was closed and boarded up. The company had gone out of business. Truly, there is something infinitely sad about going home, and finding that busy places you remember so well have disappeared, or stand as lonely sentinels to a soon-to-be-forgotten past.

At those times I always wonder: What was the point of all the hard work everyone put into them, if this was the final result. Why try so hard and sometimes worry so much? Sadly I always come up with the same rather depressing answer. Because clearly you were paid for what you did when you did it – and that was the justification for what you did. Don't expect a tomorrow; tomorrow seldom comes and, if it does, then you will probably neither recognize nor approve of it. Whoever said you can't go home was pretty close to the mark.

The next thing the Crown Agents sent me was a list of all the tropical gear I was supposed to buy. Where was I supposed to buy tropical gear in Chorley? I got smart on this one. I decided to hope I could buy it in South Africa or Northern Rhodesia. I took money instead. Luckily I guessed right: I had no trouble buying what I needed when I arrived.

Then came the medical information. Now at last, I knew why I had got the job. Northern Rhodesia had a monopoly on every incurable deadly disease in the world. They didn't seem to have the common cold, the flu or even measles. They scorned such diseases. For openers, they had malaria, blackwater fever and other impossible to pronounce ailments. But then they got serious, with things like sleeping sickness, yellow fever and smallpox. Finally, they topped off with leprosy.

Mother cried again and Dad still looked grim. Dad said he thought I was making a big mistake. I thought Dad was right. The Crown Agents, however, had no such compunction and had already arranged for me to go to the Tropical Medicine Hospital in Manchester, to receive whatever vaccinations, inoculations and assorted shots I needed. This seemed like excellent advice and, come the dawn, a thoroughly terrified young colonial servant was on their doorstep.

Fortunately, according to this venerable hospital, I had nothing to fear but fear itself. Nevertheless, during the next month, they happily stuck me with every kind of needle for every kind of disease imaginable. To this day I still maintain that I was vaccinated against swine flu and foot-and-mouth disease, but of course they denied this.

It was a miserable month. Each day, as the shots progressed, I had a different but equally unpleasant reaction to the previous day's shot. Eventually, when I refused to die, I was declared to be a bionic man, immune to all known diseases, and ready to travel to darkest Africa.

Back in 1958, air travel was still a luxury and ocean liners were the way everyone traveled. Progress had not yet reversed this fact and air travel was not the norm; while ocean liners, better known as cruise ships, became a luxury. Such is progress – and sometimes I think progress is backwards.

Anyway, it was now time to pack my steamer trunk and send it by rail to the docks, since it had to be in Southampton a week before the ship was due to sail. Steamer trunks were stored in the ship's hold and were not available during the voyage. Personal baggage needed on the voyage could accompany the passenger at the time of embarkation. Each passenger was limited to two suitcases. That was plenty for me: I only had one suit.

Luckily, I didn't need to buy a steamer trunk; my father gave me his mother's. This trunk had been in the family for more than 60 years. Apparently, my grandmother was all set to emigrate to Canada when she was about my age. She got as far as buying a steamer trunk and then changed her mind and married my grandfather instead. Yet the trunk had not been wasted. For the past 60 years it had been used to store the family's spare linen. Now, finally, it was about to be used for the purpose for which it was intended.

As I packed, I wondered if my grandmother, long dead, knew that her trunk was about to make its maiden voyage. I wondered if she would approve. I even pondered the question we all ask ourselves when we really want an Excedrin headache: 'If my granny had gone to Canada instead of marrying my granddad, who would I be?' Wisely, I decided that thinking should be left to my betters, finished packing her trunk and sent it on its merry way to the steamship Capetown Castle.

I still have that steamer trunk today. It's back to its original use of storing the family's spare linen. But it now has some very interesting stories to tell.

4. Leaving Home

On December 10th 1958, at the age of 23, I left Chorley, bound for Africa. It wasn't a dramatic leaving – my parents went to bed as usual that evening. They said that this would be the best way. They said partings are no fun. I sat alone in the living room and stroked my dog. About 11 o'clock I picked up my two suitcases and let myself out of the house. I tried to be quiet as I closed the front door. I didn't want to wake them up. I also suspected that they were not really asleep, and I knew that the door closing so softly was the loudest sound they had heard for many a year.

A door had closed on my parents' hopes and dreams of having a normal child who did normal things. They wanted so badly to have a son who stayed home. They wanted so badly grandchildren that wouldn't be strangers. They didn't want to be alone as they grew older and they wanted the warmth and comfort of my family close by. They wanted what their friends had. My mother put it best when she said: 'I didn't raise you to have you leave.' The trouble was that I didn't want what they wanted, so here I was walking quietly down our street late at night in the cold and rain with two suitcases and my dreams.

I never did go back to Chorley to live, only to visit, and visits are never the same. You've become a tourist in your own hometown. I don't think my parents ever forgave me.

Yet I had to be me and so, on that fateful night, I purposefully walked to the railway station and caught the overnight train to London. It was dark, cold and lonely and I didn't sleep much. I then caught the boat train to Southampton. This was better; the train was quite full. I wondered how many were headed for South Africa. Surely some must be. At least I was not the only person in the world who was leaving home.

These last few weeks, I had increasingly felt that what I was doing was very strange indeed. No one else in Chorley seemed to be doing it. I had begun to feel like a leper, which was doubly strange, because leprosy was an African disease, not a northern English disease. I was not supposed to feel like a leper until after I got to Africa.

Things had become very confusing of late. However, I began to perk up as the boat train neared Southampton. Once we arrived at the overseas passenger terminal, I began to realize that this really was happening. I joined the throng in the customs shed and eventually found myself on the quay with my boarding pass, staring up at a 26,000-ton ocean liner. I was getting excited now.

I bent down, touched the ground, said a quick prayer and straightened up. Then, I walked slowly up the nearest gangplank, leaving England and boarding the Capetown Castle. A steward showed me to my three-berth cabin which I was to share with two other young men. I left my suitcases on my bunk and went back on deck. I stayed there, watching the dockside activity, until the boat left port in the late afternoon. As we steamed out of Southampton and into the English Channel, the coast of England quickly faded into the mist, rain and gloom and, before long, all I could see were the rolling grey swells of the English Channel. I was on my way.

5. A Life On The Ocean Wave

The first few days of our passage to Africa exceeded all my expectations. Indeed, it was infinitely worse than any nightmare I had ever had. We encountered a force 9/10 gale. This is only one reading lower than a full hurricane. The captain said that in all his years at sea, it was the worst weather he had ever encountered.

In the Bay of Biscay, the ship was forced to run before the gale in order to try to serve meals. When we resumed our regular course, warnings were issued to hold on. The ship did everything but sink. Conditions on board were unbelievable. Two people were killed, and several more were seriously injured. Survival became a prime consideration. Foolish Old World habits like washing or changing one's clothes were abandoned and treated with the contempt they deserved. Both passengers and crew had more basic things to consider.

Among the crew, I believe most wanted to live. Among the passengers, I am sure most just wanted to die and be put out of their misery. I can honestly say that I never once thought of making it to Africa. In my most optimistic moments, I sometimes thought of making it through the next 15 minutes. Mostly, I didn't think. I suffered.

The ship was virtually deserted. Ninety percent of the passengers were confined to their bunks, unable to leave their cabins. Our cabin steward told us that conditions in most of the cabins had to be seen to be believed. People just lay in their bunks and threw up endlessly. You couldn't sleep because if you let go of the bunk rails, the motion of the boat would throw you from your perch.. Fresh air would have helped, but how can you dress and walk down passageways and up stairways to the promenade deck when you're too ill to stand? Most passengers were comatose.

While I was never actually sick, I was nearly sick, nearly every minute of every day. However, thanks to one of my cabin mates and another passenger I met on deck, I never quite gave in. Both of these friends in need were professional seamen who never had a moment's discomfort. My cabin mate was about 25 years old and, until recently, had been a cabin steward with this same shipping company. He had made this particular voyage at least 50 times in the last two years, and was en route to South Africa to work as a steward on the South African railways. Apparently he was tired of boats and needed a change of pace.

Boy, did I agree. That's also what I needed – a change of pace. Of course, right then I would willingly have volunteered for a chain gang. Anything was all right with me just as long as it didn't rock and roll in a lousy imitation of Elvis Presley.

My other companion was about 50 years of age and had recently retired as an officer in the British Navy. He had spent most of his career on destroyers and said that they rolled worse than this while at anchor in port. Naturally I didn't believe him but he certainly enjoyed his meals.

These two friends were always lighthearted and cheerful. They would not let me stay in my bunk and suffer. They dressed me and helped me stagger out on deck, where I dutifully gulped in the freezing fresh air. I believe they saved my life. They even insisted that I keep eating – a revolting thought. Food was definitely not on my agenda but I was too ill to argue. I obediently followed them to the dining saloon three times a day.

The dining saloon on the Capetown Castle was a very large room, also used as the main ballroom on special occasions. It could easily seat several hundred passengers at tables arranged in parallel rows running down the entire length of the saloon. A narrow aisle separated the rows. During the storm, the tables had only a smattering of diners. There seemed to be a definite reluctance to belly up to the trough.

In another concession to the storm, the white tablecloths which covered the tables had themselves been criss-crossed with retaining boards which divided each row of tables into many little squares. This was to stop the tableware from ending up in your lap every time the ship rolled in your direction. The boards helped, but we soon found out that it was necessary to assign each person at the table an area of responsibility. At every roll, you each grabbed the dishes in your area. It even helped, some of the time.

It definitely didn't help at lunch on the second day, when a particularly violent lurch hurled a middle-aged lady seated behind me through our table. I say through, because she picked her spot carefully and struck with precision.

She hit just to my right and she must have found a joint between two tables, because the tables parted just like the Red Sea and the lady passed through as clean as a whistle.

Unfortunately, the tablecloth did not have a joint at that particular point and accompanied the lady on her travels. In the blink of an eye, she cleared two sections of tables down to the bare wood. She came to rest at the foot of the next row of tables, covered in the contents of our table. She never did return my lunch.

Judging from the sounds coming from the kitchen the cooks were having little more success than the passengers in battling the storm. Bad as it must have been for the cooks, surrounded by flying pots and pans, it probably was even worse for the poor dining saloon stewards.

Most of these unfortunate acrobats performed like someone from a Jerry Lewis movie, as they hurled their dishes around with a seemingly reckless abandon. The amount of crockery broken was awesome. Indeed, for the rest of the voyage, there actually was a shortage of crockery and glasses at mealtimes.

At each meal, I carefully studied the menu, but only from an academic viewpoint. I wanted to see what I was not going to have. I must have been some kind of masochist. The consensus of opinion, from my two companions and the dining room steward, was that hard dry toast and black coffee was the perfect diet for my condition. For three days, I morosely chewed my crust while my friends piled up the food on their plates. I hoped, uncharitable as it seems, that they would get food poisoning. They didn't.

My hero was a young English schoolmaster who was going out to South Africa to teach the classics at a private boys' school in South Africa. He always ate at my table, and my admiration grew with every passing day. Of such was the thin red line at Waterloo. He never missed a meal. He staggered into the dining saloon as if each step was his last. He was always the last to arrive but we all felt that he had probably been on the road for many hours.

He didn't talk much, just a quiet greeting before he studied the menu with great care. He always ordered a substantial meal. When it came, he would gaze at it in horror before announcing that he had just remembered a pressing engagement. He would then leave the saloon at a medium gallop. The routine never varied. When all chairs but one were filled, our eyes would automatically swivel to the staircase leading down to the dining saloon from the promenade deck. Sure enough, holding on to the rail for dear life, here came my hero. Ten minutes later, he would be gone. I never saw him eat a bite, but he never gave up trying. As bad as I felt, I knew he was 10 times worse. In my moments of deepest despair, he stiffened my resolve to carry on – if he could, I could.

I spent most of the daylight hours out on deck in the freezing wind and rain, not because I'm an outdoors maniac, but because this was the only way to retain my toast and coffee. However, there were other rewards. Life on deck was awe inspiring. The Atlantic Ocean during a major gale has to be seen to be believed. Ours was a massive ocean-going liner, but we were dwarfed in that sea. When we were in a trough, the water towered all around us. When we rose above a wave, it was like being on a mountain top. You could see for miles.

Each time we slid into a trough, it seemed impossible that we would ever come out of it, but each time, the bow or stern would magically rise to the crest of the next wave. We were on nature's roller coaster, but this roller coaster had a corkscrew motion. Not only did we endlessly swoop up and down, but equally endlessly, we rolled from side to side. We rolled so far one way, we were convinced that we were going over. Then, just when all hope was lost, we would stop and start to roll back. What a relief that was. But the roll back would continue until we were sure that we were going over in the opposite direction.

The whole of the first day, I just hung on to a stanchion and waited for the end. By the second day, the majesty and awe-inspiring power of the ocean had reached me. I began to feel totally insignificant and I couldn't remember any of the hang-ups that had so bothered me in the past. Faced with nature in this degree of raw fury, I was totally helpless and at peace.

I also had another distraction. My retired naval officer friend had a wife and a 20-year-old daughter named Susan. He had tried the same tough-it-out treatment on his wife and daughter. His wife, being older and wiser, knew better. She stayed in her bunk and suffered. The daughter, being younger and not so wise, tried to take her father's advice. On the second day, she joined us on deck. My, she looked awful. This was not an attractive woman, but my heart went out to her, as one soul in distress to another.

For two days, we suffered together. I lost count of the number of times I held her head while she was sick over the side of the ship. I soon discovered the truth of the old axiom: 'On a ship, always stay upwind.' I'm a fast learner. Susan was never up to a visit to the dining saloon, but she sure was gutsy, although messy, in her fight for survival. It was a far, far better thing I did, than any I had ever done, as Dickens so aptly observed.

In the evenings, we were forced to retire to the lounges. These were true battlefields. If you sat in a chair and kept still, then on one roll you would slide out of the front of the chair, and on the next you would tip over the back of the chair. It was a continual battle to stay in your chair. Most of all, you could never take your eyes off the other people in the lounge. If anyone rose to leave their chair, they immediately became a weapon. One lurch of the ship and they would come hurtling across the room as a human torpedo. Two people were killed in this way and many seriously injured. When we eventually docked at Capetown, we were met by a line of ambulances that stretched as far as the eye could see. We were in the headlines in all the local papers: 'Battered liner reaches Capetown,' etc.

I myself had one narrow escape when I got up to leave the lounge just as the ship gave a particularly vicious lurch. Instantly I threw caution to the winds, or gale, and obliged with a performance of my torpedo imitation stunt. But luckily I dived into a sofa between two elderly ladies. The sofa went over backwards and the three of us rolled about on the deck. A good time was had by all. Pity we hadn't been properly introduced. I apologized and went to bed. Fortunately my fellow revelers were not seriously hurt, but nevertheless they were not happy campers.

Strangely enough, life in the cabin was almost bearable. One of my cabin mates lay with his face to the wall and moaned softly – he was no problem. My other cabin mate was the ex-deck steward. His only concern seemed to be how long until breakfast. I had a bottom bunk so if I was thrown out I wouldn't fall far. I wedged myself in the bunk each night and tried to sleep. Sometimes I did, but usually I didn't. Slowly came the dawn, one more day.

6. The Love Boat

On the fourth afternoon, two unbelievable things happened. The storm blew itself out, and we made it into Tenerife, in the Canary Islands, a day late. We dropped anchor in a lovely bay, just a few cable's lengths from the sleepy little town. Suddenly all motion ceased, and I couldn't believe it had happened. It was unreal, this stationary feeling, and I very nearly threw up. My equilibrium was shot, and I couldn't get used to the lack of lurch. Just when I had gotten my sea legs, I didn't need them. Here I was, just as in the movies, swaying from side to side on a stationary boat.

Even worse, the bowels of the ship disgorged the previously invisible passengers by the hundreds; which displeased me enormously. For I had become proprietary about the Capetown Castle. It had belonged to the hardy few. What right had all these people to walk on my decks? Strangers who hadn't left their cabins since Southampton, now excitedly crowded the rails, and shouted to the local vendors who came alongside touting their wares.

But unfortunately, because the ship was so overdue in Tenerife, there was no time for anyone to go ashore. We had to be content with what we could see from the rail. Most unusual were the young male divers from the adjacent town, who somehow managed to board our vessel. If one gave them a silver coin they would climb to the topmost deck and fearlessly plummet into the bay below, where several small fishing boats were waiting to pluck them from the water. It reminded me of the pictures I had seen of the Mexican cliff divers at Acapulco. It was all very strange and exciting.

In the early evening, we left Tenerife and sailed out into the calm, balmy and moonlit waters of the mid-Atlantic tropics. It was beautiful, just like the travel brochures said it would be. The ship's P.A. system encouraged everyone to come to dinner tonight. They also announced that there would be a formal ball in the dining saloon after dinner. The ship's band would play and we would celebrate the passing of the storm.

I went to my cabin in some shock. Did this mean I would have to shave, bathe and put on my suit? How would I ever have the courage to ask anyone to dance? What would I do if they said no? I was back to normal, inhibitions in full flower.

When I went to dinner, the place was packed. People were everywhere. It took ages to squeeze my way down the aisle to my seat. There was my hero, my school teacher friend. We grinned at each other. 'Will you have toast and coffee?' he politely asked. 'Do you intend to stay and eat what you order?' I shot back. We both laughed and the newcomers looked at us in puzzlement. We explained that it was a private joke. We felt good; we had fought the good fight. We also had a first-rate dinner. This trip had definitely taken a turn for the better.

I arrived early for the dance and took a place at the bar with most of the other young men. Prospects did not look good. There were lots of unattached young men. There did not appear to be many eligible young ladies, and competition would be fierce. Oh well, I ordered a beer and contemplated the scene. A few minutes later, a very elegant family of three came down the stairs and into the ballroom. The man looked vaguely familiar, but I had never seen either of the women before.

The older woman was obviously his wife, and I assumed the gorgeous young lady who accompanied them must be their daughter. She had blonde hair and was wearing a full length, off-the-shoulder evening gown. She really was very lovely. Sadly I realized that I would never have the courage to ask a girl that smashing to dance. 'Who is that?' exclaimed the young man on my left. 'I wish I knew,' responded his companion.

The parents spotted an empty table and went to sit down. The young lady said something to her father, and headed for the bar. I might be faint of heart but I watch well! Conversation at the bar stopped as she approached our group. She came straight up to me and said simply, 'Would you like to dance, Frank?' I knew I wasn't dreaming because I don't dream with a glass of beer in my hand. Thank God I went to a good school. I put the beer on the bar and said that I would love to dance.

As we started to dance, I confessed with some reluctance, and a definite lack of elegance, that although she seemed to know me I was afraid I couldn't quite place her face, or remember her name. This is not a recommended opening to a beautiful friendship, but it was the best I could do in the circumstances. She obviously knew me and I certainly didn't know her. Pretty girls are not easily forgotten, but this time I seemed to have succeeded.

'I'm Susan,' she said, looking at me in amused surprise. 'I'm the girl you played nursemaid to for the last two days.' 'But you don't look like Susan,' I blurted out. 'How did Susan look?' she coyly inquired. 'Sick,' I replied. As a conversationalist, I appeared to be on a downward trend. 'Well, I'm not sick anymore,' she pointed out. To a simple mind, simple explanations are such a comfort. 'I'm sorry,' I said, 'you look so lovely tonight, I never would have recognized you.' So began my first shipboard romance. The meek inherited the Earth.

The next 10 days sailing through the South Atlantic were among the happiest I've ever had. I easily fell into the restful routine of life on an ocean-going liner. In the morning, a late breakfast, around 10 a.m., followed by a couple of hours on the sun deck lazing around the pool with Susan.

A late lunch and an afternoon nap were next. For I was a gentleman now, and gentlemen take naps. Indeed, it is only the wrong class of Englishman who, as Noel Coward so aptly said, goes out with mad dogs in the midday sun. A couple of hours later, suitably restored, we would meet in one of the lounges and play bridge with her parents. It didn't seem to matter who won, it was just a pleasant way to end the afternoon, and have a few drinks. By six in the evening, it was time to head back to the cabin and dress for dinner.

Dinner was always formal and always elegant. It was a way of life soon to disappear, to be replaced by the congestion of the airport and fasten-your-seatbelt signs. I'm sorry I only caught the last few years of it, but I'm so glad I didn't miss it altogether. After dinner, the evening entertainment began. A dance, a movie or a show – each night was different.

Then, late at night, from 11 p.m. to 1 a.m., the rear lounge – the one furthest away from the cabins, was given over to the young people. All the latest rock and roll music was played and about 50 of us would rock 'til we dropped.

This was the best part of the day, and it seemed quite fitting that one of the most popular songs of 1958 was 'Wake Up Little Susie, It's Time To Go Home.' Naturally, whenever the disc jockey played that song, as he did most nights, we would all gather round and sing it for our 'Susie.' It was a good time; it was an interlude from life.

Finally, when the ship fell silent, Susan and I would stroll quietly around the almost deserted decks in the soft tropical moonlight. For the longest time, we would stand at the stern and gaze at the wake of the ship stretched out in a fluorescent trail behind us, until it disappeared into the darkness. We would talk about where we came from and where we were going – a future unknown.

Each night was bittersweet. The moment was so perfect, but each night was one day nearer to Capetown. We both knew that after Capetown we would probably never meet again. We didn't, but the memory remains. A lingering goodnight, then back to our cabins for a few hours sleep. Tomorrow we'll do it all one more time.

It was a hard life but someone's got to do it. Joy of joys, I was getting paid for this. I was on full salary from the day the boat sailed. Thank you England, your tax pounds were at work.

7. Crossing The Line

The first big event on the entertainment calendar was the visit of King Neptune, when the ship crossed the equator. That, traditionally, was a very special moment, and our crew put on a really spectacular show. About 10 victims were selected for the initiation rites, from among those passengers who had not previously crossed the equator. Those chosen were all young men or young women, which seemed rather ominous to me. Hadn't I read about Mayan pagan rites that also seemed to prefer young people?

Nevertheless, when someone volunteered my name, I calmly agreed. I began to have my doubts when the officer in charge of the ceremony told us, perhaps too casually, to put on our oldest clothes, prior to assembling on the promenade deck at the appropriate hour. Shortly thereafter, as the ship neared the Equator, we were chained together and marched around the deck, finishing up at the swimming pool where King Neptune had set up his court.

The whole place was jammed with spectators; everyone came. Passengers and crew crowded around the pool and lined the rails of the upper decks which overlooked the festivities. One by one, like lambs led to the slaughter, we shuffled forward to have our chains unhooked and meet our fate. Eager hands lifted us from our feet and threw us unceremoniously onto a table, where paste was rubbed in our hair and all over our bodies, until the attendants deemed we looked just right.

We were then carried to a poolside chair and seated in it for King Neptune's approval. When he signaled his approval, the chair was flipped over backwards and we somersaulted into the pool, where more attendants ducked us unmercifully. A good time was had by all. Actually, the paste didn't taste that bad, although it was something of an acquired taste. Personally I felt it needed a little more salt.

All in all I was glad I had been formally inducted into the fraternity of those who had sailed across the equator. It was something to be proud of, and something worth remembering. That night at dinner the captain presented to each of the victims a beautiful scroll certifying that we had crossed the equator. Susan looked proud. I still had the paste in my hair. I still have the scroll.

8. Lobster Salad

The next big event was the fancy dress ball, a firmly established

custom on all long ocean passages. Many experienced passengers
brought elaborate costumes with them.

Others spent long hours in their cabin working on their
creations. It was another aspect of a vanished way of travel. Come
to think of it, a fancy dress parade down the aisles of a Boeing 747
might not be a bad idea. It might relieve the boredom.

Anyway, on the appointed night, those of us not in fancy dress
gathered in the ballroom to watch the parade which preceded the
ball. Prizes were given for the best costumes and the competition
was fierce. There were many beautiful and original costumes and I
would have been hard put to pick a winner, until the last entrant
staggered in.

For here came the grand prize winner, making a triumphant
circuit of the ballroom to tumultuous applause. His costume was
skimpy, indeed almost non-existent. He was his own costume,
totally naked except for a pair of green bikini swimming trunks.
He had perhaps the worst case of sunburn I had ever seen and his
whole body, from head to toe, back and front, glowed. He was the
most painful shade of lobster red I ever saw. Indeed, he looked and
walked like he had been boiled alive. On his head he wore a lettuce
crown. Across one shoulder and down to the opposite hip, he wore
a sash of lettuce leaves. In his hands, he carried a small sign that
said 'Lobster Salad.'

What a perfect example of man's indomitable spirit! How I
admired his ability to snatch victory from the jaws of defeat! I also
liked his sense of humour. He was a unanimous choice for first
prize. Yet I don't remember seeing him at the ball which followed
the parade. Probably, he was not up to tripping the light fantastic.
But he had got things off to a perfect start and helped to make that
ball one of the highlights of the voyage.

9. Africa

The farewell dinner came all too soon. The voyage had passed all
too quickly, an experience never to be forgotten or repeated. In a
few short years, the Union Castle liners would vanish from the
oceans, to be replaced by three-day cruises. How sad. Our farewell
dinner was doubly special, because it was, in fact, Christmas Eve,
1958. We sang Christmas carols and said goodbye. Susan and I
walked the decks for the last time and quietly parted. We
exchanged addresses and promised to write. We did, for a while,
and then we stopped. But what we had, they can't take away.

On Christmas Day I was up by daybreak, and there it was, in the
soft early light – Africa. At 6 a. m. we glided into Capetown harbour.
I stood quietly on deck, in no hurry to start my new life. Fascinated,
I watched the morning mist, the tablecloth on Table Mountain, as it

Capetown Harbour, Christmas Day, 1958

slowly dissipated and revealed the stark outlines of that unusual mountain that towers above Capetown and its harbour. 'Merry Christmas,' I said to myself.

Activity on the quay was beginning to build, as a growing stream of disembarking passengers filled the gangplanks. It was time to go. I never saw Susan disembark. I never looked for her. What for, to say 'Have a nice day?' I think she was already a memory. I left the deck, went to my cabin, picked up my suitcases and said my goodbyes to the Capetown Castle. Then I went down the gangway and into Africa.

Looking back on this voyage, I have often wondered why it didn't have the same feel as a modern-day cruise. Perhaps it was because the old ocean liners were not pleasure ships. They were passenger ships. Their purpose was to take people where they needed to go. As a passenger you became part of this glorious tradition and I disembarked with a feeling of pride. For I had made passage on the Capetown Castle.

10. A Whole New World

Christmas in Capetown didn't look like Christmas. It looked like the middle of summer. It was hot, and the men were dressed in shorts, while the women wore summer dresses.

Christmas couldn't be Christmas without looking like Christmas, could it? But where was the snow? I knew intellectually that in the southern hemisphere, things are reversed. Summer comes in the winter, so to speak. Yet I still wasn't prepared to accept Santa Claus in a bathing suit.

Indeed, in all my years in Africa, I never grew comfortable with a Christmas barbecue, and I obviously wasn't alone in this sentiment. Many of my friends still sent traditional Christmas cards, depicting snow covered village scenes. I never did that. I sent cards showing typical African scenes. They were nice cards, but somehow they didn't seem to convey the warmth of Christmas.

Later that morning, as I stood in line waiting my turn to pass through customs, I knew that the strangeness of Africa was not my only problem with that festive season. It also didn't feel like Christmas. This holiday is supposed to be spent with your family. It's not supposed to be spent alone in a strange city. Welcome to the flip side of being a world traveler: your constant companion is loneliness.

After completing the formalities of customs and immigration, I paused to gather my thoughts and consider my next step. The Crown Agents had given me a rail voucher and told me to go to the main railway station, where I could exchange the voucher for a train ticket to Lusaka, Northern Rhodesia. My steamer trunk would hopefully be sent later by rail freight. Therefore, rather timidly, I ventured out onto the streets of Capetown, in search of a taxi to take me to the train station.

As I scanned the unfamiliar streets, I spotted a young man whom I had previously met on the Capetown Castle. I remembered that he too was a new recruit to the Colonial Service, and was also on his way to Northern Rhodesia. He looked as lost as I felt, and willingly agreed when I suggested that we team up and travel together.

Bill Curphy was a small, dark, rather intense young man from Liverpool. In due course, he became one of my best friends. Together we hailed a taxi and set off for the train station. I, perhaps wisely, was somewhat apprehensive about being in South Africa. I knew almost nothing about this country. Unfortunately, the little I knew was not encouraging.

I knew that they had something called apartheid knowing that this meant that the whites and the blacks were both restricted in where they could go and what they could do. However, I didn't know how these restrictions affected daily life. I decided to be very careful and try not to make a mistake. It would appear, since the taxi driver was black, that we could obviously ride together in a taxi. I wondered if a white taxi driver was allowed to have black passengers. Life could be very complicated.

When we arrived at the train station, I paid the driver while Bill hurried in through the nearest entrance. I started to follow him, but some sixth sense stopped me. Then I saw the sign above the entrance:

'Non-whites Only.' I froze with horror. What would happen to Bill? I soon found out, because in about five minutes, a puzzled Bill was led back out of the entrance by two very burly policemen.

They wanted to know if he knew how to read, and Bill said that he did. They then wanted to know if he was trying to make trouble, and Bill said that he wasn't. I quickly told the police that we had been in South Africa for less than an hour, and would try to behave ourselves. Somewhat mollified, they led us over to the 'Whites Only' entrance, and stood there until we disappeared inside the station. I had just had my first lesson in apartheid. 'Look before you leap' seemed to be a very good policy in South Africa.

Being sure to use the 'Whites Only' window, we exchanged our vouchers for train tickets. Still exercising great care, we made our way to the correct platform and boarded a 'Whites Only' passenger car. Safely aboard the train, we relaxed a little, as we began to realize that being a long way from home, is not just a matter of distance. You can also be a long way from home culturally. We then sat and watched the African version of Grand Central Station, for a little over an hour until, about noon, the train left Capetown and slowly headed north.

11. Riding The African Rails

A new adventure had just begun, or so I innocently thought, as we left the city behind and entered the South African veldt. However, my high expectations were quickly dashed, and this train ride turned out to be a disappointment. Perhaps I had expected too much. Perhaps I unconsciously compared it to the just completed voyage. Whatever the reasons, I remember it as being uncomfortable, unending and uninteresting. Riding the train in Africa has one great benefit: It beats walking, but not by much.

First of all, the trains were not air conditioned. If you got hot, you could open a window and let the dust and flies come in. The dust was bad enough, but the flies were in a class by themselves. African flies have a bite like the kick of a mule, and most seem to carry some exotic disease, for which there is no known cure.

You could keep the windows closed and suffer. Or keep them open and suffer. Most people seemed to alternate. When the heat became unbearable, they opened the windows. When the flies became unbearable, they closed the windows. Life was reduced to picking the form of punishment you most enjoyed. To and fro between the frying pan and the fire, so to speak.

Secondly, to compound the misery, African trains cover vast distances at extremely slow speeds. This tends to make the average train trip a multi-day odyssey. Our train took four days to reach Lusaka. It traveled so slowly that I sometimes thought of getting off

and walking along beside it for a spot of exercise. In fairness to the
railways, I'm sure that the dangers of wild animals getting on the
tracks had something to do with the speeds they maintained.

Nevertheless, by the third day, I began to imagine that I could see
the grass growing as we passed by.

Yet even though I was bored, I was still overwhelmed by the vast-
ness of Africa. When you come from a small island, you tend to have
a small mind and a small outlook, as far as distance is concerned.
When I was a child, we would not travel the 25 miles from Chorley
to the seaside resort of Blackpool, unless we went for a week's vacation. A 50-mile round trip was unthinkable, unless you intended to
stay at the beach for at least a week.

My mother's family always regretted that my mother had moved
so far from home when she got married. Mother moved two miles. I
was now discovering that I needed to expand my horizons. Africa is
a big place. It is, no offense intended, bigger than Texas. If you are
going to travel in Africa, then you are going to cover lots of territory.
By the time we reached Lusaka, I had received a forceful introduction
to African distances.

Finally, and worst of all, African travel tends to be uninteresting.
I say this with some hesitation, because I love Africa and find it fascinating, but it is the sounds, the smell, the feel of Africa that is most
compelling. African sights are magnificent but the high points are
very few and very far between. Unlike Europe or America, in which
there are many towns and farms dotting the landscape, Africa is
largely deserted. You can travel for hours and never see a village or
an animal. The terrain may not change for 2,000 miles. There is a lot
of variety, but this variety can only be seen by a traveler who covers
a vast amount of territory. Africa has many scenes in her portfolio but
she is slow to turn the pages.

Our train went north from Capetown, across the South African
veldt, for a day or so. It is a semi-arid region with scant vegetation,
that eventually gives way to the Kalahari Desert, which covers most
of Bechuanaland. The Kalahari has its own majesty but, to the
layman, there's an awful lot of sand out there.

As a traveler through Arizona, Utah and Nevada, I've often had
the feeling that a visitor from Mars, making his first landing in the
middle of one of those deserts, would probably not regard Earth as a
very hospitable planet. Perhaps I'm wrong, but I still maintain that
sand is at its best on the beach. At last, after an interminable ride
through the wide open nothingness of Bechuanaland, the train finally
left the desert behind, and entered the Southern Rhodesian grass-
lands.

The route north now began a gradual ascent to the central African
uplands, which rise to an average height of about 4,000 feet. The
considerable elevation of this vast plateau, prevents the region from
having an African jungle look. Jungles only appear in Hollywood

movies and low lying areas.

Although no longer a desert, this land is still sparsely covered with people or vegetation. It is a poor grassland, with short stumpy trees and impenetrable thorn bushes. It is a land that gets no rain for six months, and then gets too much during the monsoon, that occurs for the other six months of the year.

It is a harsh and inhospitable place. The trees are bent and wizened with the constant struggle to survive. This is the African bush. It has its rewards: to glimpse a herd of elephants in the distance, is to feel its magic. The bush, however, is endless, and you know what they say: 'If you've seen one bush, you've seen them all.'

On the morning of the fourth day we reached the mighty Zambezi, which marks the boundary between the two Rhodesias. At breakfast, in a never-to-be-forgotten spectacle, we were treated to one of those widely separated sights, which makes Africa unique. For it is here, near the Northern Rhodesian town of Livingstone, that the train crosses the Zambezi on the Victoria Falls suspension bridge, and rewards its passengers with one of the world's most awesome sights.

The Victoria Falls or 'Smoke that Thunders,' to use its beautifully descriptive African name, is not to be believed, even when seen. These falls are more than 420 feet high and more than a mile wide. They are three times the height, and one and a half times the width, of Niagara Falls. They are, perhaps, the world's finest waterfalls.

Dr. Livingstone, the first European to see them, wrote in his journal in 1858: 'Surely angels that soar in Heaven, must gaze on sights such as these.' Surely indeed, to see this angelic sight, through the window of our train, was a truly rare privilege. Suddenly, there is no more bush and your mouth goes into a fly catching routine, as you gaze, for about two minutes, in open-mouthed wonder, at that incredible wall of water. Thank God, the train moves so slowly! Thank God, the tracks parallel the falls, so very close to their splendour. Just as suddenly, it is gone and the scenery is back to more bush. You ask your friends, if they saw what you thought you saw, and they did.

Still in shock, you make a mental note to return as soon as possible and to stay for as long as it takes, to really see the falls. I did, about two years later, with a girl I almost married, who happened to grow up in Livingstone. The Victoria Falls is a most romantic place in the moonlight. It makes a pretty girl even prettier, but that's another story.

After 12 more hours, and endless more miles across the semi-arid lonely plains of the central African bush, the train finally wheezed into Lusaka, just before dark. Thankfully, but a little fearfully, we descended to the little platform in the tiny station. This was not a metropolis, but we were home – our new home. What would we find here? Would I be glad or sorry I had come? There was no turning back now. I picked up my suitcases and trudged towards the exit, and my new life.

12. A Gentlemanly Game Of Bridge

I've saved one small vignette from my train ride until last. It concerns the desperate, amusing and unusual lengths we went to in order to relieve the monotony of the trip. It starts with one of the other passengers surreptitiously showing me his deck of playing cards. He did this with a sly smirk on his face, the reason for which was apparent, as soon as I saw the first card, which featured a naked woman in an extremely unusual and athletic position.

Quickly I scanned the entire pack. Each card had a different woman in a different pose. The photographer was a man of exceptional imagination. I scanned the pack again, more slowly this time, in growing excitement. Just as I had hoped, not only were all 52 cards present, but in a prosaic deference to custom, the top left and bottom right hand corner of each, clearly showed its nominal value.

Beauty is in the eye of the beholder. Joyfully I turned to my new friend, and pleaded with him to lend me his cards. 'You like them that much?' He asked. 'Oh yes,' I replied, 'Now we can play bridge.' Nonplused, he looked at me in total amazement, and, probably because he was unable to think of a reply, gave me the cards and wandered away, shaking his head in bewilderment at the vagaries of human nature.

Posthaste I rounded up three other passengers and we then adjourned to the lounge car, where we spent many delightful hours playing bridge, with the most pornographic deck of cards I had ever seen. Yet I had searched high and low on that train, and failed to locate anyone with a normal deck of cards. Much as I wanted to play bridge to help shorten the trip, I couldn't, until that student of the female figure saved the day.

Passers-by who paused to watch our game, would see nothing unusual as a hand was dealt and bids were made. But once play began, this tranquil scene was abruptly shattered. A gasp of horror would greet each pasteboard as it was laid upon the table, and revealed in all its dubious artistic glory. Outraged, our audience would tarry no more, and hastily departed from our den of iniquity. Usually they left muttering something about, 'What is the world coming to?' or, 'They looked like such nice young men.' For my part, I guess I must have been undersexed: it was the aces and kings in my hand which caused me the most excitement.

I still remember that deck of cards with nostalgic affection. They were used to play some of the best bridge I've ever played. Sad to say, I can't remember any of the ladies who adorned the pack, but I wish them well. Perhaps the moral of this story is, that things are often not what they seem to be, especially at first glance. Certainly this is true of Africa, as I was soon to discover, as I began to adjust to life under the African sun.

Chapter 2

Early Days In Lusaka

1. The Stamp Man

My career as a British colonial civil servant began, and almost ended on December 29, 1958, the day after I arrived in Lusaka, the capital of Northern Rhodesia.

The previous evening Bill Curphy and I had been met at the train station by a small Afrikaner whose name was Johannes Uys. Yonnie, as we called him, was a native of Lusaka, having been born on his father's enormous ranch, some 70 miles south of the town.

After we had waved the train goodbye, or perhaps good riddance, Yonnie had driven us to the government rest house, where we were to live temporarily. Before leaving he promised to return early the next day and take us to work. True to his word, he came to get us at 7:30 the following morning, and delivered us to the Ministry of Finance, where we had been told to report for further instructions.

Ministry of Finance in Lusaka, 1959

After completing the necessary paperwork, I was assigned a junior clerk's job as a cashier and receptionist at the ministry's front desk, while Bill was banished to the Ministry of Native Affairs. By late afternoon, I was well into my career, writing receipts for the various people who came in to pay their bills.

Around 4 p.m., a distinguished elderly man came up to my window and politely asked if I had any stamps. Well, it was my first day at work. I was tired and hot and it seemed like a silly question to me. So I looked at him cheerfully and imprudently said, 'push off mate, this is the Ministry of Finance. You need the Post Office if you want stamps.'

My customer looked at me in total astonishment and then, deciding to heed my advice, left at a brisk clip to seek his stamps elsewhere. A few moments later, the first day's work successfully completed, I locked my safe and wearily walked the two miles back to the government rest house.

The next morning, I rose early and pretended to enjoy the two-mile walk to work. This was not easy, for it was quickly becoming clear that the combination of no buses, no car and not being able to drive, could prove to be a tad inconvenient. But at least the sun was shining and eventually, only slightly the worse for wear, I arrived at work, where my new boss was waiting to see me. Apparently he had news, and in a strangely somber voice, he told me that the Permanent Secretary of the Ministry of Finance would like to see me in his office.

I was not surprised – true talent is obvious – and I had clearly done a good job of giving change the previous day. Unfortunately, my supervisor did not share my enthusiasm. He advised caution. Rumour had it, he said, that Mr Lewis the Permanent Secretary was seeking permission to have me shot.

In a thoughtful mood, I approached the Holy of Holies, and in due course, was ushered into a large wood-paneled office, where I was introduced to a distinguished middle-aged man, who sat at the opulent desk which stood in the middle of the room. On the wall behind him was a picture of the Queen. To his left rear stood the British flag. It was all rather grand. I sat in the chair before his desk and politely waited to be shot. Happily I wasn't, and instead played a minor role in the following conversation:

P.S.:   'So you're Bennett.'
Me: 'Yes sir.'
P.S.:   'How long have you been with us?'
Me: 'This is my second day, sir.'
P.S: 'I see.'
         After a pause, he continued in a soft voice.
         'I have been a colonial officer for almost 30 years, and have done quite well. Last year I was awarded an M.B.E., (Member of the British Empire, a prestigious award), and two years ago I became the Permanent Secretary of this ministry.'

Me:	'Yes sir.'
P.S:	'See that phone on my desk?'
Me:	'Yes sir.'
P.S.:	'If it rings, I will pick it up.'
Me:	'Yes sir.'
P.S:	'If it is Mr. Nicholson, the Minister of Finance, on the line, and if he asks me for stamps, do you know what I will say?'
Me:	(As the light began to dawn), 'No sir.'
P.S.:	'Well, Mr. Bennett, I shall say – 'Yes sir, Mr. Nicholson' – and hang up the phone.'
Me:	'Yes sir.'
P.S.:	'Then, Mr. Bennett, I will go and get the Minister his God damned stamps.'
Me:	'Yes sir.'
P.S.:	'If, after 30 years in the service, I am prepared to get the minister his bloody stamps, is it asking too much of you to do the same? At least, until you've been with us a few more days.'
Me:	'No sir.'
P.S.:	'Good. Could we, perhaps, even persuade you to modify your behaviour, and extend to the third most senior colonial officer in the colony the respect he deserves?'
Me:	'Yes sir, but, sir, I didn't know who he was.'
P.S.:	'Everyone knows the minister.'
Me:	'Not everyone, I didn't.'
P.S.:	'So I've decided to believe, which is the only reason you are still in the colony!'
Me:	'Thank you, sir.'
P.S.:	'Welcome to Northern Rhodesia. Now go away and try helping us run the empire, in preference to destroying it.'
Me:	'Thank you, sir, I'll try.'

On the surface it may seem that my offense was trivial, and perhaps it had been, but in those days, dignity was paramount. The Colonial Civil Service resembled an old guards regiment, and you had to mind your Ps and Qs. Yet, I don't honestly believe I could have been fired for my faux pas. That was not the service's way. They preferred to mold recalcitrant officers into the corporate image, kind of like the modern day Marines would tend to do.

Trivial or not, my fame as the stamp man rapidly spread throughout the territory and stuck to me, pun intended, for the rest of my career. This notoriety even reached Kasama in the Northern Province, as I discovered some four years later, soon after I became the province's provincial accountant. When I arrived there, I went to pay my compliments to the provincial commissioner, he grinned from ear to ear before asking me to sit down. He then offered me a cup of tea and said, 'so you're Bennett, the stamp man. I'm so glad to meet you. Wish I'd had your kind of nerve. Nicholson was a sanctimonious old prig and I'm glad someone finally told him to go take a hike.' On such fleeting moments of insanity are futures built.

2. Grounded

After such an auspicious start to my colonial career, I managed to pass the first few weeks of 1959 in total obscurity. At work, this was fine, but in my private life the results were not so fine and I rapidly became a social hermit.

The problem was mobility, or rather the lack of it, and came as a complete surprise, since in England, I had always lived in a small pedestrian-oriented town, with about as many buses as people. Lusaka, on the other hand, had virtually no buses, especially in the white suburbs, where most of the streets didn't even have sidewalks. Therefore if you didn't own a car and drive, you walked, and if you walked in Africa, you quickly became hot, dirty, tired and demented.

At home, in England, I never needed a car, because the bus was always available. None of my friends drove or had cars and the only time we rode in such splendour was at weddings and funerals. Cars were a luxury reserved for posh people and, unbelievable as it may now seem, I was 18 years old when I first rode in a private automobile. I remember that ride well. It was from Preston to Chorley, about nine miles, and the car belonged to Johnny Walker, the actuary of the bank where I worked.

It was well after dark, and I sat in the front passenger's seat as he drove us home. I can still see the way his headlights reflected back from the rows of cat's eyes which marked the middle of the highway. It was so fascinating and beautiful that I sat spellbound, while my heart ached to own a car. But in those days it was only a pipe dream. Ordinary people didn't have cars.

Yet now, when I appeared to be stuck, quite literally, right in the middle of Africa, owning a car no longer seemed like a dream. It had become a necessity. Unfortunately for me and my legs, a car would have to remain a dream, until I could save enough money to buy one, since 'drive now, pay later' was not a central African slogan. To us, schooled in a puritan ethic, if you couldn't pay for something, then you didn't need it, and only the rich could borrow money. Consequently, I spent the next several weeks living in the government rest house and daily walking the two miles to work, and back, on increasingly tender feet.

Practically, I really had no choice but to stay in the rest house, because it was the only place where I could live and commute to work on foot. However, it did have other advantages. Rooms were adequate, although small, and the veranda was an ideal place to sit and relax. The dining room was definitely first class, with surprisingly reasonable prices, and coffee was served each night, after dinner, in a very pleasant lounge. But best of all, there was no lack of excellent company, since most of the other residents were also confined to barracks by a similar lack of transportation. The weekends however, dragged interminably, as I made Scrooge seem like a spendthrift, hoarding my funds like a miser, and dreaming of the day when I would be free at last.

3. Me And My Whistle

Still, all was not boredom, for during my first few weeks as a Northern Rhodesian foot soldier, I had one experience which combined farce and terror in equal proportions, while sharpening my interest in staying alive. This happened when, shortly after my arrival in Northern Rhodesia, the colony experienced its first guerrilla sabotage scare. Apparently, the incipient African struggle to achieve independence had turned to more violent ways to express its point of view.

To meet the challenge, the colonial service came up with two ideas, one good, one bad. The good idea was that all important installations should be guarded 24 hours a day. The bad idea was that all young male officers would be drafted to do guard duty, and that included me. No stone had been left unturned in planning to meet this emergency, and we were each issued with an armband to give us authority, a whistle to sound the alarm – if anything should go wrong – and a truncheon to protect government property. Move over John Wayne, here I come.

Unfortunately, this farce had a sober side that quickly turned my casual fear of the future into active terror. For after I was assigned to protect the main radio transmitter tower, I soon began to realize, to my horror, just how serious my plight could be. Not only was this tower a prime sabotage target, but it was four miles out of town, in the middle of the nowhere bush. And, if that was not bad enough, the final nail in my coffin came, figuratively speaking I fervently hoped, when I was told that I had won the honour of being the Queen's representative on the 4 a.m. to 8 a.m. shift.

Since I had no car I tried to have my assignment changed. But unfortunately all my protestations fell on deaf ears. Perhaps this was Mr. Nicholson's revenge! Anyway, after telling myself all new experiences are fun, I now began to set my bedside alarm for 2:30 a.m., and prayed that this early bird would be spared an encounter with anything or anyone.

Having unwillingly joined the nocturnal set, I soon discovered the flaw in another popular adage. If anyone ever tells you 'Early to bed, early to rise, keeps a man healthy, wealthy and wise' then he is a fool. It kept me terrified. This may, in part, have been due to my being quite new to Africa and not familiar with the sounds of an African night. Perhaps so, but as I walked the four miles to my guard post, feverishly clutching my whistle, I trembled with fear at every rustle and cough that came out of the surrounding darkness.

Once I had reached the radio transmitter hut, and sadly watched the midnight to 4 a.m. guard drive off in his car, I would try, every night, to conquer my fears and ensure the survival of the fittest. After giving the matter much thought, and secure in the knowledge my mother did not raise a fool, I had reluctantly resolved, the first night, to face my Hobson's choice head on, and apply some good old Lancashire cunning.

They say fear sharpens the wits, and I quickly decided I feared the bush at night less than I feared a terrorist attack. Accordingly, I opted to be sensible and leave the lights on in the transmitter hut each night, while I went and hid in the bush. I figured I would give an eyewitness account of any terrorist attack, and to hell with my whistle. Yet even though I had chosen my favourite type of terror, I still spent a considerable portion of my life ignoring the sounds of wildlife at play and praying for sunrise.

Reports of the beauty of an African dawn are not exaggerated. It is also safe to say that during this period I never missed a single one, although my appreciation of their beauty was overshadowed by heartfelt relief when the early morning sun signaled the end of another uneventful watch. After I could see clearly, but never before, I rose from my hiding place in the bush, which I varied nightly, and bravely assumed my guard duties in the transmitter hut.

At 8 a.m., the engineers who worked at the radio tower arrived and then, in a fair imitation of John Wayne, I ambled off into the wilderness. Some three hours later, having enjoyed a four-mile saunter through the countryside, a leisurely shower, a delightful breakfast and a two-mile stroll to work, I would be ready to begin what I had innocently hoped was my normal work day.

It now appeared to me as if the colonial service contained aspects I was not adequately prepared to handle. At the very least, I ought to have been advised to buy several pairs of combat boots. I even pondered the possibility of getting some kind of on-foot mileage allowance. But this last idea was one I wisely kept to myself.

Luckily the guerrilla scare only lasted for about five weeks before it fizzled out. Shortly thereafter my guard duty career came to an end, when I received a nice certificate of appreciation from a grateful governor and, in return, happily surrendered my armband, whistle and truncheon. It also began to look, since I hadn't been killed, as if my concerns during the emergency may have been groundless, and I should therefore have more faith in higher authority. Obviously 'they' knew best, yet I still harboured doubts about the effectiveness of my whistle.

Suppose, for instance, the tower had been attacked and I had stoutly served my queen by blowing my whistle. What good would I have done? I was four miles from town and only the terrorists could have heard me. Perhaps that was the answer! Perhaps all official whistles possess magic powers, which are strong enough to make an enemy flee in terror! Thankfully, the true value of my noisemaker was never exposed, and my entire stint of guard duty was uneventful, but fear banished boredom.

4. My First Home

Just when I was beginning to despair of ever leaving the government rest house, Bill Curphy came, like an angel of mercy, to my rescue. He too was confined to barracks by a lack of wheels, but apparently had been more resourceful than the rest of us, because one night at dinner, he proudly announced that he had bought a car and rented a house. This was great news and I even felt a twinge of jealousy, until he politely invited me to come and live with him. Somewhat mollified, I asked him how on earth he managed to pull off these twin feats.

He told me he was buying the car from Ken Bayman, with whom he worked, and renting the house from Bill Taylor, a senior member of the Ministry of Finance, who was going on overseas leave and needed a caretaker for his government-owned house. That car is a painful subject about which I will have much more to say a little later. But the house was a Godsend.

Normally a junior, unmarried officer, such as Bill, would never have qualified for a government house and would be condemned to a life in the rest house, or a nearby block of Spartan one-bedroom apartments. However, there was one unique situation which made even the best of our homes available to the lower ranks. Bill had learned of this loophole and utilized it to his advantage.

At this juncture, and in order to better understand what Bill had done, you will have to bear with me while I explain the intricacies of British Colonial Regulations, insofar as they apply to overseas leave. Luckily, although the subject was complicated, its basic provisions were not, and revolved around the fact that each expatriate officer received five days a month of foreign leave for every month served in Northern Rhodesia. This leave was accumulated over a three year period, the length of an average tour of duty, and then had to be taken, outside of Africa, in a temperate climate.

Thus, after three years a colonial officer would have 180 days of leave accumulated, to which was added 42 days of travel time, for a grand total of 222 days. All of this leave was, of course, on full salary, and the government also picked up the tab on all travel expenses incurred by an officer, his wife and his children. These expenses usually included first-class return rail fare to Capetown South Africa, and passage by sea, to Europe and back, in a grade of accommodation whose quality was determined by an officer's rank. However, even the humblest clerk received one of the better berths on the Union Castle liners, while the Governor of Northern Rhodesia always received a luxury suite and ate at the captain's table.

It was a tough job, but someone had to do it, which is probably why we also got two weeks of local leave, plus about 12 days of public holidays each year. Sometimes it seemed as if life was one long rest cure and we really had to struggle to find enough time to take all of our vacations. But we tried.

Having so much foreign leave meant that once every three years each of us was gone on a very long sabbatical. This forced the service to have about 15 percent more employees than it actually needed, since every officer on leave had to be replaced by a new officer freshly returned to duty. There was therefore a constant turnover of experienced personnel and this was good for the service, because no one ever got too deeply embedded in his favourite rut. Small wonder, that with benefits like these, most of us considered the British Colonial Office to be the world's premier employer. And just in case we got tired, retirement on full pension was mandatory at age 55.

Although there was no real down side to our incredibly long leaves, they did raise the possibility that an awful lot of houses were going to sit empty for seven and a half months, at three-year intervals, and this was precisely what the government would not allow. Thus, each time an officer went on leave he had to move out of his house, which meant he also gave up his furniture, and each time he came back from leave he had to move into a different house with different furnishings.

However, since it was a tad inconvenient for the senior echelons of the service to play musical houses, there had to be some way they could avoid taking their turn. Consequently, colonial regulations stipulated that senior officers could keep their houses and furniture during their leaves, provided they found another officer prepared to accept a temporary seven and a half month tenancy, of the senior officer's house and furnishings. Which is exactly what Bill had triumphantly arranged with Bill Taylor, who was going on long leave the next month.

Now I must admit, that the idea of baby-sitting a house has its drawbacks. Obviously, you are going to lose it after a few months, and it is never really home, since you didn't choose the pictures on the walls. Nevertheless, on balance it was worth it, when you weighed the considerable advantages the arrangement delivered.

In the first place, it enabled a junior officer to get a much better accommodation, with much better furniture, than his rank would warrant. Secondly, the house would usually be in the best part of town, with extensive grounds and, if you were lucky, a swimming pool. In addition, the house would probably have three or four bedrooms, thereby giving you the option of inviting several friends to come share the luxury and help reduce your expenses. But best of all, the rent was determined by the temporary tenant's modest junior officer salary, and not by the quality of the house provided, which allowed serfs like me to live like lords.

Bill Curphy, Moses and Family

All in all, house sitting was a very attractive proposition, and in my early years in Northern Rhodesia I did a great deal of it with no regrets. Indeed, many of my fondest memories revolve around the friends I made during those caretaker days, which passed so quickly and yet, on reflection, may well have given me my most enjoyable African experiences.

However, when Bill Curphy first broached the idea, I was somewhat reluctant to leave our present quarters, since I had no car and no way of getting to work from a house in the suburbs. But this was no problem, Bill assured me, as he kindly offered to take me to work each morning and bring me back home each afternoon. He then craftily clinched the deal by reminding me that his car would also be available in the evenings. 'Perhaps we could even go to a movie,' he said, knowing how seldom we had been to the cinema in the last few months. 'What's a movie?' I asked, before delightedly accepting his offer and acknowledging my new role as a de facto member of the middle class.

Having made our decision, we could hardly contain our impatience until the big day came, some three weeks later, when we moved into a nice two-bedroom house with a view, for which Bill paid the princely sum of eight pounds – or 15 dollars – per month in rent.

Our first priority was to acquire a cook and so, after consulting a local pastor, we hired a mature middle-aged African named Moses for this vital position. A few days later Moses, his wife and seven children, moved into the servant's quarters immediately behind our home. This was the normal practice in Northern Rhodesia, where all European houses had their own African house, built behind the main house and separated from it by a fairly large backyard. Both families would grow flowers, vegetables, corn and even bananas, in the communal yard where the children of both would roll around in the dirt together. A good cook would cost, in 1960s money, about $20 a month. But, it must be remembered, that in our society, the job also provided a house, free water and sewage, free electricity and a plot of land to farm. It was a different society with different rules.

I don't know if it was a just society. I have conflicting emotions on this particular issue. However, I do know that it provided a better standard of living for African servants than any to be found in their home village. I also suspect that it provided a better life than any to be found in central Africa today.

Moses was a tyrant. He immediately took full control of our lives and ran them with an iron-fisted discipline my mother would have envied. He was implacable and would not tolerate any deviation from the standards of civilized society to which he was apparently accustomed. We endured him, much as I suspect he endured us, for one simple reason: comfort.

Under Moses' iron rule, Bill and I lived considerably better than any of our friends or acquaintances. Moses was a veritable Jeeves. All my friends stood in awe of him. His dinners were productions of gourmet delight and under his stern eye, the house boy and garden boy kept our home in immaculate condition. I lived in greater comfort and elegance than any I could ever have imagined and if there was a stiff price to pay, I willingly paid it.

The extent to which our lives had changed was brought home to me about three weeks after Moses took over our home. By this time I had already discovered that I was unwelcome in the kitchen, without his invitation. The kitchen was his kingdom – stay out! On this particular evening, I invited Moses into the lounge about 5 p.m. and innocently told him that tonight we would be doing our first entertaining and had invited two guests to come to dinner.

Moses responded by politely inquiring about my sanity. He explained that guests could not be invited without his approval and certainly not without at least a week's notice. He informed me that even if I had no position to maintain, he certainly did not intend to allow me to bring dishonour on our household and shame to him and his village.

I ate crow and begged him to produce a few sandwiches and I would take the blame. He said he would produce a miracle. He then asked for the sex, age and rank of both our guests. It now began to dawn on me that life with Moses was going to be no bowl of cherries. 'Why do you want to know?' I asked. Silly me, the answer was obvious. Seating arrangements for dinner and the order in which our guests would be served would be determined by strict rules of etiquette and courtesy. I apologized once more and provided the information. Moses advanced back into the kitchen and I retreated into my bedroom.

If this was African culture, then I was a barbarian. I hoped fervently that Moses was an exception. I also had enough foresight to call our friends and remind them that in our home we always dressed for dinner. Then I hunted for my one good suit and tried to make myself presentable. I also diffidently suggested to Bill that prudence would dictate he do the same. At 7 o'clock, our friends, newly washed and groomed, arrived for dinner and inquired as to whether I had gone mad or got married. 'Worse,' I replied. 'A new cook hired us.' They stared and I gave them both a stiff drink.

Precisely at 7:30 Moses entered the lounge, and announced that dinner was ready to be served and would we please adjourn to the dining room. We meekly followed his lead and after being seated according to his rules of protocol, were treated to a superb meal. Apparently, Moses had been to the local Indian store and charged what he fancied to our account.

By the third course, I had decided against my original idea of getting a second job. Might as well face the problem head on. Go for the jugular, so to speak, and rob a bank! Our friends remained quiet throughout the meal. Moses and the house boy attended with solicitous regard to their every want. I think they suspected we'd borrowed Moses from the Governor's mansion. I'd had that thought myself. It was a memorable evening and a fine introduction to my accidentally acquired new lifestyle.

All went well until the meal was ended. I then politely inquired if Moses would be good enough to serve coffee in the dining room. He gave me a drop-dead look and obediently served the coffee. Strange, I thought. Shortly thereafter, our guests departed and I asked Moses to step into the lounge, where I tried to praise him to the skies for his sterling performance. Moses brushed aside my praise and inquired as to how long I thought it would take before either of us could again be seen in polite society. In short he was not amused, and I cautiously probed further.

Me:	'What happened, Moses?'
Moses:	'The coffee, Bwana.'
Me:	'I enjoyed the coffee.'
Moses:	'Bwana, how could you shame me so?'
Me:	'What are you talking about, Moses?'
Moses:	'We served coffee in the dining room.'
Me:	'So?'
Moses:	'Coffee is *never* served in the dining room. Coffee is *always* served in the lounge.'
Me:	'So, why didn't you tell me?'
Moses:	(in horror) 'Bwana, in front of our guests! That would have been even worse.'
Me:	'Moses, I am going to try to do better.'
Moses:	'Please, Bwana.'

And better I did. Under Moses' tutelage, I acquired whatever semblance of refinement I possess. He took a small town boy and built a colonial gentleman. Of course, some of my friends disagree with this assessment. They say that he took a fundamentally nice man with problems and produced a raving maniac. Whatever the truth I am eternally grateful for the light he brought into my life when he showed me the joy of doing what is done.

Moses, I must confess, was probably something of an extremist, insofar as he followed his customs, not as rules or guidelines, but as an unwavering path through life. But, he certainly made our table famous and was in high demand for special events throughout Lusaka.

He was unique in my experience, and, to complicate our relationship even further, my feeble attempts to communicate with him were often frustrated by my inadequate command of the English language. Africans tended to speak English correctly and have trouble with idiomatic phrases and convoluted usage of the double negative. I often recall with pleasure, a conversation we had, early one evening, just before sundowners. It all started when I went into the kitchen looking for the garden boy, and was horrified to see my favourite family heirloom, my mother's teapot, lying shattered in the kitchen trash can. The attempted conversation went as follows:

Me:	'Moses, you didn't break my best teapot, did you?'
Moses:	'Yes, Bwana.'
Me:	'God, Moses, I wish you'd be more careful.'
Moses:	'I am careful, Bwana.'
Me:	'Like hell you are – look at my mother's teapot.'
Moses:	'I didn't break it.'
Me:	'You just said you did.'
Moses:	'No, I did not.'
Me:	'I asked you if you broke it and you said you did.'
Moses:	'No, Bwana, you asked me if I didn't break it and I said yes – yes, I didn't break it.'
Me:	After a long and painful silence, 'Moses, what are we having for dinner?'

So, you see, even when everyone tries their best, misunderstanding and confusion often reign supreme. To Moses, I was always the 'little Bwana,' and I always suspected that the 'little' referred to his opinion of my intellectual capacity.

But I certainly was not too dumb to know that life with Moses was infinitely better than life back at the government rest house. The Colonial Service was finally beginning to live up to its brochures: Bill and I now had all the blessings of married life – except a wife and children – as we entered the routine of the white colonial officer in central Africa.

Sundowners on the veranda soon became a high point of our

evenings, while meals were varied, formal, and always served in the dining room, where flowers adorned the table. In the mornings we were gently awakened with our ritual cup of tea and clothes ready to be worn that day were neatly laid out at the foot of the bed. All our shoes were kept spit polish clean and dirty clothes were washed three times a week. It was the 'life of Reilly' for a small town boy of humble origin and I began to feel both elegant and pampered, as I easily slid into the culture I had obviously been born to enjoy.

It was into this genteel atmosphere that Bill introduced his philosophical approach to the flu, when he came home early one evening with a big bottle of whiskey and a look of impending death. This was definitely not the Bill I had grown accustomed to, so I politely inquired as to whether he had developed a personal problem. My question seemed to cause him additional grief, yet he still took the time to reply, 'No, I have the flu,' before disappearing into the kitchen still nursing his whiskey. Full of curiosity, I followed.

Ignoring my presence, Bill quickly set to work, with all the grace of one of Macbeth's witches, to work his magic and produce his brew. He began by pouring a third of the bottle of whiskey into a large beer tankard. Next he added a similar amount of boiling water and sugar to taste. Finally, he topped his mug off with a little nutmeg and a squeeze or two of lemon juice, before pausing to admire his handiwork with a sigh of satisfaction. It was all very mysterious, especially since Bill remained wordless throughout the whole procedure, and even Moses was moved to silence by the sight of the professor at work in his laboratory.

At this point in the drama an incantation would certainly have been in order, but apparently Bill disagreed, for he now picked up the tankard and reverently bore its lethal brew to his room where, still clutching his salvation, he took to his bed. Sure that I was about to learn some great truth of Liverpudlian folk remedies, I eagerly followed Bill to his chamber and watched as he happily emptied the tankard. 'How does it work?' I asked. 'How does what work?' he responded. 'Your folk remedy, does it cure the flu?' I explained. 'No, of course not,' he crossly answered. 'Then, why did you make it and drink it?' I queried.

Bill looked at me as if I was a little dense, then condescended to answer. 'I made it and drank it because I like it – and anyway, its also by far the best way I know, to have fun being sick – which is why I usually have at least one glass each time I'm ill.' Nothing further needed to be said, and I quietly withdrew as he settled down for a good nights sleep.

Judging from the results, it must have worked, for by the next day Bill was much better and, in two days, he was fully recovered. But, even if Bill's brew had no therapeutic benefit, I still really admired his approach, since the world would obviously be a happier place if more of us could learn to enjoy being miserable. There was also the added benefit that his obviously original mind would in the future have further entertaining gems to display, and this was a thoroughly delightful prospect.

Now, as I have previously explained, I had remained with the Ministry of Finance, in its main headquarters, while Bill was on loan to Native Affairs. Of course neither of us had been consulted prior to these postings, which were made by our superiors, who, I believe, used a specially designed dartboard to guide our careers. However, the immediate practical effect was that we worked in different buildings and moved in different circles, thereby enabling each of us, through the other, to broaden his range of friends.

About a week after Bill recovered from the flu, he introduced me to Ken Bayman and Peter Van Eden, two fellow officers he had met at the Ministry of Native Affairs. Little did I then realize how soon these two new acquaintances, together with Ken's wife Olive, were to become really close friends of mine. Nor had I the slightest suspicion of the extent to which they would be involved in some of my wildest African escapades.

Ken Bayman was a small, plump, red-faced and very blonde young man, who in 1959 must have been about 35 years old. He was, you may recall, the previous owner of Bill's new car, and was teaching Bill to drive. His background was similar to mine, since he was born in Wigan, a town which is only about nine miles from Chorley, and it was this common heritage which forged the first link in our chain of friendship. It is always nice, in a foreign land, to meet someone from a town so close to home.

He had not come to Northern Rhodesia as an expatriate officer of the Colonial Service, but had followed a more circuitous route. Apparently, he had emigrated from England to South Africa with his parents while still a teenager, and over the years his family had migrated north through the Transvaal and the Rhodesias before somehow finishing up in Lusaka. Ken had subsequently applied for a job with the government, in the normal way a hometown boy joins the civil service. After being hired, he had been posted to the Ministry of Native Affairs as an accountant and that, of course, was where he met Bill.

I have dwelt at some length on the details of how Ken joined the civil service because, in the wisdom of the Colonial Office, this was an important point. Ken was a local officer. He had not been recruited and vetted in London, as I had been, and was not a true colonial civil servant. He was a local recruit and, as such, a second-class citizen. His conditions of service, especially his leave and pension rights, were inferior to mine. In some ways, he was almost treated as if he were black. It was all so foolishly proper, and it led to some friction within the service. It never led to any between Ken and me, for we had worse things to do.

Ken's wife, Olive, was a tall, slender, attractive young lady. When we met she must have been about 30 although, of course, she looked considerably younger. She was an Afrikaner by birth, her maiden name being Krause, and the 10 years of her marriage to Ken had produced four extremely blonde and very pretty little daughters.

The Baymans did not live in government housing, but had their own small farm on the outskirts of Lusaka. They had put down roots, and this was their home. Indeed, I believe that Olive was born in Lusaka, since both her parents and two older brothers had large farms in the bush just outside of town. To this day, I often wonder what happened to them in the years following independence, when so many of us climbed on the boat and left Northern Rhodesia to its future.

My third new acquaintance, Peter Van Eden, was everything I wanted to be and, strangely enough, I was everything he wanted to be. With such a mutual admiration society, we had to become firm friends, although I still believe my taste was better than his. Peter was lethal to women. You only had to mention his name in polite society and all the young ladies would swoon. He made Rudolph Valentino look like a coarse and vulgar lout.

At the time our paths first crossed Peter was about 20 years old, 6 feet 2 inches in height, slim, graceful and very elegant in the Michael York tradition. His smile opened bedroom doors, and his eyes had the kind of attentive innocence of a docile cocker spaniel. He was the ultimate lethal weapon and, by rights, should have been banned as a potential menace to the public good.

Consequently, I admired him immensely, for it was a joy to watch him work the ladies. But Peter was more than a pretty face, and one day as we sat drinking our sundowners, he told me how glad he had been to find in me such a delightful breadth of vision into the unacceptable. On reflection, I think he meant that with my ideas and his delivery, we could probably destroy the colony. Certainly, I know how hard we tried.

Peter was a hybrid South African. His mother was English and his father was Afrikaans. However, by upbringing and culture he was more English than Afrikaans. Like most people raised in a bilingual household, he was fluent in both languages and seemed to have combined them together in one gigantic vocabulary. Therefore, even though he spoke mainly in English, his sentences often included a phrase or two in Afrikaans.

But Peter's linguistic abilities were not his most useful attribute, for he was the best, and most cautious, drunk driver I ever saw. Thus, at parties, we always made it a rule that he drove us home. Sometimes we had to help him to the car and position him behind the wheel, yet he never failed us, and once in motion, Peter was a model of decorum. He would stare woodenly through the windshield and never exceeded 15 miles per hour. At all crossroads, he came to a halt and rigorously inspected the intersecting highway. Quite often this examination would take five or more minutes, since he would only venture further if the other road was deserted.

Though it could take hours to get home we always felt safe, and no one ever accused Peter of reckless driving. Drunk, he drove like a neurotic 90-year-old maiden aunt. Sober, he drove like Fangio having a bad day.

He had much in common with Olive Bayman, because he too was a native of Lusaka. His parents and sister lived on a farm just outside of town and, before he came to stay with me, that was where he had been living. Peter, like Ken, had joined the civil service as a local officer and also had second-class citizen status, but, unlike Ken, he was an African in the truest sense. His whole family for many generations past had been born, had lived, and had died in Africa. Peter knew only South Africa and the Rhodesias. He had never visited Europe and had no wish to go there. His roots were not in the old country; he was a true white African. I wonder where he is today?

5. Take Me Out To The Ball Game

In early July of 1959, about two months after Bill and I set up house together, we had our first misadventure. It began innocently enough when Bill suggested we take a trip in the large American Chevrolet he had just bought from our friend Ken Bayman. Perhaps I had a premonition of things to come, because I immediately told Bill to avoid putting too much faith in his new set of wheels, since nothing sound had ever come out of Wigan. Bill ignored me, and promised to make our first excursion outside of Lusaka a moving experience.

Cautiously, I asked him if he knew where he wanted to go, and Bill responded by triumphantly announcing that he had purchased four tickets to a soccer match in Ndola, in the very near future. 'Where is Ndola?' I asked. 'Oh somewhere to the north,' Bill confidently answered. 'Who is playing?' I continued. 'Bolton Wanderers,' he smugly replied, as he gave me the last answer I had expected to hear. Apparently Bolton, my favourite team, was making an off-season goodwill tour of Southern Africa this very month. Joy of joys, they were due to play a Northern Rhodesian international team in Ndola next weekend and Bill had bought tickets.

Deeply touched, I unwisely agreed to go. Yet how could I have said no? Bolton is only 10 miles from Chorley and Dad and I had stood on the terraces of Burnden Park for many a year. What a thrill it would be to see my local team, and Nat Lofthouse, my childhood idol, playing a soccer match in darkest Africa!

Later that evening, while dinner was being served, I suddenly remembered Bill's reference to having bought four tickets to the game. 'Who are the extra two tickets for?' I curiously asked. 'Ken Bayman, because he sold me the car and Moses, because he's our cook,' Bill replied, as if it should have been obvious. 'That's nice,' I said, making a mental note to avoid logic since it was evidently not one of my strong points.

After dinner, we got out a map of Northern Rhodesia and quickly determined a route to Ndola, which, according to our calculations, lay some 250 miles due north of Lusaka. It also seemed as if the road was mostly paved with very few miles of dirt. It looked like a five-hour drive each way and an exciting introduction to the African veldt. We agreed to leave on Saturday morning at 6, which ought to get us to Ndola by 11, in plenty of time to find the stadium before the game's 2 p.m. kickoff. Assuming all went well, we intended to start back about 6 that evening and try to be home by 11. A long day but not unreasonable, and I would get to see Nat Lofthouse and all my other heroes who played for Bolton. Boy, I could hardly wait till Saturday and, as I conquered my fears, I felt sure it was going to be a wonderful experience.

A few days later, at the crack of dawn, we four musketeers loaded ourselves into Bill's new old car and bravely headed north. For the first three hours, it was like a dream come true. Bill drove and I sat beside him. We relished our first trip outside of Lusaka and excitedly drew each other's attention to all the strange new sights that unfolded around us. It was a beautiful winter day and the car was running smoothly and quietly, God was in Heaven and all was well on Earth.

I believe we first realized the possibility of some slight inconvenience when the car threw a rod and its engine disintegrated. Philosophically, I have always been amazed at the speed with which a wonderfully efficient and vitally useful piece of machinery can become a useless pile of junk. Because that is what we had when Bill steered his exploding bomb to the side of the road and brought it to a halt.

One look at the tangled wreckage under the hood was all it took to understand the full extent of our problem. Undoubtedly this engine would take days to rebuild, perhaps even weeks, if you included ordering all the spare parts we definitely needed. I then reminded Bill about the problems associated with Wigan and he, quite predictably, told me to drop dead.

It's truly amazing how the opportunity we now had, to take a closer and more prolonged look at the African bush, failed to fire our enthusiasm. We somehow didn't wish to commence our first hiking safari. So instead we held a quick council of war and produced our plan of attack. First, we would all try to hitchhike the remaining 80 miles to Ndola, and, if lucky, get there in time to see the soccer match. Then, we must all hitchhike back to Lusaka, hopefully, without too much inconvenience.

Next week Bill, accompanied by Ken (who sold him this lemon) intended to borrow a truck and drive back to our rest stop to retrieve the wreckage. If they were lucky and scavengers, animal or human, had not stripped the car, they could then tow it back to Lusaka. Once there, Ken, who was very embarrassed by the turn of events, had volunteered to rebuild the engine with help from Bill.

The plan was sound and it worked faultlessly, depending on one's perspective. Besides, it was probably the only thing to do, especially if we wanted to make any effort to see the game. For you must remember that wrecker service, police patrols and fellow travelers are, on African roads, conspicuous by their absence.

To ensure fair play we ceremoniously drew lots, to see who would take the first ride we managed to get. I won, Bill drew the second ride, Ken, the third and poor Moses, the fourth. Fortunately, we did have some reasonable hopes of thumbing a lift, since we were on one of Northern Rhodesia's main highways and there had to be other soccer fans heading for the big game. Sure enough, within half an hour, a small two-seater sports car came over the horizon to our rear and slowed to a halt when its sole occupant saw our disconsolate group.

I rapidly explained our predicament and plan, before asking the driver if he could kindly give me a ride towards Ndola and the soccer match. He smiled rather strangely and said, 'My pleasure, I'm going to Ndola, hop in.' Jubilantly, I jumped in the passenger's seat and after telling my erstwhile companions, 'Have a nice day,' I left them to their luck.

My good Samaritan, who was obviously English, merely nodded when I expressed my gratitude for the ride. He appeared to be about 50 years old, and judging from his car, he was obviously well heeled. I also got the feeling, from his comportment, that he was probably well placed. Nothing much was said until we had driven a few more miles, and then he started the following, somewhat amazing, conversation:

Good Samaritan:	'Rather a shame, what happened to your friend's car.'
Me:	'Yes, it was, rather. I do so hope I can make it to the stadium in time for the match.'
Good Samaritan:	'Oh, you should have no problem.'
Me:	'I'm not sure. How close to the stadium can you take me?'
Good Samaritan:	'All the way.'
Me:	'I don't want to inconvenience you, but, if you're also going to the game, that would be great.'
Good Samaritan:	'Well, actually I am.' A long pause and then he added, 'You see, I'm one of the officials. I'm one of the linesmen.'
Me:	(In astonishment) 'You're what?'
Good Samaritan:	'A linesman.' Another long pause and then he said, 'What kind of a ticket do you have?'
Me:	'One of the cheaper seats, I'm afraid.'
Good Samaritan:	'Would you like to sit in the main grandstand?'
Me:	'Who wouldn't?'
Good Samaritan:	'Good, I'll give you a ticket. You see, they gave me several complimentary ones.'

| Me: | (Beginning to doubt my ears) 'That would be nice, thank you.' |

He then lapsed into silence and nothing more was said for about another hour as I waited to wake up from the ridiculous dream I was obviously having. Finally he resumed our conversation:

Good Samaritan:	'How are you going to get back to Lusaka?'
Me:	'I'll try and thumb a ride in the parking lot after the game. There's got to be some people going to Lusaka.'
Good Samaritan:	'I'm willing to take you, but there's one problem with that idea.'
Me:	'What's that?'
Good Samaritan:	'I'm not going home right after the match. I have to attend the post-game banquet and dance.'
Me:	'I don't mind waiting in your car. You're doing so much already.'
Saint:	'Oh goodness gracious no, I'll give you a ticket to the banquet.'
Me:	'That would be nice.' (A poor response, the best I could manage until the shock wore off.)
Saint:	'I'm afraid the ticket won't be for one of the better tables.'
Me:	'I'll manage.'
Saint:	'Well, that's settled. Let's hope Northern Rhodesia wins.'
Me:	'This will be the first game I ever went to, where I won't criticize the officials.'
Saint:	'Unfortunately, you'll probably be the only one who doesn't.'

We rode the rest of the way to Ndola in silence and, try as I might, I never woke up. But maybe the dream was real, because when we got to the ball park my friend was true to his word, and nonchalantly handed me a ticket to a seat in the main grandstand. He also suggested we meet at his car one hour after the match and, once I agreed, he hurried away. Dazed, I stood and watched as he headed for the player's entrance and then, made my way into the stadium.

It felt a little strange sitting in the best seats, and I got some puzzled glances for continually singing the praises of our excellent officials. However, it was a very good game, and the English profes sionals had to pull out all the stops in order to beat the colonial amateurs.

Northern Rhodesia led at half time, and narrowly lost, 4-3. George Sharp, a white striker from Lusaka and a lieutenant in the local police force, was the star of the match and scored all three of Northern Rhodesia's goals. It was a marvelous afternoon and I was so glad I decided to come on this trip.

Yet the best was still to be, for when we met in the stadium parking lot, an hour after the game had ended, my sainted linesman casually handed me an engraved invitation to the post-game banquet. I suppose my embarrassment must have shown, because the moment I began to stammer my thanks, he quietly said, 'Get in the car, we need to hurry, we don't want to be late.'

We weren't. It was wonderful, and the banquet was pure delight. Not only did I get an excellent free meal and all the champagne I could drink, but I also got to meet all my boyhood heroes. I even had a chance to chat with King Nat Lofthouse. It was better than I ever would have imagined and, to put it mildly, totally unexpected, unplanned and undeserved. Time flew as I ate, drank and talked soccer for about five hours, until my friend decided it was time to go home. So, sometime shortly before midnight, we both climbed into his car and he started the long drive back to Lusaka.

I was exhausted from my exhilarating day and consequently I slept all the way home. Therefore, I didn't have a chance to see if Bill's ruin still stood in the bush. It made no difference; I couldn't have done anything just by seeing it and, anyway, in the dark it probably would have been difficult to find. Whatever, I slept the sleep of the just and woke with the dawn as we neared the outskirts of my new hometown.

A gentleman to the end, this good Samaritan followed my directions to our house and kindly deposited me on my front doorstep, just after sunrise that Sunday morning. Again I tried to express my thanks, but he said they were not necessary. He also said he was sorry Northern Rhodesia had lost, and I reminded him they'd come close. Smiling, he agreed, and politely said good morning before driving away. Suddenly I felt humbled to have been in the presence of such kindness and determined to do better in the future. Then, tired but happy and content, I turned and entered our deserted house.

I had not expected to be the first one home since by going to the banquet I had stayed in Ndola far longer than we had planned. Still, I was sure they would all be along soon, so I fixed and ate a leisurely breakfast and settled down to wait for my friends' return. It was a long wait, and by the time I started to lock up to go to bed that night, I began to have my first twinges of concern.

The following morning I almost didn't make it to work on time, when Moses forgot to wake me up. Now to be fair, he may not have forgotten, since there was no way to be sure, because Moses was still out in the bush. So, it seemed, were Bill and Ken, who both appeared to be taking a rural vacation. I therefore was forced to fix my own breakfast and hitchhike to work, which was very inconvenient.

Being by nature a shrinking violet I tried to postpone the inevitable as long as possible. But, when Monday noon arrived without either Bill or Ken answering any of my frequent calls to Native Affairs, I was forced to telephone their supervisors and politely inform them that two of their officers may have gone native. They were not amused and said they hoped the damn fools would come home soon. I said I shared their hope and kept on waiting.

By Monday evening, both Ken's wife, Olive, and Moses' wife were getting hysterical, and beginning to drive me crazy. They were also getting close to the logical decision that it was all my fault. I wished someone else would come home. All was surely forgiven and the prodigals would be welcomed back. At last, late Tuesday evening, Bill staggered in, glared at me and slammed his bedroom door as he went wordlessly to bed. Yet at least he was home.

On Wednesday things continued to improve when Olive called to tell me her husband had returned to the fold, but refused to come out of the toilet. Two down, one to go. Where was Moses? Apparently, he must have decided to emigrate and renounce his Northern Rhodesian heritage because he remained conspicuous by his absence.

Unfortunately our misadventure was not yet complete, since Bill, with Ken's help, still needed to retrieve Bill's car from the place it was decorating in the African bush. The day after Ken's return, they borrowed a truck, and, taking a day's leave, drove back towards Ndola to rescue Bill's albatross. They also promised to keep a sharp lookout for the missing Moses and, if possible, persuade him to come back with them.

This time, things went much better. I waved them goodbye in Lusaka at about 6 on Thursday morning and by 5 that afternoon, they were back home with Bill's car in tow. However, there had been no sign of Moses, which was becoming something of a mystery. Why was he so long overdue? Still they did have some good news, for Bill's car had not been stripped, and all it needed was a new engine. Now, if only Moses would return, we could all relax.

At long last, some 10 days after our ill-fated trip began, Moses limped back home and announced he would no longer be amenable to suggestions of travel to distant parts. He told us quite forcefully he had decided to become a recluse, and live out the rest of his life in our kitchen. Gradually, our lives returned to normal and Bill and Ken rebuilt the Chevrolet engine. I'm glad to say the car gave Bill no further trouble but he never suggested another extended trip. Once bitten, twice shy appeared to be the prevailing attitude.

Despite my gentle probing, I was unable to get a complete explanation of where everyone had been and why it took them so long to get home after our breakdown. In Bill and Ken's case, it seems as if they just didn't have much luck hitching rides on the sparsely traveled African roads. When I asked them if they got to the game in time, they said something extremely crude about my parents, which I interpreted to mean that they had not seen any of the soccer match. In a spasm of sensitivity I admitted only that I had seen the whole game, and did not mention the post-game banquet I had been forced to endure. Silence, in this case, was obviously both wise and golden.

Regrettably, Moses' story was infinitely sad and illustrated some of the worst features of life in central Africa in the 1960s. For even though he endlessly tried, Moses never found anyone willing to give him a ride. He had therefore to walk the whole 170 miles back to Lusaka, from the place where Bill's car broke down. It took him a week and a half to walk that distance, with very little food to eat or water to drink. At night, he was forced to sleep in the bush and, one night, was almost attacked by lions. All in all, a dreadful trip which Moses had no wish to repeat.

The reason he got no help was simple – he was a black African. The whites would not help him because he was black. The local blacks would not help him because he was not from their village or tribe and did not speak their language. He was an outcast in his own land. He had left his tribal area and everyone, black and white, regarded him with intense suspicion. I now felt very guilty that we had not been aware of this problem. My only defense was ignorance. In those early months in Africa, I had not learned the subtle nuances of how a fragmented society worked. Well, now I was wiser and I didn't like what I had learned.

I don't know why Bill and Ken failed to spot Moses when they went to get Bill's car. Clearly Moses wouldn't walk all day, so perhaps he had been resting in the shade of a roadside tree as they passed him by, or perhaps they just didn't recognize him. Certainly, on the day he arrived home, he didn't look much like our Moses, but seemed to have more in common with a refugee from a Tarzan movie. Anyway, it was good to have him back, and in charge of our home.

6. The Deans

During the next couple of months, Bill and I restricted our adventures to the drive to and from the office, as we became sedate suburban commuters who traveled together in their own small African car pool. Our trips were usually quite uneventful, until early one morning on the way to work we passed a lone European tramping along the highway and, remembering our own months on foot, we stopped to offer him a ride.

He was a tall, bearded, skinny, disheveled, bespectacled Englishman from London. His name was Dixie Dean, and he was destined to become one of my closest friends. Dixie was new to Northern Rhodesia and, as we had surmised, was in his pre-driving phase. He was not a colonial officer, but had been recruited by the local radio station as one of their sound engineers, and was married to a Southern Rhodesian girl from Bulawayo whom he had met in London. Her name was Sally and apparently she had wanted to go home, but so far Lusaka was the closest they could manage.

However, when I first met Dixie, he was not thinking of leaving town, since Sally was six months pregnant and in due course gave birth to a beautiful baby daughter. This child later became my one and only godchild, when, some six months after she was born, the Deans invited me to the baby's christening and asked me to be their daughter's godfather. It was an honour I greatly appreciated, as they were a family I cared for deeply.

Yet even by English standards, the Deans were truly eccentric, and if Dixie was out in left field, then Sally was a full five miles removed from the stadium. They were so weird that I was, by comparison, quite normal, and they also seemed to relish some of the impossible situations in which we constantly managed to become embroiled.

But if variety is the spice of life, then certainly the Deans were a hot tamale, as they proved one winter's evening when I dropped by their home, and found them both on their knees in the backyard, carefully examining the woodpile. Not wishing to intrude, I waited a few moments before asking politely what on earth they were doing and, with equal politeness, Dixie told me they were looking for insects. I then queried them as to whether they had gone native, and Sally replied by pointing out how cold the evening had become. At this point, knowing my friends well, I kept my peace and waited for a fuller explanation of their nocturnal activities.

Nothing was said for the next 10 minutes until Dixie broke the silence to explain that Sally wanted to light a fire in the lounge fireplace and, obviously, they couldn't burn logs which were covered with insects. Sally then amplified Dixie's reply by delivering a brief lecture on the insensitivity of those who would roast an innocent insect, just to keep warm, and I gave a noncommittal response.

Surely it is friends like these who make life worth living, and for about an hour I stood in the cool moonlight of their small backyard, watching in fascination as they deloused a small pile of logs. When my feet grew chilled, I bid them a pleasant good evening and went home to roast some insects. I never did find out whether or not they ever lit their fire but I determined to buy them a small electric heater for Christmas.

It was impossible not to be impressed by the schemes the Deans came up with. One day, about a year after we met, Dixie told me that he and his wife were going to become the first people ever to canoe the Zambezi River from start to finish. When I pointed out that the Victoria Falls would prove to be an interesting diversion, he caustically explained their intention to portage past certain problem areas. I then asked him who would inherit my godchild, and he told me they were going to leave her with Sally's mother in Bulawayo.

The Deans were careful planners. They even knew where the source of the Zambezi River was supposed to be located. Apparently, it was in a remote corner of the northwestern province of Northern Rhodesia, some 300 miles from Lusaka and about 40 miles from Mwinilunga, the nearest government village. Now this was about as isolated as you can get in central Africa, and was right in the middle of a narrow finger of Northern Rhodesia which juts up between the Belgian Congo to the east and Portuguese Angola to the west.

To make matters worse, the Zambezi entered Angola some 20 miles from its source and flowed through that country for 150 miles before coming back, in a loop, into Northern Rhodesia. No wonder they'd be the first – they'd probably be the last. This was an extremely dangerous expedition they were about to undertake and certainly not one I would recommend.

Undeterred by my doomsday forecasts, they delivered their daughter to Bulawayo and, probably as an afterthought, bought a canoe. Dixie then took a leave of absence from the radio station and bright and early one morning, they tied the canoe to the top of their car and left Lusaka for Mwinilunga. It was agreed that after about two months, I would get a friend to drive me to Mwinilunga to retrieve their car, which would be left in the District Commissioner's care. Boy, was I looking forward to that trip, over some of the worst dirt roads in Africa. But the Deans would have done as much, or more, for me, so I tried not to think about my coming vacation.

Meanwhile, back on the ranch, two more weeks passed without so much as a 'wish you were here postcard,' but of course this was no cause for concern, since postcards were not generally available where they had gone. In addition, nobody, including the Deans, had any idea how long this trip would take. Perhaps, as little as two months, then again, perhaps 10 years. Who knew?

Regrettably, things did not go entirely as the Deans had planned, and early in the third week of their expedition, they were back in Lusaka, thinner, wiser and sans one canoe. A more mature Dixie now allowed as to know how it was a jungle out there. After much prodding, he gave me a brief summary of their voyage of exploration, which evidently went from bad to worse as the trip progressed.

Indeed, their troubles seemed to begin at about the same time as they did, since they had a great deal of difficulty finding the source of the Zambezi and, once there, sadly discovered that the river's head-waters were too shallow to float a canoe. Consequently, they were obliged to spend two arduous days walking their craft downriver, while all the mosquitoes in central Africa had a field day.

In due course they reached deeper water, where they had a couple of day's restful canoeing past sleeping crocodiles and frolicking hippos. Unfortunately, this tranquility did not continue, for on the fourth morning, a playful hippo stomped their canoe and brought the expedition to a conclusion almost before it started. They now had the time to enjoy a few days leisurely stroll through the delightful countryside of the northwestern province, before returning, lean and mean, to the metropolis of Mwinilunga. Thankfully, they saved me the chore of fetching their car by using it themselves to get home to Lusaka.

I was, of course, relieved to see them alive, a possibility I had not really considered. Swallowing his pride, Dixie returned to the radio station after only a three-week leave of absence. The following weekend they drove to Bulawayo to retrieve my goddaughter and, as soon as they got back, began to plan their next madcap scheme. What wonderfully exciting friends they were and how glad I am that I got to share in some of their more mundane activities.

For the next two years, I enjoyed the Deans' approach to life until they ignored my pleas and returned to England by the overland route. Naturally, they prepared for this adventure in their own inimitable style, by buying an old Land Rover from Lusaka Airport. This vehicle had belonged to the airport fire marshal until it had become too decrepit for further use. It was then sold to the Deans for about $500, being absolutely ideal for a cross-Sahara jaunt.

Dixie spent a couple of months overhauling the Land Rover's mechanical parts and converting its body into a fairly primitive imitation of a pickup truck, with a camper shell. Finally, he announced himself satisfied and, bright and early one morning, he, Sally and my godchild drove out of my life and into my memories. I never heard from them again, so I don't know what happened. I hope they made it safely to England. I trust that, in this case, no news was good news, but it would have been nice to have received a postcard from London.

The trip they took was not completely unknown during the years I lived in Africa. Civil wars had not yet closed Ethiopia and the Sudan to the occasional tourist. Libya was still a sleepy Arab kingdom, while most of Africa remained under colonial domination, and, paradoxically, was comparatively safe to travel. Their projected route, for the first few weeks of their African odyssey, lay mainly to the north, through Tanganyika, Kenya, Ethiopia, Sudan and Egypt. They then intended to turn west and mosey through Libya, Algeria and Morocco, to the Mediterranean port of Tangier. A brief ferry ride across the Strait of Gibraltar would land them in Europe, in the British colony of Gibraltar. From there, it was a piece of cake through Spain and France to a channel port and its ferry to England and home.

I'm not sure exactly how far that is, particularly on Africa's bone-jarring dirt roads, where one definitely doesn't drive as the crow flies. But it has to be several thousand miles. Quite a trip, for a young unarmed English couple and a two-year-old daughter, especially when you consider the rickety old Land Rover on which they relied. Yet that was the Deans, and I'm glad I had the privilege of experiencing their point of view for a couple of enjoyable years.

7. Where On Earth Is Petauke?

Bill and I had met the Deans about halfway through our tenure in Bill Taylor's home and nothing much happened during the next three months until, a month before our tenancy expired, Moses resigned and poor Bill was posted to a backwater of the empire. In neither case was the departure totally unexpected, but, taken together, they sure rang the curtain down on a phase of my life.

This parting of the ways began one morning at breakfast, when Moses either gave up in disgust or responded to a higher calling. Whatever his reason was, he spoilt our eggs and bacon by giving one month's notice of his intention to resign as Lord of our kitchen. He said that he had decided to accept a call to become the presiding deacon at his local Baptist church, which, since he was very active in religious circles, seemed like a wonderful opportunity. Accordingly, we wished him well, and it was agreed he should leave our service in one month's time, which fortunately would coincide with the end of our stay in Bill Taylor's house.

The very same afternoon, when Bill picked me up after work, he gloomily announced that the worst had happened and he had been posted to the bush. Although I was disappointed I was not surprised, because this was the norm for anyone who worked in Native Affairs. The bush was where most of the natives had their affairs and, in order to supervise them, one had to adjourn to the bush. Thus, Bill had been given four weeks' notice to settle his debts and buy insect repellent, after which he would leave Lusaka to become the district accountant in the government village of Petauke in the eastern province.

Now, rumour had it that Petauke had never previously been visited by a white man, and was permanently off limits to all white women. Nevertheless, such were the exigencies of colonial service and, with heavy hearts, we arranged Bill's going-away party. Still, it could have been worse: it could have been me, and I thanked God it wasn't, not yet, for the Sword of Damocles hung above all our heads.

I hope our party was a success, but to me it was sad, more like a wake really, since in the following week I was due to lose Bill, Moses and my home. However, we servants of the Queen are made of stern stuff. Five days later, shortly after Bill Taylor reclaimed the keys to his castle, Bill cheerfully said goodbye to Moses, me and the house, as he made ready to explore the future. Sadly I watched him climb into his Chevrolet and start its engine. He gave me a cheery wave, to which I responded by wishing him good luck as I stood with Moses on our stoop for the last time and, moments later, we watched him drive away from the big city's distractions, towards the tranquil life of a country squire.

Finally, once Bill's car had disappeared down the street, I turned, shook Moses' hand and, after wishing him all the best, got into the car of a friend who was kindly taking me back to the government rest house where I, of course, had been forced to return.

At the time, I confidently expected that Bill and I would meet again but we never did. Our short acquaintance was at an end and from now on, our lives took different paths. Yet, from time to time, I did hear a little of Bill through the colonial grapevine. To my great surprise, I learned that there was a white woman in Petauke who was, apparently, the head nurse in a local mission hospital. According to my rumours, she was considerably older than Bill, but undeterred, he had pursued her and, within a year of his leaving Lusaka, he had himself a wife. This merely confirmed my suspicions that the African bush is a dangerous place to live, and I resolved to avoid it as long as I possibly could.

I now need to return to the beloved Colonial Regulations, to more fully explain how, and when, Bill Curphy left Northern Rhodesia. These regulations required all officers to serve a three-year probationary period before becoming permanent and pensionable. The end of this first tour of duty was therefore a watershed, whereby both the service and the officer could carefully weigh their options. Life in central Africa was never easy, and lacked most big-city amenities, and thus a considerable number of officers chose to leave Northern Rhodesia once they had completed their first three-year tour.

Apparently, that was the path Bill followed. After two years in Petauke, he resigned from the service and took his wife home to Liverpool. In retrospect I don't think Bill ever really fell in love with Africa, but then again maybe he just had itchy feet and needed a new adventure. Whatever his reason, I felt a twinge of regret when I saw in the Colonial Gazette that he had left the colony. Now I knew our paths would cross no more and, sure enough, they never did.

And so my first set of adventures in Northern Rhodesia drew to a close. Moses was spreading the faith, Bill was in Petauke and I was back in the Government Rest House, where, as long as I didn't have a car, I was destined to remain. But it had been lots of fun and I had made many new friends with whom I would share many future adventures. I had much to be grateful for, including the fact that I had finally saved $1,000 and intended to get me some wheels.

Chapter 3

Games People Play

1. My *Alma Mater*

I wish I could say that I returned to the government rest house in Lusaka with boundless enthusiasm, but then again, if wishes were wings pigs would fly, and I did enjoy renewing acquaintances with some of the permanent residents who had become my friends.

It also felt a little like *déjà vu* when I first entered the dining room, after an absence of almost eight months, and saw once again the eager young faces of all the raw recruits to Her Majesty's service. How innocent they all looked, and how difficult it was to admit to having been one of these solemn white faces just a few short months ago. Now I was deeply tanned and walked with the confidence of the great white hunter.

As I surveyed the familiar scene I realized that this, my *alma mater*, was a rite of passage which must be endured by all newly arrived colonial servants in the capital of Northern Rhodesia. This was where everyone had their first home and got their first look at Tarzan's Africa. And yet, in all fairness I have to confess to finding my return quite delightful, especially since I had been in Africa for almost a year, and could lord it over all the tenderfoots from England. I must have been insufferable as I shared my vast collection of African lore, but I enjoyed myself so much that dinner in the rest house rapidly became the highlight of my day, while I continued to hoard my pennies. However, the end was in sight; I had begun to look for a vehicle to fulfill my dreams.

2. P 371

What words can I use? How can I best convey my feelings on the day I bought my first car? Perhaps it is best not even to try to describe the indescribable and so I will merely repeat one of Jackie Gleason's most famous lines – 'How sweet it is.' I had never expected to own a car, and had been tramping around Northern Rhodesia far longer than I, or my aching feet, cared to remember.

When I finally got my wheels it was a truly momentous occasion, which took place, co-incidentally, almost a year to the day from when I first arrived in Northern Rhodesia. This awesome Christmas present cost 525 pounds, a considerable sum of money and was purchased from Bobby Strachan, a Scottish friend of mine.

My vision of loveliness was a six-month-old, sky-blue 1958 English Ford Consol. It was love at first sight. Earth did not have anything more fair to show and I thoroughly enjoyed standing in the rest house's parking lot while I gazed adoringly upon my salvation. For, of course, since I didn't know how to drive, I still was bound to *terra firma*. But I was making progress.

Over the next several weeks, Bobby Strachan taught me to drive. I was a very good student, a very careful and attentive listener to all his instructions and, in particular, I well remember the first instruction he gave me on the first day I drove. Bobby said 'I advise you to drive this car as if you will be paying for all repairs.' Slightly puzzled, I replied, 'But I will.' Bobby smiled and said, 'Exactly – now start the engine and be careful.' The penny dropped and has kept on dropping. That first piece of motoring advice has always been my driving creed. I have always treated a car as if it was a fairly delicate and expensive lethal weapon. Well, almost always. And I try to drive like Scrooge and keep my money out of the repairman's pockets.

At long last, one glorious morning, I reached sexual maturity, for I passed my driving examination and became a man. Now I could drive alone – a wonderful feeling of control and power. I could even go to work in dignity and style. Perhaps I could even find a girlfriend. But at least I could go to a movie. The world was my oyster, I was free to roam. I was so excited I almost cleaned my car.

Maybe my first car meant more to me than it normally would, because I was 24 years old before I got it and learned to drive. Maybe it was such a big event because I came from a society where none of my family or friends had ever owned a car. Whatever the reason, I never forgot my first set of wheels. Nor, strangely enough, have I forgotten my first license plate number, P 371, which still remains clear in my mind.

My faithful chariot was also the only car I ever owned in Africa and I loved it through a wide variety of good times and bad until the time came for me to leave. Yet I still can recall, on the day I left the country, how sad I was when I handed the keys over to the African police lieutenant who bought it. I suspect his feelings and background were similar to what mine had been seven years before. I even remember that he, like me, was unable to drive and had wisely brought along a friend, who drove the car away. Hopefully, he had more luck with wrecks than I did, but most of all, I hope the car served him as well as it served me.

I suppose, since I just alluded to misfortune, that this is as good a place as any to explain how I nearly broke my insurance agent's heart with an incredible run of bad luck. It all started a year or so after I got the car and lasted about four months. For during this period my car and I experienced more adversity than any God-fearing African should ever be forced to endure.

Quite naturally, like all good stories, this one begins when I fell in love. Her name was Wendy and I met her in Lusaka some six months after I bought my car. She was a pretty girl and, when I first saw her, she was walking down the street with Peter Van Eden. It was, as with the car, love at first sight. But that is another story for a later chapter.

She was, at the time we first met, 19 years old, with long dark hair, a wide smile and a good figure. She was intelligent, popular and good fun, and I was smitten. By birth she was a Southern Rhodesian, and had grown up in Livingstone, Northern Rhodesia, where her parents still lived, while Wendy, who now worked for the Federal I.R.S., had recently been transferred to Lusaka.

Now perhaps I'm a nice guy or perhaps I'm stupid, but, one weekend about three months after we started dating, I lent her my precious car so she could drive to Livingstone to visit her parents. In retrospect, it was not one of my better ideas, since Livingstone is almost 300 miles from Lusaka, mostly over very bad dirt roads. Although Wendy was an experienced driver, she had never owned a car, so probably it was a chance I should not have taken. Still, I did it, and she almost reached the outskirts of her hometown before she rolled my car, three times.

Wendy escaped with multiple bruises but my beloved car was in serious need of extended traction. To this end, it was towed the remaining 10 miles into Livingstone and then ignominiously shipped back to Lusaka on a flatbed rail car, while a chastened Wendy came back by passenger train. Manfully, I managed to restrain my tears when my girlfriend returned to the fold, but I broke down and wept like a baby when my car came home.

It must not have been as bad as I feared, because the insurance company opted to rebuild it rather than bury it. This meant that I returned to my pedestrian lifestyle for the six weeks it took Lusaka's only body shop to work a minor miracle.

Wendy, to her credit, was very considerate. Some evenings she even walked over to my house for dinner and, some evenings, I would return the compliment by walking the two miles to her apartment. It was all good, clean fun but not exactly what I had intended when I bought a car.

Eventually, the great day came when the Italian body shop had promised the resurrection would be complete. Accordingly, shortly before noon on that fateful day, Bobby Strachan kindly drove me the three miles from our office to the downtown repair shop, and I nervously went to look at my car. It was a miracle, it was beautiful, perhaps even more so than Wendy. I was so happy I almost kissed the owner and his two sons before leaving to triumphantly drive the few miles back to work.

Like Wendy, I almost made it. I managed a good two miles before my boss's car came out of a side street and rammed me amidships, with a seemingly complete disregard for the rules of the road. For the second time, dignity escaped me as I wept tears of bitter grief, while my boss was relieved to see I was uninjured and alluded to the fact that I must have been in his blind spot, which was why he never saw me before he attacked.

Thankfully (strange word), I had less to bewail this time, because once we got my car out of the roadside ditch, it seemed to be, by my standards, only slightly the worse for wear and by 1:30, it had been towed back to my Italian friend's body shop. I went into his office and politely asked if he would like to repair my car. This question seemed to puzzle him and he told me I must be confused, since all the repairs needed on my car had already been done. I then had to explain that I was talking about new repairs while he was talking about old repairs. Yet still he didn't believe me, until we went outside and studied the evidence. Then, beginning to believe, he quietly turned to me and said, 'I giva you some advice, you sella this car'.

Naturally, I was not going to do anything so foolish, so he reluctantly agreed to devote another two weeks to another minor miracle. Meanwhile, I tried to explain to Wendy why we never went anywhere, and she inelegantly mentioned the possibility of my having to choose between her and that monster of a car. I looked hurt and reminded her of my complete innocence in this tale of woe. She looked hurt and apologized. Now we both looked hurt.

Again, in due course, the big day came and I got my car back. But, prudent to a fault, I returned to my office by a secret route and managed to get there with my car still in mint condition. However, fate was wiser than I, for one week later, as I read the evening newspaper in my lounge, I heard the familiar sound of rending metal, coming from my driveway. Not wishing to investigate, I read on, until a downcast Dixie, who had recently bought an old VW Beetle, entered the house to tell me his brakes just failed and he had used my car as an emergency anchor. I cried. Then it was back to the local body shop for me.

This time, I was greeted like an old friend who has stayed away too long. After all it had been a week. One of the sons told me their father was thinking of expanding his business and bringing in more relatives from the old country. Smugly, I replied that I was doing my best and they agreed to give their Number One customer a high priority. Evidently, I was on a descending scale, for the repairs were quite minor, and within a week I had my curse back on the road.

Ever the optimist, I now decided to take Wendy to a movie and, the very next evening, full of high spirits, we drove unscathed from her apartment to the theatre. Hardly able to believe our good fortune, we thoroughly enjoyed a bad movie and, when it ended, wandered arm in arm into the theatre's parking lot, only to be greeted by the empty space where my car had been parked, before someone stole it. We then spent a delightful hour with the British South African police, who thoughtfully took us both home once they had secured all the pertinent details.

The following morning, I took off work and, using a friend's car, went to see my long-suffering insurance agent, who, when I was ushered into his office, visibly blanched, so I hastened to assure him that my car had not been in an accident. Somewhat mollified, he risked a cautious smile before asking why I had come to see him, and I replied as gently as possible that my car had been stolen.

For a moment or two, he stared at the picture of the Queen on the wall, then he opened up his desk drawer and took out my file, which, to ease the burden of handling my claims, was apparently kept in as convenient a location as possible. Reverently, he began to leaf through this bulky folder, until his growing sense of horror became more than he could bear. He then quietly laid down the file, took off his glasses, lay back in his chair and roared with laughter, as the tears started to stream down his face.

Being by nature sympathetic, I let his grief run its course, until eventually he regained enough of his composure to apologize for his unprofessional conduct and tell me why my problems were, in essence, a boon to the insurance industry. This last remark was not exactly what I had expected him to say, but I was pleased to be such a valuable client and happily gave my consent when he asked if he could write an article on the wisdom of insurance, with my experiences as the proof of the pudding. Evidently, I was not a bad risk or a bad driver, just living proof that the law of averages does not exist. Finally, he told me my premiums would not be raised or my policy canceled and, as I was leaving his office, he sadly supposed I would stay in touch.

Yet, to every cloud there is a silver lining and the next day the police found my car sitting demurely by the side of the road, some 10 miles from where it had been stolen. It was, they said, almost totally undamaged and early the next morning, they delivered it to the Ford dealership for minor repairs. These, it turned out, were limited to the ignition switch, which had been broken when the car was hot wired, and a new driver's door air vent, which had been broken to gain access to the interior.

Car theft was very rare in Northern Rhodesia. In the first place, most Africans didn't drive and, even if they did, a new car in the village would stick out like a sore thumb. Secondly, the European population was very small and widely scattered, which greatly restricted the market in stolen vehicles. Thirdly, distances were so vast and roads so poor that the idea of taking a stolen car out of the country was not really practical. Therefore, in all probability, my car was stolen by a couple of teen-agers out for a good time, who drove it around Lusaka for an hour or so before going home to mummy.

Nevertheless, my feelings of relief were tinged with some anxiety when I went to the dealer the next day to retrieve my car, because I was beginning to agree with Wendy that this car was jinxed. However, with one notable exception, I never again had the slightest problem with my faithful chariot, although I kept it and drove it over some of the world's worst roads, for another five years. Indeed, as I previously noted, it was the last thing I sold on the last day of my life in Northern Rhodesia.

3. Martin Crosby

I really don't know which of the friends I made in Africa was the most delightful, but I do know that Martin Crosby has to be near the top of the list. We first met, by accident, in the government rest house where we just happened to share a table for dinner one evening. It was about two months after I bought my car. At the time I was no longer living in the rest house, having recently exploited my new-found freedom by moving into a one-bedroom apartment in the nearby three story government single-officer housing complex. But I still occasionally went back to my *alma mater* for a meal and it was there that I made the acquaintance of this 23-year-old tenderfoot, so fresh off the boat.

Martin was definitely not the rugged outdoors type, being instead a small, plump, red-faced and very blonde young man from Yorkshire. I immediately took to this fellow northerner with his impeccable public school charm and engaging manner. Unfortunately, although he too was an employee of the Ministry of Finance, he had, like Bill, been seconded to Native Affairs, and I therefore took great delight in explaining to him at dinner, on the evening we met, the main reasons why his stay in civilization would be brief.

'Martin, my boy,' I told him, 'You, like all of Native Affairs, are destined for the great outdoors.' Martin was appalled but bore my dire predictions with fatalistic grace and I had a lovely evening, while Martin allowed as to how he should have stayed in Bradford, his hometown. When we parted much later in the evening, after several cups of coffee, the seeds of our friendship had already been sown, and we soon took to eating dinner together in the rest house dining room whenever we both could spare the time.

For Martin, of course, time was not a problem. Like all who came before him, Martin was going through his ambulatory phase. His horizon was limited to the government rest house, the Ministry of Native Affairs and the verge of the roads that ran between these two tourist attractions. Consequently, Martin was far from content and said so on numerous occasions.

I helped as best I could, by getting in the habit of picking him up outside the rest house most mornings, and giving him a ride as far as the Ministry of Finance. One morning, he asked if there was any way I might agree to letting him share my apartment. I reminded him that it only had one bedroom and he reminded me that I could cut my expenses in half. Why not, I thought, and so I asked the housing officer for an extra bed and, as soon as this arrived, Martin moved in to share my home.

4. Valhalla

Never in my life had I met anyone to whom Africa showed the degree of enthusiasm that it reserved for Martin. Every insect in Northern Rhodesia appeared to have sworn a solemn oath to eat as much of him as time would permit. Each morning when we arose from our beds, Martin's body would look like a battlefield. Yet, what infuriated him most was the fact that Africa's voracious hordes seemed to have excellent taste, and scrupulously avoided my undesirable body. Martin tried every remedy possible, including a mosquito net, but nothing seemed to work. He was gradually being eaten alive.

One evening, Martin came home in triumph, clutching a brown paper bag and announced that his problem was now history. He had been given the cure. 'What is it?' I innocently asked.

'Vinegar,' Martin replied.

'Vinegar! What the hell do you do with vinegar?' I queried in surprise.

'You rub it all over your body with a sponge,' he shyly explained, showing me the contents of his paper bag. Sure enough, he had a large bottle of premium malt vinegar and a nice soft sponge. He was ready to take the cure.

'Not in my apartment you don't – this is not a bloody fish and chip shop,' I said, as I firmly rejected his remedy.

'But Frank, I'm being eaten alive,' he pleaded, and so I relented, and our nights became unbearable.

Still, I must admit that Martin maintained his sense of decorum, as, last thing each night, he adjourned to our bathroom and gave himself a thorough sponging in vinegar. Unfortunately he didn't stay there, and when he eventually entered the bedroom to wearily lie down on his bed, he brought with him an accompanying unbelievable stench, which nightly purged my sinuses and brought tears of genuine pain to my eyes.

However, the effect on the Northern Rhodesian insect population was dramatic. They immediately sent urgent wires to all their cousins in distant lands that Valhalla was to be found in my humble abode and, consequently, the fury of the assault on Martin's table almost doubled, as the vinegar loving insects rewarded his efforts. Martin nevertheless stuck to his guns, by unwisely deciding to give the vinegar a little while longer to pickle his skin, and solemnly continued his nightly sponging.

It now became apparent that stern measures were called for, since Martin's aroma had become more than I could bear. He had to be brought to his senses before I died of vinegar poisoning. I therefore took my problem to an objective source, the Deans, who had never met Martin. Together, once I had convinced them that I was not stark raving mad, we developed a plan of revenge.

The following night, after Martin and I had retired, I quietly opened the bedroom window, which fortunately was close to my bed. I then lay down and waited. About 2 a.m., I woke with a start when I felt the prick of Dixie's toasting fork in my left shoulder. My co-conspirators had arrived and were lurking in the bushes beneath my bedroom window, through which Dixie had prodded me into action. A few whispered words passed between me and the bushes, before I crept from my bed as our plan unfolded. I first tiptoed to Martin's bed, to make sure that he was fast asleep, and primly covered by his blanket and sheet. Satisfied that all was now well, I quietly left the bedroom and stole down the hallway to the front door, where I slowly drew back the deadbolt with a minimum of sound, as I made ready to entertain my friends.

At this point in the story, it is important to remember that Martin had never seen or heard of the Deans. They were an unknown element, about to fulfill his every fantasy. At the same time as I had been moving to open my outside door, they had stealthily crept from the bushes at the rear of our complex, to the verandah which adorned its front. Consequently, when I finally opened the door, the Deans were waiting, and quickly slipped through the doorway and into my apartment. So far, so good. Now for the climax of our little charade.

While Dixie and I lurked in the hallway, Sally crept into the bedroom where Martin innocently slept the sleep of the just. She knelt beside Martin's bed and gently ran her fingers through his hair. Next, for extra effect, she seductively whispered sweet nothings in his ear, while she told him of her joy at being able to come to his room. Regrettably, Martin's reaction did not live up to our high expectations, because according to Sally's subsequent account there was no reaction at all from Martin. He seemed to be ignoring her and pursuing the even tenor of his ways.

Meanwhile, out in the hallway, Dixie and I waited for World War III to begin. But all was quiet on the Western Front. Neither audible sounds nor movement came from the darkened room at the end of the corridor. Puzzled and a little concerned about his wife's fate, Dixie determined on a brilliant improvisation to our plan. He raced into the bedroom, threw on the light and confronted the cavorting couple. In horribly dramatic style, he then shouted at the top of his lungs. 'Ah, ha – just as I suspected – now I have all the evidence I need to obtain a divorce.' Yet still we played to an unappreciative audience and, as he later admitted, Dixie felt like a fool as Martin continued to ignore our pantomime. Indeed, although obviously no longer in the land of Nod, Martin still appeared to be treating the whole event with the supreme contempt it so richly deserved.

Perplexed, and beginning to fear that something was going terribly wrong, I abandoned my post in the hallway and joined the merry troupe in our bedroom, where Martin, with a look of total uncomprehending horror on his face, still refused to join in the festivities. He lay in his bed like a corpse, and both of his eyes bulged from their sockets, as though they were ready to part company with his ashen face. He was not a pretty sight, and I immediately decided to lighten the situation by explaining to him that he was the victim of our finely honed sense of humour.

Martin, however, unkindly ignored my comments and it now began to look as if he had suffered some kind of an attack, since he appeared to have all the symptoms of shell shock. I therefore sat on his bed and talked reassuringly, until I succeeded in convincing him that he hadn't died and gone to Hell.

Eventually, I managed to help him stagger into the lounge where he collapsed into an easy chair and, wearing his bed sheet as a cloak, sat and stared at Sally. At my prompting, he finally accepted a large glass of whiskey and his eyes retreated into their sockets as he sipped the restorative brew. Yet it still took another hour before Martin's face resumed its brick-like hue and he was able to tell us how he felt. His explanation of his reaction to our prank was simple, for he apparently was quite unable to believe his senses when he awoke to the touch of Sally's fingers and the sound of her voice. Thus, his body and mind rejected the reality of his nightmare, since they had no previous measure against which to compare current events. 'I was,' he explained, 'totally unable and unwilling to accept the truth of what I was seeing and feeling.'

After it became clear he would survive our lunacy, I belatedly introduced Martin to the Deans, in order to cement their relationship. But Martin's response, although polite, was formal and cold, which may have been why the party broke up a few minutes later, when the Deans decided to go home. However, since we all had undoubtedly earned an hour or two of innocent sleep, I made no attempt to dissuade them. Martin said he understood and please come visit again.

Once our guests had left, I solicitously inquired of Martin as to how his insect bites were feeling, and to my relief he looked at me in puzzlement before he replied, 'What insect bites?' Secretly pleased that my cure seemed to have worked, I said something noncommittal and went to bed. Martin, on the other hand, stayed in the lounge to brood with his whiskey and sheet, as another uneventful night came to a close in the central African bush, where the white man's civilization continued to pacify the colony.

It must have been pure chance but shortly after Martin met the Deans, he discontinued his ritual ablutions in vinegar. Happily, he seemed to have outlived his charm for African insects and they began to leave him alone. He was now able to get a good night's sleep and wake in the morning with skin as pure as the driven snow. And I was able to sleep without the stench of vinegar clogging my nostrils, while I dreamt about my next intelligent idea.

5. Look Mummy, A Plane

I can't really explain why we got up to such elaborate practical jokes but they were a common feature of our daily lives. Perhaps it was because we were young and foolish, or perhaps it was because we were restless and far from home, or maybe it was simply because we were bored. Yet I didn't think I was bored, even though we definitely had nowhere much to go for a day trip, and life tended to follow a fairly narrow routine. Certainly there was very little in the way of passive entertainment, since in Lusaka, we had no TV, only one radio station, three cinemas, three nightclubs and about 10 restaurants.

We were therefore not spoiled for choice, which may well explain the enormous popularity of Sunday brunch at the airport's rooftop restaurant and lounge where, if you wanted to eat lunch on Sunday, it was always necessary to book well in advance. Was the food good? No, not particularly. Was the view spectacular? Only if your fetish is airport runways! Then what was the big attraction? The answer was the VC-10. Each Sunday afternoon at precisely 1 p.m., the weekly VC-10 jet-engined airliner from London arrived at Lusaka's International Airport.

Imagine, if you can, the incredible excitement of watching a big plane land. This was the only jet-engined plane that came to Lusaka and, if you excluded Southern Rhodesia, it was also the only external flight that landed at our airport. That weekly VC-10 was our one link with civilization. Many were the times I stood on the airport restaurant's viewing platform and watched with excitement as the big bird screeched to a landing.

There was also the joy of being able to watch the 50 or 60 passengers disembark from the plane and cross the tarmac, as they headed for the arrival lounge beneath our rooftop vantage point. These people came from Europe and had been to the Promised Land. So they were obviously sophisticated, wealthy and wise, since they had flown halfway around the world in a luxury jet plane. Consequently, it was always a privilege to hobnob with the jet set, while one marveled at how similar to us they looked. And, with thrills like this, was it any wonder that we sometimes resorted to homemade pleasures of the weirder kind?

6. Never Judge A Book By Its Cover

It was, therefore, with a deep sense of pride that I related Martin's nocturnal adventures to Ken and Olive Bayman a few days after the blessed event. Unfortunately their reaction was not what I had expected. To put it mildly, they were disappointed at having been excluded from such an opportunity! They even inquired as to whether I doubted Olive's sexual prowess, and had decided she was too staid to play with Martin's hair. Now, obviously, I had in no way intended to distress these two close friends, so I hurriedly sought to make amends by formulating my next venture into lunacy and, somewhat mollified, they eagerly agreed to participate in my planned attack on the Deans. Once again, a crucial element of the plan was dependent upon the Deans being completely unknown to, in this case, the Baymans.

Luckily, that was not a problem, since the Baymans and Deans moved in different circles, except for me, and had never met. Thus, I confidently proceeded with phase one of our plan. I telephoned Dixie at work and gave him my splendid news. 'Dixie, I'm in love,' I told him. 'Not again,' he replied wearily. 'Dixie, this is the girl! Lucinda is unbelievable. You and Sally have got to meet her,' I enthused. Dixie relented and said he would speak to Sally. A couple of days later, he called back and invited Lucinda and me to dinner the very next night. I, of course, graciously accepted and immediately called Ken to tell him the Deans had taken the bait.

Early the following evening, I drove out to the Bayman farm to collect Lucinda, a.k.a. Olive Bayman. She looked magnificent; not a hair was out of place. She was the most sexually provocative tramp I ever saw. Her clothes were so tight, I swear she must have been born in them. Indeed, she looked so bad that even her four little daughters were appalled at Mummy's appearance, which Ken gallantly tried to explain away as being necessary for a grownup game. Regrettably, neither the daughters nor I believed his explanation.

Finally, just before we left for the Deans with exhortations to be bad, Ken sprinkled whiskey down the front of Olive's undersized sweater, because, as he confidently explained, women like Lucinda always smelled of booze. Yet in doing this he may have made a mistake, since Olive now smelled a rat and immediately demanded to know how he came by that snippet of information. That was a question Ken had no wish to answer, so he wisely restricted his reply to 'Have a nice evening.'

On this thoughtful note, I drove Olive to the Deans for a quiet, friendly dinner, in the full and blissful realization that Sally's only failing was her tendency to be somewhat old fashioned, maybe even a little prudish, and definitely not an admirer of Lucinda's lifestyle.

Accordingly, when Olive and I arrived at the Deans and slowly ascended the veranda steps to their front door, I knew our reception would be uncertain. Therefore, when I knocked on their door and Dixie came to greet us, I was not totally surprised at the look of horror with which he responded to my enthusiastic introduction of my new fair lady. However, having no choice, he quietly ushered us into the lounge where Sally was waiting. I did the honours with all the élan I could muster. Lucinda gushed. Sally almost died.

Dinner itself was a great success, or failure, depending, like all of life, on your point of view. The Deans were gracious hosts, since they had been raised in the traditions of polite society. Although it was obvious that the effort taxed them sorely. Lucinda, to my considerable relief, was magnificent and even to my untutored eye she was a perfect tart. Her appearance was truly awful, her manners appalling and her conversation suggestive. She was almost good enough to embarrass me, and I could easily have fallen in love with this outrageous creature.

From time to time, I caught the Deans glancing my way with puzzled expressions. But these were few and far between, as they spent most of their time staring at Lucinda, like a couple of mice bewitched by a snake. I, of course, played it cool and said very little. I just danced attendance on my lady's every whim and made it plain that I was totally under her spell. Eventually, when we had outstayed our welcome by about three hours, we mercifully left the Deans to their thoughts and I took a gleeful Olive home to Ken and their children.

Right on schedule the next day, Dixie called me at work. He had three pieces of information to give me. One, Sally would no longer speak to me. Two, my dinner pass to their table had been revoked. Three, they intended to take legal advice and see if they could abort my position as their daughter's godfather. In a nutshell, they were not amused, but, fortunately, did not possess a vocabulary rich enough to adequately describe their views on Lucinda. Thus, Dixie merely said they considered her unsuitable and, when I innocently asked him what she was unsuitable for, his response appeared to indicate she was unsuitable for the human race. The bottom line was that, since my sanity was obviously in doubt, please leave them alone. They seemed to feel as if my sickness might be contagious, and this was a possibility they wished to avoid, along with me. I feigned hurt and shock at Dixie's remarks and the conversation ended on a rather cool note.

So far, so good, and, with all the groundwork laid, it was now time for Part Two of our prank. I called Ken at work to tell him that the Deans were both gaffed and ready to be landed in the boat. This, naturally, was the news he had been waiting for and we agreed to administer the *coup de gras* on the following Sunday afternoon, directly after Morning Prayers at Lusaka Cathedral. Accordingly, we rendezvoused in the church parking lot at about 1 p.m. on the chosen day, and the Baymans followed me in their car as I ignored my banishment and drove to the Dean's castle.

Once again, Olive and I slowly ascended the veranda steps to the Dean's front door and, once again, I knew our reception would be uncertain. Yet this time, we had a different image to project. I was in my Sunday suit. Olive was decorously dressed to the nines as a conservative, young church-going matron. Plus, for added effect, her husband Ken, also in his Sunday suit, and her four delightful daughters, also beautifully attired, stood beside us, as I knocked on Dixie's door.

To be honest, I was slightly disappointed in Dixie. He really ought to have learned his lesson, and should not have been answering knocks on his door. But apparently he was a glutton for punishment, and a few seconds after I rattled his cage, he opened the door to the assembled throng. Quickly, before he changed his mind, I fervently apologized for my unannounced visit, and went on to say how dearly I wanted to introduce them to some new friends of mine, whom I was sure they'd love to meet. I also ingenuously added, that since the Baymans had four little girls, wouldn't it be nice, if my goddaughter could meet some new playmates?

Dixie, impolitely I thought, ignored my speech. And for some strange reason, he seemed content to stare at the Bayman family, with an expression that he seemed to have borrowed from Martin. Evidently, he was having trouble reconciling Olive, Ken and the girls with his jaundiced opinion of Lucinda. Not wishing to disturb Dixie in this reverie, I politely said no more and, within a minute or so, Sally came to the door to see what was intriguing Dixie. She saw, and joined him in his ponderings.

Olive, as befits the seasoned performer she had become, innocently pretended that nothing was wrong and sweetly asked Sally if she could see my goddaughter, of whom I had often spoken so proudly. Trapped again, the Deans woodenly invited us to enter their home. Once inside, I courteously made the necessary introductions. The Deans expressed delight at meeting the Bayman family. The Baymans returned the compliment, and I spent a few minutes introducing my goddaughter to four new playmates, before cheerfully accepting Sally's offer of a nice cup of tea.

The five of us then adjourned to the lounge, where we drank our tea and exchanged the requisite pleasantries. The Baymans and I had fun. The Deans did not. They seemed preoccupied and no longer interested in my declining mental health. Judging from their expressions, I deduced that they now intended to devote the bulk of their interest to monastic pursuits. It seemed as if they were weary of the vagaries of the world and wished only to be left alone.

Being gentlefolk ourselves, sensitive to their needs, the Baymans and I took our leave after about an hour's worth of idle chatter. It had been such a nice way to spend a restful Sunday afternoon. That's what friends are for, to make one's life a misery.

Just like clockwork, Dixie was back on my office telephone on

Monday morning to tell me how much they had liked Ken and the four daughters, even though their respect for Olive-Lucinda and I, had reached new lows. They now seemed to believe that Olive-Lucinda was a split personality and while Ken was happily married to Olive, I was happily having an affair with Lucinda. Naturally, I solemnly agreed with everything Dixie said, and sincerely congratulated them for having so easily solved the puzzle.

Finally, by way of a parting shot, I carefully turned the knife in the wound by pointing out how, since all four of us were happy, we may have achieved something close to Utopia, in an otherwise sordid world. Dixie, thank God, was not amenable to this line of reasoning, which he summarily rejected, before angrily hanging up his phone. This was, for him, an unusual display of emotion, and the perfect ending to our prank. With nothing left to achieve, I immediately called Ken with the good news, which I asked him to relay to Olive.

A week later, after a suitable period of mourning, Ken, as our chosen representative, called Dixie and told him the whole story. Dixie was enchanted. He loved the idea and was very flattered by the time and effort we had all devoted to setting them up. Sally was not amused and it took perhaps another month before she saw the joke. Martin was ecstatic. He said it could not have happened to a nicer couple. He did however, noticeably refrain from telling me of the hopes he entertained for my immediate future. I therefore determined to watch Martin closely and never again trust his friendly face.

7. Bridge Is An Easy Game

Having thus exhausted my fevered mind, I now became a model of circumspection and played no more pranks on my friends for the next several months. Apparently, my humour was like baseball; we both had an off season. Yet peace was hard to find, especially when one was forced to endure, on a daily basis, Martin's enthusiasm for the game of bridge. To be fair, I acknowledge it as a game I enjoy playing. But Martin went much further – he loved to play bridge. He ate, drank, smoked, slept and talked nothing but bridge. Indeed, he almost always carried a pack of cards and, at the drop of a hat, he would deal, bid and play all four hands of an imaginary game, which, to say the least, was a noteworthy performance.

Naturally, he always began at the beginning, by shuffling his deck of cards prior to dealing the requisite four hands, which he then solemnly picked up and bid, each in its turn, after carefully discussing its options with himself. This unusual process would continue through as many rounds of bidding as the hands seemed to warrant, until eventually Martin triumphantly announced the winning bid.

Then came the moment of truth. For Martin now had to both make and defeat the contract he had worked so hard to establish.

Therefore, he carefully played out all four hands, picking each one up and laying it down as the sequence of play demanded – except that the dummy hand was displayed face up, as the rules required. Accordingly, the other three hands maintained their secrecy as Martin played them all and ensured that the value of each hand was never revealed to the other two hands.

It was all rather weird, especially since Martin sometimes failed to make his bid, and then deftly completed the charade by holding an extensive post-mortem with himself, as he tried to determine which hand he had bid or played badly. As if this was not enough, he often became incensed, when he bid a contract and then defeated himself as he played the cards.

Bridge was close to being his religion, and he approached each hand of these solitary rituals, with all the solemnity of a bishop celebrating High Mass on Easter Sunday. And so, I wisely noted that Martin and bridge were definitely not a combination to be trifled with and I prudently decided to exercise caution by avoiding any involvement with his obsession for the game.

Unfortunately, all my good intentions came to naught when Lusaka hosted an international duplicate bridge tournament. Martin, of course, was elated, and decided to enter the tournament, if only he could find a suitable partner. Since this seemed like a good idea to me, I politely wished him luck, without much interest, and thought no more about it. This, in hindsight, was a fatal mistake, for within a week he casually announced that he had entered the tournament with me as his partner. Naturally, I did not greet this news with overwhelming joy, and, hoping that I had heard a phantom voice, I somberly asked him to repeat his announcement.

He did, and it sounded much the same the second time around. 'Why me?' I plaintively inquired. Sadly, just as I had feared, I received the insulting reply – 'Because I couldn't find anyone else.' Desperate, I tried one final gambit – 'What if I say no?' But Martin was ready for me and triumphantly declared, 'You can't say no. You owe me. Look what you did to me with those fools, the Deans.' Sorrowfully, I acknowledged the merits of his argument and, trapped by my own past, I reluctantly agreed to be sacrificed on the altar of the god of bridge.

Victorious at last, Martin now began to make joyful preparations for my demise and, since the tournament was not to take place for another month, he devoted all of our spare time to making me a better bridge player. He made me read every bridge book ever written, and also insisted on my presence as an observer at his nightly game of Solitaire Bridge. Martin was calling in his chips and I had to pay the price.

Just when I began to give up hope of ever going to a movie again, the big day finally arrived, and resplendent in our Sunday suits, we drove to the tournament hall. Suddenly, with our destination already in sight, Martin belatedly asked me if there was any chance that he may perhaps have tried to teach me too much too fast, and could I possibly have become confused. Possibly, no. Definitely, yes. At the best I hoped to do no harm, and at the worst I would surely disgrace us both. Gloomily he agreed that disgrace was what he expected and, on this cheerful note, we arrived at the torture chamber where the tournament was soon to begin.

Nevertheless, we were both determined to go down with our colours flying and, with more bravado than sense, we marched resolutely into the hall. It was, I noted with dismay, surprisingly well filled with prosperous-looking people, who milled around the numerous card tables which stood ready for use. Our tickets were taken by a very pompous-looking official, who escorted us to one of these tables and proudly introduced us to our first opponents – the current South African champions of duplicate bridge. Martin, to say the least, was suitably impressed and showed it by looking slightly sick. I, with less to lose, merely looked thoughtful. Still, they seemed harmless enough, and for the next few minutes we exchanged idle pleasantries, until the room was called to order with the news that play was about to commence.

Now came the moment of truth. It was time to shuffle and deal the first hand, and, when no one did, I almost offered to do so myself. But then, just in time, Martin's lessons paid a dividend, and I remembered being told that in duplicate bridge all hands are pre-dealt and laid before each player's place on the table. Hence there is no dealer and, after every game – as the word duplicate suggests – the next game's hands are constructed to be identical to the first game's hands.

Consequently, all players at a given table play with the same hand as the previous occupants of their seat, which thereby compels each player to change tables at the end of each game. North and south may, perhaps, go clockwise around the room while east and west may go counterclockwise, thus ensuring that on every hand, each pair of players faces a different opponent and plays a different hand. However, as previously stated, at each individual table the four hands dealt for the first group will remain the same for each subsequent game. Eventually, at the end of the evening, there will be a north and south winner and an east and west winner, who will both have scored more points than any other north/south or east/west tandem. Or, so I understood; this, along with most other aspects of my first duplicate bridge tournament, was still somewhat unclear.

Anyway, having avoided making a fool of myself by volunteering to shuffle and deal, I carefully picked up my cards, glanced quickly through them, and then soberly replaced them face down on the table. At first I thought I may be sick; surely I was hallucinating. Slowly I took several deep breaths before daring to pick up my cards and re-examine their contents. And, sure enough, I soon confirmed my earlier suspicion. I was hallucinating. But with no other viable option, I reluctantly decided to believe my lying eyes, and gently laid my hand down, while waiting for the bidding to begin, since I, as the fourth player, would bid last.

Thus, without warning, I joined that select group of pilgrims who have seen the perfect wave, and I shall never forget the excitement I felt, as I bid and played my first hand of Tournament Bridge in the following extraordinary manner.

First round:

South African champion No. 1:	'No bid.'
Martin:	'No bid.'
South African champion No. 2:	'No bid.'
Me:	'Seven no trumps.'

Judging from Martin's reaction, this may well have been one of the few opening bids that he was not emotionally prepared to respond to, with anything more positive than a wild-eyed stare. Apparently he lacked confidence in his own ability as a teacher and had come to the conclusion that I was about to commit the unpardonable sin of embarrassing us both in public. With no indication of any help from my partner, I had pre-emptively made the highest possible bid in the game of bridge and, to compound my folly, I had done this as an opening bid.

He was also handicapped by the fact that no bridge book he had ever read had a chapter on this approach to bidding. Possibly a textbook on the criminally insane may have broached the subject but, judging by his expression, Martin was not a devotee of the lunatic fringe, and wisely held his peace as the tableau continued to unfold.

Second round:

South African champion No. 1:	'Doubled.'
Martin:	'No bid.'
South African champion No. 2:	'No bid.'
Me:	'Redoubled.'

But this time, after I bid, Martin avoided my eyes, for his pain was too deep and personal to be shared. I had started as a quiet lunatic and had now reached the frenetic stage by making my second bid, without ever taking the time to re-examine my cards. This did not exactly inspire confidence in my partner, whose depression increased substantially when the opposition challenged my bid, and I confidently challenged their challenge, easing into the highest conceivable contract under the rules of bridge without the slightest help or encouragement from my partner.

Yet even that was not the worst of it, for not only was I below average as a bridge player, but this, frighteningly, was also the first hand I had ever played of tournament bridge. Thus, in essence, I was confidently trying to hit a home run off the first pitch of my major-league career, and my self-evident foolishness easily proved to Martin that his fears had been well founded. Quite clearly to him, I was hopelessly confused. He, equally clearly to me, wished he was home alone, and nicely tucked up in his warm little bed.

However, since the bidding was now complete, it was time for the denouement, whereby I would reveal the state of my mind by playing my hand. But, before I bared all, I still had one more twist to turn on Martin's screw of pain. Therefore, with impeccable grace, I turned to South African champion #1 and, smiling my sweetest smile, said, 'We'll play the hand if you wish, but it really is a waste of time, for you see, I have a lay down.'

Mercifully, Martin had by now lost all interest in the tournament which is why, in the interests of his sanity, he ignored my remark, because one can take only so much abuse, and Martin's cup was full to the brim. Even the gentleman to whom I had spoken betrayed a little surprise, as he said, 'Oh dear, you do understand the rules of a lay down, don't you?'

I nodded my understanding. If you claim a lay down, then everyone places their cards face up on the table and the opposition controls the play of all four hands. In that case, all the South Africans needed to do was examine our hands and then play them in such a way as to make us lose just one of the 13 tricks available. Not only had I gone out on a limb, but, as an encore, I was now about to sever the limb from the tree.

Apprehensively the two South Africans locked eyes and then #2 turned to me and said, 'Please show us your hand.' Ever the showman, I relished the moment and said politely, 'My pleasure.' I then picked up my hand for the first time since the bidding began and, card by card, I laid face up on the table, pure perfection in bridge.

In spades, I showed ace, king, queen and jack. In hearts, I revealed ace, king and queen. In diamonds, I displayed ace, king and queen. Finally, after a pregnant pause, I introduced the ace, king and queen of clubs. Now, at last, I dared to smile at Martin, who was looking smug. For, hadn't he taught me all I knew? I was merely the clay, and to the potter in Martin was the glory due.

At first no one spoke, until, after the longest pause, South African champion #1 turned to me and said, 'Thank you for making my trip to Lusaka so very exciting. I've been playing bridge all my life and now at last, I've seen the perfect hand.' His friend added, rather ruefully, 'Of course, it would have been much nicer if it had been mine, but the next best thing is to play in a game where someone else is dealt it.' Charmed, I thought how courteous they both were, and said so. Then we called the tournament director to our table and asked for his advice.

Of course, the game could not be allowed to stand. Tournament bridge loses its meaning when someone, literally, holds an unbeatable hand. So after everyone had gathered around our table and shook my hand, as they oohed and aahed, our cards were reshuffled and redealt. We then sadly, for me, replayed our first hand as the other tables quietly waited until we caught up. Shortly thereafter, the musical progression began and my moment of glory was over.

Unfortunately, I don't remember how well Martin and I did in the tournament. But I'm sure we didn't win and I'm equally sure we didn't disgrace ourselves. In addition, I seem to recall the South African champions winning their half of the tournament which was, perhaps, only to be expected.

Lastly, by way of a postscript, I also remember how, as we drove home from the fray, Martin broke a long silence with a heartfelt plea. 'Why on earth did it have to be you who got dealt the perfect hand?' Smugly, flaunting my superior knowledge of music, I haughtily replied, 'For the same reason that Mozart was a better composer than Salieri.' And, on that perfect note, we went home.

8. Another One Bites The Dust

Once more, calm descended on my life until, sadly enough, my forecast for Martin's future came true and only a few months after our foray into competitive bridge, his luck ran out. One evening he came home and dolefully announced that Native Affairs had transferred him to Livingstone, to be that small town's district accountant. 'Still, Martin's fate was better than Bill's, and even though Livingstone was merely a shadow on a map, at least it had the Victoria Falls. So, once again I attended a best friend's farewell party and soon thereafter, Martin was gone from my life.

Fortunately, I did not immediately lose total contact with my roommate, because later that year I went and spent Christmas in Livingstone, with the parents of Wendy, my Demolition Derby girlfriend. But that's another story and I'll get to it in due course.

Regrettably, however, Martin's career followed the same path as Bill's. Thus, when his first tour of duty was over, he resigned from the service and returned to the warm embrace of Yorkshire bridge. Perhaps, as was the case with so many of my friends, he rejected African life because it was different from home and, if different, obviously bad. But whatever his reasons were, I never heard from Martin again once he had left the service. Consequently he, like Bill, disappeared without trace from my life, although I still enjoy my memories of his delightful company and always keep an eye open for books on the rules of Solitaire Bridge.

And thus ended the first half of my first tour in Northern Rhodesia. For it was now almost 18 months since I had arrived in the protectorate, and I was rapidly becoming a devotee of colonial life. Indeed, with each day that passed, I became more and more of a white African. My interest in events beyond our horizons gradually diminished until eventually, horror of horrors, I ceased reading the overseas press, and really began to spread my wings in the tropical night.

Chapter 4

Daily Life Under The Colonial Flag

1. Lusaka, A Garden City

There is a poem I know well which propounds the theme that someone who is born blind will never regret being unable to see, since they
never could, and cannot miss something they have never had. Now,
while I do not accept this idea in its entirety, I do agree that it is very
difficult to understand an environment you have never known. Thus,
although I will do my best to give some idea of the way we lived in
Lusaka in 1959 through 1962, I do realize that my picture will be
seen dimly, as through a cloud.

To begin with, Lusaka itself was a very pleasant surprise and
turned out to be a modern, spotlessly clean city with an abundance of
parks and gardens. Indeed, it was much nicer than any of the dirty
Lancastrian towns with which I was familiar. Sometimes, as I sat
drinking a beer in a restaurant on the second-floor balcony of a
downtown office building, I would wonder if somehow things had
become confused, since the colony seemed to be far more amenable
to the good life than was the mother country. Most assuredly, if this
was darkest Africa, then I fervently hoped that no one ever bothered
to turn on the lights.

This oasis was, by central African standards, a fairly large town,
with an elite white population of about 12,000, who, in the main,
were colonial civil servants and very well educated. In colonial Africa,
there were no blue collar jobs for white men, since this kind of work
was almost totally reserved for the local black population. Therefore,
in essence we had a caste system, in which the blacks did the work,
the Indians and Pakistanis ran the commerce and the white man ran
the country. But, most of all, as recent events in Africa have so tragi-
cally illustrated, the white man kept the peace. Ours was a gentle,
tranquil land in which murder and theft were almost unknown.

The Asiatic and native populations lived in their own part of town
in much the same way that American cities are divided along ethnic
and racial lines, although many of the richer Indians had moved out
of their area and into the predominantly white suburbs.
Consequently, on one occasion, my next-door neighbours and very

good friends were Pakistani owners of a downtown department store. This was not unusual, since the relatively small Asiatic population of about 5,000 had a virtual monopoly on Lusaka's retail trade. Naturally, this was resented by the 70,000 black Africans who comprised the bulk of our towns total population of about 90,000 and, not surprisingly, after independence much of the Asiatic population of central Africa followed the white man into exile.

Lusaka's amenities were reasonable. Our three cinemas were all multiracial, but each catered to a different segment of society. One was primarily white, one white and Asiatic and one Asiatic and black. 'Bitter Rice,' with Sylvana Mangano, came to the native cinema, and on that occasion, two of us went down to the township to see this film and had a very steamy evening, in every sense of the word, since the theatre was jammed and very poorly ventilated. That was an experience I never chose to repeat and in future I confined myself to the white and Asiatic theatres.

In addition, as befits a capital city, we even had a drive-in movie where we could all pretend to be Americans as we watched teen-age American films featuring bobbysoxers. For the more sophisticated, we also had four nightclubs, one of which – the Blue Angel – always had a live band playing dance music on the patio behind the lounge. This was my favourite watering hole, where I loved to sit at a patio table and relish the African night, or, better still, if I had a date, to dance on the patio dance floor beneath an African moon.

Yet it was our restaurants that were our main attraction, for we had the best Indian restaurants in the world and ours were not specialty bistros. Instead, they were Indian restaurants run by Indians, for Indians, and any other customer who happened to chance by. Their curry was truly out of this world and, if you were brave enough to order their really hot items, you would cry like a baby as dinner burnt with all the fires of Hell as it tortured your throat and stomach. Naturally, this was a problem easily handled by the connoisseur. My friends and I always consumed many tankards of beer with our curry, in order to adequately douse the flames. Thus, after an evening meal of hot Madras curry, it always fell to Peter Van Eden's special talents to safely deliver us to our respective homes.

For recreation, we chased girls at the city's large open-air swimming pool, which was, in my day, a whites-only facility and my favourite place to relax and contemplate African wildlife. When I got tired of this spectator sport, I could always go and practice my soccer skills at the Lusaka Central Sports Club, where I played – rather poorly – on their whites-only soccer team, in a whites-only soccer league, comprised of about seven local amateur teams. Of course not everyone believed in such strenuous exercise, so the city had an exclusive country club with a beautiful 18-hole golf course. I, being unexclusive, never played there. But this was no great handicap. We also had a very nice municipal golf course, where I incessantly hacked my way through the tropical rough as I ignored the normal path from tee to green.

However, in one delightful way, Lusaka lagged severely behind the rest of the civilized world. We had virtually no commercial advertising, since we, to our undying shame, had no TV, no billboards, no clearance sales, and only one government-run, non-commercial radio station. Our lives were devoid of endless opportunities to save money by spending ourselves into bankruptcy. Additionally, we even had the distinction of living in the only part of the world where Coca Cola was outsold by one of its subsidiaries. Here, in southern Africa, Fanta Orange was king and Coke was an insignificant drink.

Ironically, and perhaps unfortunately, it was in per capita cigarette consumption that we led the world, since our locally manufactured cigarettes were made from the best locally grown Virginia tobacco and were very inexpensive. Three of our brands that I remember well – Peter Stuyvesant, Carlton and Life – came in 50-cigarette boxes and could be bought in 500-cigarette cartons at the grocery store. A box of 50 cigarettes cost about 25 cents and everyone at work always left an open box on their desk so that anyone passing could just help themselves to a smoke, for cigarettes were so cheap as to be of inconsequential value. Of course, all this was before smoking was deemed hazardous to your health and none of us dreamed of the problems our habit could cause.

Our cigarettes were also tax free, since in this uncivilized part of the world we almost entirely dispensed with civilization's scourge of taxation, and lived on the bounty of our mineral resources. Accordingly, with commendable restraint, our leaders wisely reserved the privilege of taxation for our three or four large copper mining companies, who made us the world's third largest copper producer in the early 1960s, and paid the bulk of our taxes.

Unfortunately this idyllic situation did not persist and world copper prices plummeted, by coincidence, at about the same time as Northern Rhodesia achieved independence as Zambia. Yet in my day, ours was a rich colony with no budget imbalance and almost no personal taxation. We were, in fact, an African version of Texas in its glory days, and our butcher always had a liberal supply of South African lobster on ice.

Nevertheless, although we ate, drank and played with the best, there was still one other modern amenity, besides the electric toothbrush, which passed us by. Happily, we were spared from the absurdity of diet foods with low-calorie content, since this was an idea whose time had not yet come in central Africa. We came from a simpler world where food was meant to sustain life and, if we didn't want the extra calories, we ate less, which still seems to me to be a practical answer to the problem of overeating.

This simple approach to the dangers of overindulgence well illustrates the difficulty we had in our isolation, as we tried to understand what the rest of the world, and the U.S. in particular, was trying to accomplish.

Sometimes the American way was quite incomprehensible to me and most of my friends. Martin Luther King and the civil rights movement in the U.S., were emerging in the early 1960s, and received extensive coverage in the African press. As the story unfolded, Lusaka's only newspaper gave copious reports on what was happening. From our viewpoint, it seemed like the U.S. was about ready to embark on its second civil war. And this we could not understand since we did not, in any way, appreciate how segregated the U.S. had remained despite its championing of the causes of life, liberty and the pursuit of happiness.

Therefore, when we saw pictures of people being attacked by dogs and read about demonstrators being shot, we could not believe that these events could be taking place in the land which gave us John Wayne and all those lovely Hollywood musicals. Consequently, we just shook our heads and tried to remember that we were the ones, or so we had been told, who needed to improve our manners.

Still, in spite of my confusion, I did eventually realize that Martin Luther King had become the first black man to achieve world-class status in the white man's world and had clearly shown all black Africans how much it was possible to accomplish. As a result, his influence in colonial Africa was enormous and probably much greater than has ever been acknowledged. For he was the one who stiffened the resolve of our independence-minded politicians, as they renewed their struggle to supplant the white man and become the new kings of the hill.

We were also confused by the well-publicized execution of Caryl Chessman in California, on May 2, 1960, some 12 years after he was first sent to death row for aggravated kidnapping. This too, was exhaustively covered by our media and the consensus of opinion held, that to keep a man on death row for so many years before finally executing him, was more barbaric than anything to be found in darkest Africa.

As in most things, I'm sure we oversimplified but, to us, justice delayed was justice denied and a civilized country ought to have been able to kill or not kill, with a little more expediency. Of course, I have since come to realize how strenuously the American system of justice labors, as it tries to be scrupulously fair to all of its defendants. But at the time, from the wilds of Africa, it seemed to me and everyone I spoke to, that this was a particularly cruel variation of the Chinese water torture idea. Admittedly, this probably proves my point: a little knowledge garnered from afar can be a dangerous thing. Yet I can still remember how hard I tried, and failed to understand what on earth was happening.

Happily, my final anecdote about my lack of understanding of life on a distant planet called the U.S., is less serious and concerns my inability to believe that the Americans had invented a hot coffee machine. This mind-boggling piece of information was relayed to me by a colleague who had just been to America for an inter-government conference and came back suitably impressed.

Me:	'So, how was the States?'
World Traveler:	'Not bad, quite interesting really.'
Me:	'What was so interesting?'
World Traveler:	'Their hot coffee machines.'
Me:	'Their what?'
World Traveler:	'Hot coffee machines! They have machines that sell you a cup of coffee for a quarter.'
Me:	'That's impossible.'
World Traveler:	'No it's not. They have them.'
Me:	'They can't have them. How would the machine know who takes milk and who takes sugar?'
World Traveler:	'It has a button for milk and another for sugar.'
Me:	'I don't believe you.
World Traveler:	'Oh yes it does. And, get this, it also has a button for extra milk and another for extra sugar.'
Me:	'Get lost.'

Now, although this story seems trivial, it does serve to illustrate the gulf which separates different cultures and, as such, it deserves consideration. I might also add that I never believed my friend's story until I came to America many years later and put my hand in the wound, by buying a cup of coffee from one of those incredible coffee-dispensing contraptions.

Anyway, back to my overview of Lusaka, where life often seemed to be one long party as we all struggled to adequately toast our Queen, and avoid malaria by drinking liberal quantities of gin and tonic. For certainly it is true to say that we did have a great number of parties, perhaps because we were mostly young and foolish, or perhaps because we all had numerous servants to help clean up the mess. However, we often had a much better excuse to make merry, since at most parties the guest of honour was usually about to disappear into the bush, or was about to leave on a seven-and-a-half-month vacation, complete with two luxury cruises at taxpayer expense.

Therefore, in the first case, it was traditional to help the unfortunate nascent hermit drown his sorrows while, in the second case, it was equally traditional to help the fortunate parolee celebrate his forthcoming re-entry into western civilization. As a result, it is possible to claim that our transitory lifestyle was largely responsible for our social gatherings and intemperate attitudes. At least that is what we always said and tried to believe.

For more formal recreation we also had a first-class hotel and a thoroughbred racecourse. The hotel was called the Edinburgh Hotel.

I don't know why. It was much too rich for my blood except for lunch on Sunday, when the masses were served chicken in a basket on the patio which overlooked the hotel's lily pond. This was a wonderfully elegant lunch. Often I could be found at the Edinburgh after church on Sunday, eating my chicken and drinking an ice-cold beer, while the frogs in the pool joined the incessant African crickets in providing a musical background for our entertainment.

Speaking of entertainment, I now turn to the racecourse, which was a little less elegant than the Edinburgh Hotel but a whole lot more profitable for me. A very good friend of mine, Mokie Mendelsohn, worked there as a turf accountant, or bookmaker, with Ken Bayman as his clerk. Thus I had inside connections, through their influence becoming the head parking lot attendant for the 10 to 12 race meets per year.

This meant that I didn't see too much of the races but I did make enough money to eat Sunday lunch at the Edinburgh Hotel. Yet all was not lost, since after the sixth race we stopped charging admission in the parking lot and I therefore could go and watch the last three or four races of each meet. It was a nice little racecourse and I always enjoyed being part of its background. Poignantly, in that wonderful way we decide who does what, the jockeys were almost all black, but then so was a large proportion of the crowd, since the Africans seemed to enjoy horse racing as much as anyone else, especially on a warm sunny afternoon.

Because it was the capital of Northern Rhodesia, Lusaka's ambience was enhanced by the usual fine buildings: the High Court, the Parliament Building, the Governor's Residence, the Church of England Cathedral and numerous monuments and statues which lent elegance to our tree-lined boulevards. In addition, even though our streets were not paved with gold, they were nevertheless paved with asphalt, which has to be the next best thing.

Throughout most of the town we had street lights and even traffic lights, while almost all of our homes had running water and electricity. But, regrettably, air conditioning was unknown in our society. Neither our cars, nor our offices, nor our stores, nor our homes, were air conditioned. We let it all hang out. We sweat.

So there you have it. That, to the best of my ability, is what Lusaka was all about in the early 1960s. Today? Who knows? But I fear the worst, since I recently read an article which reported AIDS as being rampant in central Africa and I doubt that Lusaka is an exception. Yet I cling to the hope I am wrong, and continue to remember a vibrant little town, with a main street named Cairo Road, which proudly proclaimed that to the south lay South Africa, while to the north lay Egypt on this, the main Cape-to-Cairo Highway.

2. Remittance Men

Though at first it may seem odd, it really is only to be expected that there should be a significant number of odd people in odd parts of the world. This is partially because the backwaters of empires have always been used as dumping grounds for the motherland's misfits. Consequently, there were in Northern Rhodesia, just as there were in the rest of colonial Africa, a fair number of remittance men who received a substantial allowance from their British families, on the sole condition that they never again darken the shores of the British Isles. In a delightful twist of fate, Europe's loss was often Africa's gain, since most of these prominent black sheep became the backbone of their transplanted societies and brought many innovations to the African bush.

In particular, I remember how the District Commissioner of Lundazi, an extremely remote village to which it was rumoured he had been banished, built a very nice 12th-century castle for his home. He did this, so I was told, merely because he preferred to live in a castle and, to me, that is by far the best reason to build one. Unfortunately, I never visited his district nor saw his folly. Friends of mine who did, however, said it was quite a sight and very substantial. He was also reported to be one of the best hosts in the Protectorate and giver of the best parties.

Still, even if most of my friends and acquaintances were not so strikingly different, there were, to say the least, some very interesting people who worked in the Ministry of Finance. Definitely we were not dull. Especially in the payroll department. As I soon found out when I was transferred to that unit some six months after I corrected Mr. Nicholson's misapprehension about stamps. Many of the following stories took place during the year I spent in payroll, and I can honestly say I was seldom bored.

3. Is He Really One Of Yours?

My first story begins early one February morning in the middle of our summer (and the European winter) when the telephone rang on my desk and I innocently said, 'Hello'. To my amazement, I found myself talking to an English police inspector who wanted to know if he had reached the Ministry of Finance in Lusaka, Northern Rhodesia. I said that he had and he went on to ask me if I knew so and so. Carefully, I admitted I did, since the gentleman in question was one of my friends.

The policeman then asked me if I had any suggestions as to what he should do with him. Startled, I asked for further details and was told that the officer in question was currently sitting in the policeman's office, nattily attired in colonial white shorts and sports shirt, which seemed inappropriate attire for a snowy winter's day in old London town. According to the policeman, my friend was demanding to be returned to Lusaka, Northern Rhodesia, and the policeman was not sure if such a place existed. Wisely, I expressed my condolences to the London police and speedily had the call transferred to the Permanent Secretary, Ministry of Finance. This gentleman was undoubtedly due for a knighthood, and had therefore earned the opportunity to handle this minor inconvenience.

Much later, when the dust finally settled, I got the full story. It began, naturally, in the Lusaka airport bar, where my colleague got smashed and came up with the idea of going home to England for a few more drinks. Amazingly, he managed to get on board our weekly VC-10 and apparently sobered up at about the same time as he was deposited, in his tropical gear, into the welcoming snow of an English winter.

Like the Marines, the British Colonial Service took care of its own and my friend, still in tropical gear, but shivering and sober, rode the next week's VC-10 back to Lusaka. He was then, as were all sinners, rewarded with a posting to the remotest boma the Permanent Secretary could find, and his salary was reduced significantly – for however many months it took the service to recover the out-of-pocket expenses his brief flirtation with freedom had engendered. Plus, I'm sure, he was forbidden ever again to drink in an airport bar. But at least he saw the Promised Land and, as Andy Warhol said, for 15 minutes he was famous.

4. Mr. And Mrs. Lewenstein

The Lewensteins were old, or seemed so to me in my youth, when first we met, and I never did get the full story of where they came from. However, from things they said, I came to believe they were White Russian aristocrats who had fled their homeland in 1918 at the time of the Bolshevik Revolution. Both were local employees of the Ministry of Finance and worked in the Internal Auditing Department. Their English was atrocious, with a heavy eastern European accent, but their manners and comportment were a delightful glimpse into an elegant world that no longer existed, and I loved to sit and listen to the tales they spun.

Yet it is not for their romantic reminiscences that I best remember them, but for a piece of advice which old Mr. Lewenstein gave me as we shared a quiet cup of coffee in his Spartan office. 'Frank,' he said, 'imagine how much knowledge you would gain if you read 30 minutes of good literature each and every day.' Well Mr. Lewenstein, you struck a responsive chord and I've tried to follow your advice. Of course, I'm not very wise, since I've mainly learned how little I know, but thanks to you, my life has been fuller and I've had a lot more fun.

This, I'm sure, would have pleased those two lonely old Russians, who lived out their lives in an alien society, so very far from their beloved homeland.

5. Sleep No More, Macbeth Hath Murdered Sleep

Larry Beck, who was in his mid-30s, was a big, burly, typically Afrikaans South African, with a dark complexion, brown eyes and jet black hair. He had a loud, deep voice and an explosive temper. In short, Larry was loaded for bear and not to be trifled with. Unfortunately, at the time of this anecdote, Larry, Bobby Strachan and I shared a large office in the payroll section of the Ministry of Finance and, during his afternoon nap, Larry was wont to snore rather loudly, which tended to disrupt the even tenure of our working environment. Naturally, Bobby and I broached this subject with him, and politely pointed out the virtues of a more peaceful nap. But he was adamant in denying he ever slept and stubbornly continued to saw logs in the late afternoon sunshine.

To the connoisseur, his technique for taking a nap was a thing of beauty. He would sleep sitting bolt upright at his desk, with his pen dramatically poised above an open file and, if it was not for the vocal accompaniment, a casual glance would leave the impression that Larry was hard at work on a difficult problem. Usually, indeed unfailingly, he napped from around 2:30 to 3:30 p.m. When he awoke his pen would furtively descend to the file before him, as Larry surreptitiously rejoined the working class. The snoring then ceased abruptly, although, of course, according to Larry it had never started in the first place.

For weeks, Bobby and I lived in fear of the Permanent Secretary coming into our office to be greeted by two wide-awake clowns and a sleeping joker but, luckily, this never happened. However, enough is enough and one afternoon we decided on stern measures when, precisely at 2:30 p.m., Larry entered the land of Nod and his daily serenade began to saw through the somnolent air. We rose stealthily from our desks, and each of us gripped one end of Larry's desk. Slowly, with infinite care, we gently eased the desk away from our resting workmate, before quietly carrying it out of our office and down the adjacent hallway to the janitor's storeroom, where we happily left it amid a collection of mops and brooms.

We then spent the next hour contentedly pretending to work on our files, while Larry sat midway between us, bolt upright in his chair, pen dramatically poised over thin air, as he slept the sleep of the just. It truly was a beautiful pastoral scene. Yet it ended rather abruptly when, right on schedule at 3:30 p.m., Larry woke from his nap and fell from his chair, as his pen came down on a non-existent file on a non-existent desk.

Like most Afrikaners, Larry was bilingual and thus was able to curse us fluently in two languages in a raucous bellow for the next 10 minutes, without ever once having to repeat himself. Nevertheless, when a crowd began to form, he wisely managed to calm down and, with our willing help, dourly set out to retrieve his desk from the storeroom where it had been stashed. Soon, before our dreaded Permanent Secretary appeared, we got everything back in place but not, thank God, back to normal. Because from that day forward, Larry Beck successfully resisted the urge to nap in the office, and never again did his snores disturb the late afternoon calm of the colonial civil service, as it administered the Empire.

6. So What Is The Question?

It is said that a leopard never changes its spots, and this may well be true. But, in the case of John Clayton, another of my colleagues in the payroll section of the Ministry of Finance, it was definitely untrue. In him, I witnessed a metamorphosis more complete than any I could possibly have imagined.

John, at the time we became colleagues, was about 30 years old and was the loudest-mouthed, most profane, dirty-minded, drunken lout I have ever met. He was also a barrel of fun and generous to his friends but, according to rumour, was not good to his wife and two children. Quite clearly and beyond doubt, this tall, angular, blue-eyed, very blonde and balding Yorkshireman was not exactly what every mother seeks for her daughter. Even though, to go with his other faults, John was undoubtedly eager to please every mother's daughter as well as, in all probability, the family pets. He was, indubitably, an obnoxious man and one of my closest friends.

Some six months after we began to work together, John's story almost ended in the tragic way so many other similar stories have ended. As he drove home late one evening, drunk and incapable, he lost control of his Volkswagen Beetle, which bounced off a tree, flipped over, and came to rest upside down in the roadside ditch. Slowly, by the grace of God, John climbed out of his car's rear window completely unhurt, and miraculously, he emerged into his new life: a sober, strait-laced, born-again Christian.

The changes in John were awesome. He never again swore, his demeanor was always gentle; he never again drank and was transformed into an ideal husband and father. In addition, he became a religious zealot, whose sole purpose in life was to save souls for Christ in his own inimitable style. Intriguingly, this particular facet of the new John soon became a feature of the men's bathrooms in the Ministry of Finance, where John now spent long hours unwinding our toilet rolls and then rewinding them with small religious tracts, strategically located every two or three feet in the roll.

Thus, when one reached the critical stage in a visit to the toilet, a gentle religious reminder would flutter to your feet. This good idea had apparently been revealed to John when he realized that most people, like him, did most of their serious reading on the throne and, therefore, he leapt at the opportunity to provide suitable reading material.

But, this was not the only way in which John reached out to an unwary public. Some years later I visited him in Abercorn, a remote boma on the shores of Lake Tanganyika, the site of John's banishment by an unsympathetic Permanent Secretary. By now John had refined his technique adding a new weapon to his arsenal. It was a large gold question mark, which he wore prominently in the lapel of his white tropical shirt, and he proceeded to ensnare the boma's unsuspecting customers as follows:

John: 'Good morning, Sir.'
Victim: 'Good morning. May I please buy an elephant license?'
John: 'Certainly sir. Please fill out this application.'
Victim: 'Thank you. Excuse me, but is that a question mark you are wearing in your lapel?'
John: 'Yes sir.'
Victim: 'Why?'
John: 'To ask the question.'
Victim: 'What question?'
John: (Leaning forward eagerly as he sprung the trap) 'Are you saved?'

Of such men as these is the kingdom of Heaven on Earth dependent and, although his path was unorthodox, John Clayton enthusiastically devoted himself to spreading the Gospel to all who would listen. Yet, for those of us who had known him so well, both before and after he rolled his V.W., his most effective ministry was the incredible changes he made in his own life when he found the Lord.

Naturally, once John had been sent to the outback, our meetings became more and more infrequent, until eventually we lost touch with each other. However, I did hear from him one last time, shortly before Northern Rhodesia became Zambia, and that conversation will serve as the perfect opportunity for me to share some thoughts on how the western press covered events during the turbulent days just before African rule was established.

One afternoon in 1963, when pre-independence problems in Northern Rhodesia were at their worst, the telephone rang on my desk and, when I answered it, I immediately recognized the voice of John Clayton, calling me in desperation from England.

'Frank,' he said, 'Please tell me the truth. Is it safe to come home?'

Oh Lord, I thought, he's started drinking again! 'Why wouldn't it be?' I cautiously asked.

'Well,' he answered, 'According to the English papers, you're all barricaded in your houses with your bathtubs filled with drinking water, as you wait for the local freedom fighters to attack.'

'John,' I assured him, 'Come home, they're crazy. The only attack that will take place here today is due to begin as soon as I can get you off the telephone, when Bobby and I are going to attack the golf course for a murderous nine holes!'

Relieved, he hung up and, in due course, came home. But, the moral of this story is the extent to which the press can, insidiously, create a totally false picture. Often they do it with a subtle use of words, through which a point can be made without ever being said. For instance, in stories about Southern Rhodesia, the government became a 'regime' and the authorities never 'announced' anything anymore, but rather they 'said' or, even worse, their comments were prefixed by the delightful phrase 'according to.'

Indeed, on occasion, after listening to the BBC or reading Time magazine, I would go outside and gaze in bewilderment at the tranquility that lay before my eyes. Then, still searching for an answer, I would say to myself, 'Maybe I'm dreaming. Maybe this is not Northern Rhodesia. Maybe I'm not here!' That was the only explanation which made sense, since I could in no way relate what I read to what I lived. Sadly, I learned the hard way to be very cynical of press reports, and henceforth I could never again listen to the news with an unconditional belief in the truth of what I was being told.

Perhaps the best illustration of my point occurred when one of our high court judges addressed this same issue, just a few weeks after John Clayton called me from London to discuss our civil war. Strangely enough, the vehicle for this particular judge's remarks, was his official report into a reputed case of police brutality, which was supposed to have taken place during a political demonstration.

Apparently nothing of the kind ever happened and, in some exasperation, the judge summed up his findings with an eloquent complaint:

> 'The face of Helen of Troy, as we all know, was reputed to have launched a thousand ships, but to me, the accomplishment of Rosie Matwetwe's toe is equally impressive. For it launched a Royal Commission of Investigation into police brutality, which is no small achievement for such a tiny toe.'

That was it. That was the sum of the judge's finding. One African lady had her foot stood on, by one policeman. A trivial incident, yet according to foreign press reports, one would have assumed that World War III had broken out. Now, how can such wildly exaggerated stories gain credence in other lands? Quite easily, I believe, provided these incredibly inaccurate stories came from a little known, or visited, Third World country.

The temptation in the supposedly more civilized world to sensationalize, or editorialize, the facts coming out of the more remote corners of the globe, appears to be almost irresistible. This is especially true when there is very little chance that anyone else will be able, or inclined, to prove you wrong. Thus, I and all my friends, like John, spent a good deal of our time, trying to explain to our overseas families why the picture they had of life in central Africa differed so markedly from the truth. But, in the end, we just gave up on the western tabloids and John went back to the bigger question, while I continued to attack our unfriendly golf courses.

7. Some Little Foreigner

The 1920s and 1930s, were marked by an influx of white settlers into Northern Rhodesia. They came by ox wagon, and soon established themselves as farmers or ranchers, in much the same way as the American west was settled during the 19th-century. The majority of these voortrekkers – their Afrikaans name – were Afrikaners from either South Africa or Southern Rhodesia, and they were truly the ones who, for better or for worse, opened up central Africa to western influence, in a 20th-century version of 'How the West was Won.'

By chance, one of these first voortrekkers had settled near present-day Lusaka, and that was how I came to know his youngest son who, to his father's dismay, did not want to be a farmer but had become instead a lowly payroll clerk in our Ministry of Finance. This was the same young man, Johannes Uys, who had kindly met me at the train station on the evening I first arrived in Lusaka.

Yonnie, as we all called him, was a small, vivacious 25-year-old Afrikaner, without a care in the world and very little concern for what the future may bring. He was, of course, by birth a Lusakan, having been born on his father's ranch, where he still lived and daily commuted to work in his VW Bug. But sometimes, if his father was in a mellow mood, Yonnie borrowed one of the family's fleet of Rolls Royces, for his father had prospered, and then he came to work in a manner more befitting the King of England than a junior clerk in the colonial administration.

In addition, since Yonnie was young and had a finely tuned sense of humour, he always endeavoured, on his Rolls Royce days, to park his Silver Cloud right next to the Permanent Secretary's rather plebeian transport, to the consummate delight of all the junior staff. However, I doubt if this charming little gesture of comparative social status sat as well with our beloved leader, who was reputed to resent subordinates who drove Rolls Royces to work. Yet Yonnie's wealth was only skin deep, since his rather dour father kept him, his sister and three brothers on a very tight rein.

Yonnie, to his dismay, was expected to make it on his colonial service pay, and because Yonnie always had trouble doing this, I was continually forced to lend him money to bridge the gap he inevitably encountered between paydays. Naturally, each payday, he always squared the account and, just as naturally, before the next payday came around, he would be back in my debt. It was an ironic situation that often made me wonder who was the millionaire's son. But, given Yonnie's plaintive lament that the old voortrekker would probably kill him if he asked for money, I probably didn't have much choice. And so I happily served as his financial consultant for more than a year.

My only visit to the family farm took place when I was invited to attend his sister's 21st-birthday party, to which several of Yonnie's friends had also been invited. I left Lusaka early one Saturday evening, bound for the Uys' ranch and an overnight visit, because I, as Yonnie's banker, had even been invited to stay the night and return home on Sunday morning. Amazingly, it was only a one-hour drive from my world to a world that I had only previously visited at the movies.

Yet that was what it felt like when I reached this central African estate. I was instantly reminded of the Texas-style ranch where Rock Hudson held court in his epic film, Giant. Both had the same kind of imposing gateway at their entrance and the same kind of winding dirt road, passing through fields of corn and herds of cattle until, some 20 miles later, the ranch house itself was finally reached.

Once there, this fairy tale atmosphere continued, especially when the party began. Whole sides of beef were roasted over open pit fires in a courtyard festooned with Chinese lanterns and filled by a vast throng of guests. Nearby, in the shadows, stood a small army of uniformed servants, who unobtrusively attended to each reveler's needs or whims with unfailing courtesy.

It really was an incredible extravaganza, and it lasted until dawn. Just like in the movies, a good time was had by all. Much later that morning, after several hours sleep, Yonnie gave me a tour of this private kingdom and then I went home, happy to have seen Shangri-la but sad because I felt that the winds of change would soon blow it away.

My premonition proved true and when Northern Rhodesia became Zambia a few years later, the Uys family retreated to South Africa after selling their ranch to the new government, who immediately turned it into the Zambian Camp David. To some, this new use for their ranch was undoubtedly just and perhaps a definition of progress. Nonetheless, it clearly illustrates the very great difficulty the Afrikaner has in gaining acceptance on a continent he has called home for at least 300 years. In particular, we tend to forget that his African roots are almost as old as those of the white man in the United States of America and, as such, the Afrikaner is a true native in Southern Africa.

Almost farcically, the most poignant denial of this truth that I ever witnessed occurred one day when I was having lunch with two new arrivals from England. Casually I inquired as to who had met them at the train station and, equally casually, they replied that it had been 'some little foreigner.' That was Yonnie Uys, a native-born Lusakan whose father was one of the first white men to settle in the territory. Yet to these two Englishmen, with less than one week's residence in Africa between them, Yonnie was the immigrant.

Blissfully, on such arrogance, our Empire was built, as we happily referred to anyone non-British as a foreigner in the land of his birth. I wonder where Yonnie is now; indeed I often wonder where all of my friends and colleagues in that time warp have gone. I still miss them, but I am everlastingly grateful for having known them. They were the salt of Northern Rhodesia, just before the lights went out.

Chapter 5

It Helps If You're Also Crazy

1. Mrs. Townsend's Envelopes

I have long been an admirer of Murphy's Law and have often been comforted by its stark acceptance of disaster as a bulwark of life. However, I have also been helped by my own contribution to realism, which I now modestly present as Bennett's Law: 'Chaos is the norm and any deviation from chaos is a temporary aberration from reality.' Thus, by always accepting life's little foibles as the basis for our existence, I had very little trouble coping with the British Colonial Civil Service.

But from time to time our leaders sorely tested our resolve and, on one memorable occasion, a colleague named Mrs. Townsend almost failed to rise above the challenge she encountered. In a never-to-be-forgotten bout with authority, the good lady nearly bit the dust as she struggled to comply with a new directive from the governor.

It all began innocently enough when, in response to our master's voice, the Chief Establishment Officer kicked off an economy drive by issuing a four-page memorandum of ideas. It contained many noble precepts and was undoubtedly worthy of the Good Housekeeping seal of approval. Happily, most of these pearls have been erased from my memory by the merciful ticking of the clock. Nevertheless, a few of the gems have survived, indelibly seared in my mind:

1. When you go home in the evening, turn your stamp pad upside down. This will enable the ink to drain to the top of the pad. Therefore, the pad will not need replacing or re-inking as frequently, and the Empire will be prolonged.
2. Use paper clips instead of staples to fasten multiple sheets of paper together, since paper clips are re-usable while staples are not. Thus vast quantities of staples will be saved, without a corresponding increase in the consumption of paper clips.
3. Inter-office and inter-ministerial mail will use old envelopes, which must be retained for this purpose. Old addresses will be crossed out and the new addresses sandwiched in, by hand, on any

available space remaining on the envelope. This new procedure will reduce our consumption of envelopes dramatically, perhaps by 50 percent.

Faithfully, once this epistle had been received, the whole service entered upon a frenetic compliance with its doctrine. But no one outshone Mrs. Townsend, the mailroom supervisor in the Ministry of Finance. This small, ancient, dogmatic, crusty, opinionated and lovable lady was determined to excel and be a beacon to the surrounding darkness. To her, the Governor was God, and all correspondence now left our office in old, tattered, multiple-addressed envelopes, whose tops were stapled shut.

Yet that is precisely where she sinned, because about one week into the program, the Government Printer came to see our Permanent Secretary and showed him one of our envelopes which Mrs. Townsend had correctly re-used. Unfortunately, she had used two staples to secure the envelope. This, of course, was a major sin, since one whole staple had been wasted and the entire program jeopardized. Accordingly, Mrs. Townsend was rebuked by the Permanent Secretary and told to mend her ways by showing better judgment in the conservation of government property.

Bravely, she took her medicine like a man, which in those days was permitted, and retired to her office to brood. The following morning, with a steely glint in her eyes, she came to work primed for leopard, with her houseboy and cook in tow. Firmly, she escorted these two elderly gentlemen into her office, where each deposited a large stack of old newspapers and several balls of string beside her desk. Solemnly, she then thanked them both and, after escorting her staff out of the building, returned to her desk to begin the day's work.

As luck would have it, I happened to be in the mailroom collecting my mail when Mrs. Townsend began to get even, and thus I had a front row seat as the old warrior bent to her task. Primly, she selected a large sheet of newspaper from one of the stacks at her feet and carefully spread it on her desk. Then, with the same prim care, she gently laid an outgoing memorandum in the middle of the sheet of newsprint. Next, as a wolfish grin spread across her face, she gleefully wrapped the memo in the newspaper, tied up the resulting package with a length of her string, addressed it with a felt tipped marker, and happily deposited her fish and chip look-alike into her out basket.

Suitably impressed, I queried her as to whether she had fully thought through her idea. 'Oh yes!' she proudly replied. 'This is my bloody paper and my bloody string, and I'm going to save them more money than they ever dreamed possible.' Sadly, I mentioned the similarity our ministry had assumed to the neighborhood fish and chip shop but still she remained faithful to her vision and I prudently went back to the payroll section.

By mid-afternoon, most of the ministry had stopped by to reason with, or congratulate Mrs. Townsend, as she continued to fold and wrap our outgoing mail. Finally, the Permanent Secretary came down and bearded her in her lair. Vainly, he pleaded the prestige of the Service, and manfully she continued to wrap, until eventually they found common ground. She, for her part, agreed to abandon this bold new venture and he, somewhat reluctantly, agreed to ask the Government Printer to abandon his staple-counting career.

Thus, calm returned to central Africa, as this outpost of civilization concentrated on keeping its stamp pads moist, and Mrs. Townsend went back to second-hand envelopes, with full discretion over the number of staples needed to secure the Empire's secrets.

2. If You Can't Win, Lose Gracefully

A few months after Mrs. Townsend's tour de force, it was my turn to challenge authority. But this time, since I did not possess any of her masculine characteristics, I took a more subtle approach to the problems I encountered. It all started when the whole colonial service in Northern Rhodesia was awarded a cost-of-living pay raise.

At first, like everyone else, I gleefully greeted this news by immediately adjusting to a more affluent lifestyle. Plus, since the pay raise had been made retroactive for six months, I developed lofty plans to spend the considerable sum I would soon be receiving in arrears of pay.

Unfortunately, my joy was short lived and rapidly turned to horror when I, with one helper, was given the task of implementing the new pay scales for all the 7,000 officers involved. In addition, as a bonus, I was asked to do it as quickly as possible, because everyone was anxious to receive their arrears and begin to be paid at the new rates. Desperately, I tried to point out to my superiors that my section was slightly understaffed – by about 50 was my conservative estimate – but my pleas fell on deaf ears I was told to get on with the job.

Frantically, I did some calculations and discovered that, on average, each officer's new salary and arrears would take about one hour to process. Therefore my one clerk and I could each do about eight conversions a day. However, since every conversion had to be double checked, we would, in reality, each do four conversions, and check four conversions, per day. This gave us a combined output of 40 conversions per week, which translates to about 2,000 conversions a year. The conclusion was obvious: A realistic time frame for the whole project, was three and one-half years, and that was certainly at least three years longer than my life expectancy, if these figures ever reached the unsympathetic mob.

Still, it was also abundantly clear that there was nothing more I could do to change the situation and so, calmly and quietly, we set to work. It was a nightmare, especially the arrears, since each officer's salary determined his rent and pension deductions. Thus, as we calculated arrears of salary, we also had to calculate arrears of rent and pension deductions. Plus, if an officer had been promoted during the past six months, we had to calculate arrears on two different pay scales.

Worst of all was the case of an officer who was acting in another officer's position, because then the acting officer received, as an allowance, 95 percent of the difference between their two salaries. Accordingly, we now had to calculate the new rate for both officers, in order to determine what 95 percent of their new difference was worth. Finally, in tears, we were able to calculate the arrears of difference, by subtracting the old difference paid, from the new difference due.

Hopefully, unless you are a relative of Einstein, all of the above is very confusing. If so, then welcome to the club, where two lonely servants daily toiled with pen and several sheets of paper per conversion, as they heroically struggled, without computers, to accomplish a task which threatened to be a lifelong project.

Happily, succor came when, some two months after our struggle began, the Governor, thank God, made an inspection tour of the Ministry of Finance. Foolishly, the Permanent Secretary brought him into our office, to see the proletariat at work.

The Governor:	'Good morning.'
Me:	'Good morning.'
The Governor:	'And what exactly is your job?'
Me:	'I'm converting everyone's salary from the old to the new pay scales.'
The Governor:	'Oh really, then you must be the most popular man in the territory.'
Me:	'Perhaps, sir.'
The Governor:	'How is it going?'
Me:	(Seizing this once-in-a-lifetime opportunity), 'Quite well, really. My assistant and I hope to finish Agriculture and Education this year and, with luck, should be well into the Army and Police by the end of next year.'
The Governor:	(Silence)
Me:	(Silence)
The Governor:	'Are you a comedian, young man?'
Me:	'No sir, a realist.'
The Governor:	'Please explain.'
Me:	'Well, your Excellency, there are only two of us assigned to the task and we are averaging eight conversions a day. Therefore, since there are 7,000 officers whose pay scales need converting, simple arithmetic gives a time frame of three and a half years to complete the project.'
The Governor:	'That is unacceptable.'

Me:	'Yes, Your Excellency.'
The Governor:	'Do you have any suggestions?'
Me:	'Yes sir.'
The Governor:	'Speak.'
Me:	'Well sir, we could put an advertisement in the Colonial Gazette, offering to pay five pounds an hour, evenings and weekends, to any colonial officer who wants to come and help me during his spare time. And, sir, I don't mind working evenings and weekends to get the job done.'
The Governor:	'That is unacceptable.'
Me:	'Yes sir.'
The Governor:	'You know the Service doesn't pay overtime. Next thing you'll want is a trade union!'
Me:	'Yes sir, on both counts.'
The Governor:	'Have you any other suggestions?'
Me:	'Yes sir, give me a staff of 50.'
The Governor:	'That is impossible.'
Me:	'Yes, Your Excellency.'
The Governor:	'Any more ideas?'
Me:	'No, Your Excellency.'
The Governor:	'You did say three and a half years?'
Me:	'Yes, Your Excellency.'
The Governor:	'That is unacceptable.'
Me:	'Yes, Your Excellency.'

And so our interview ended and the Governor made a strategic but thoughtful retreat from my office. However, about 10 days later, my telephone started ringing off the hook, and I was deluged with volunteers who all wanted to come share in the pot of gold the Colonial Gazette was cheerfully promoting.

Patience and virtue had prevailed, for there, in the latest issue of our Bible, was the startling offer I had proposed, of five pounds an hour, evenings and weekends, payable to any officer who volunteered to help me convert the Service from the old to the new pay scales.

Unbelievably, the Governor had bought my idea, lock, stock and barrel. Within a week, I and my one qualified assistant had a conference room full of bedlam, and 60 to 70 amateur accountants, busting their anatomies to get the job done. It was, I must admit, the nearest thing to organized anarchy that the Service had ever seen. Nevertheless, within three months, my rag-tag army had successfully converted the entire government payroll to the new rates, and had also paid all arrears due to the more than 7,000 anxious paupers who haunted my dreams.

Thus ended the only time in my career that the colonial service in Northern Rhodesia paid overtime and I got to return to the quiet life of a junior payroll clerk. But at least for a little while, I had my place in the sun, since I was the only clerk in the colony's history who ever persuaded a governor to advertise his willingness to pay by the hour.

3. Doing It The American Way

As previously noted, I was, for some considerable time, a payroll clerk and, as such, together with a raft of friends, I was responsible for the payroll of the entire colonial service. In all truth, we were an important part of our ministry. Indeed, perhaps I was lucky to be transferred to Payroll from my cashier's job, particularly after my fiasco with Mr. Nicholson.

Then again, maybe it was felt that I would be less dangerous if I was moved away from the public gaze and into the bowels of Finance, where I could more easily be watched by a bevy of senior accountants who, by and large, were crazier than I. Luckily, I happily fit in with this merry band of vagabonds, and consequently spent a delightful 12 months in Payroll before being transferred to Passages, which is another story that I will get to shortly.

Now, in general, life in Payroll was calm if, of course, we had no generic pay raises to disturb our peace. Usually, we managed to pay our fellow officers a close approximation of the salary they had probably earned. Yet this admirable level of accuracy was easily destroyed, as we soon discovered to our sorrow, when our chief accountant went to America for a course in computerized accounting and came home imbued with the spirit of progress. Inspired to do good, he immediately changed our time-honoured method of doing one month's payroll each month, and the whole department collapsed into chaos.

This most regrettable event occurred mainly because the new system was totally driven by little pieces of variously coloured paper, officially known as payroll control slips, and all changes to an officer's salary or deductions had to be processed, in their entirety, immediately as they were received. Thus, in our brave new world, most normal transactions now mandated a wide cross-section of forms for a wide variety of months, which, unhappily, was the sting in the tail of an otherwise sound idea and the cause of our department's decline.

For example, let us consider the case of an officer who, in December, had a temporary staff advance of 100 pounds, repayable over the next three months, and beginning with a deduction of 33 pounds and 33 pence, from his January salary. In February, naturally, the same deduction of 33 pounds, 33 pence would apply but, in March, the deduction would be 33 pounds and 34 pence and, in April, the deduction would cease. However, in order to accomplish this fairly routine transaction, three payroll control slips must be prepared. One for January, to set up a deduction of 33.33. One for March to change the deduction to 33.34. And one for April to cancel the deduction. Quite simple really, if you have a mind like a steel trap.

Yet that was not the worst part, for I have still to explain what we did, or didn't do, with all those damnable change slips which littered our desks. Without them there was no system. They were the lifeblood which drove it and eventually destroyed it. The whole process depended upon each little slip being carefully filed in one of the 12 payroll control bins, which had just been installed in our boss's office.

In theory, but alas, never in reality, each of these bins was meant to contain all of the changes for a specific month of the year, and therefore, under our leader's watchful eye, we amateur mailmen tried faithfully to deposit our various control slips, in the correct month's pit. So, in the example just described, I would, in January, put one slip in each of the January, March and April bins.

Therefore, according to the rules, each of these leering bins should always contain every appropriate change needed to produce a perfect payroll in its ordained month. Of course they didn't, since this is an imperfect world, and many slips were, perish the thought, misfiled. Plus, it was almost impossible to undo something we had already done, which, to continue my previous example, would be necessary if my mythical officer repaid his loan in full in early January by personal cheque, thereby making invalid my January, March and April changes.

But these little memos had long since gone to their respective boxes, and so I would be reduced to raiding the control bins, in the hope of finding and destroying my inappropriate changes. Usually, I would succeed, but sometimes I would not, since each box contained many hundred pieces of confetti and guarded its secrets well. Consequently, with the passage of time, the contents of the control bins increasingly diverged from reality and served only to confuse the issue.

However, as detailed above, these bins were the vital crux of the new system and, at the end of a payroll period, the relevant month's bin was ceremoniously wheeled to the computer room for processing against the payroll register. Now in theory, this was a great step forward, because in the past, keypunch had been forced to re-key, each month, the entire deck of payroll computer cards from our payroll ledger sheets. But now all they needed to key were computer cards for the changes, which was a significant plus for keypunch, since it drastically reduced their workload. Nevertheless, like all of life, there was a flip side, and the new system soon revealed two fairly significant disadvantages.

One: We in payroll were overworked, undersexed and lost in a world of pink slips. Two: The payrolls produced had to be seen to be believed.

Naturally, since this is the way my life has always evolved, my most imaginative pay slip was reserved for our beloved governor and, in the first month after we went to the new enlightenment, I paid him an allowance equal to the rent he owed on Government House. Plus, to make amends, I also discontinued his rental deduction in its entirety. Damn those little pieces of paper. Guess I must have used the wrong colour or filed it in the wrong box. In any event, when this minor mistake was politely brought to my attention by the Chief Establishment Officer, I confidently predicted a different result next month.

Boy was I right. As soon as the following month's payroll hit the fan, the Chief Establishment Officer politely took the time to visit my office, and hysterically informed me that this time I had tripled the Governor's fictitious rental allowance, while still refusing to charge him rent for Government House.

Sadly, I tried to explain to my inquisitor the reasons why I could no longer forecast exactly who would get what each month. Sadly, he rejected my arguments, until I showed him those leering payroll control bins, each filled to the brim with multihued garbage. He then offered to discuss this great leap forward with our chief accountant and suggested I pray for guidance before any more payrolls were produced.

In addition, in case my prayers went unanswered, the C.E.O. arranged to have the Governor's next pay slip intercepted and sent to my office for manual verification, before he allowed this monthly flight of fancy to be mailed to Government House. That is what saved my bacon, for as soon as I saw my next offering, I saw my mistake. Still, I was getting closer, because this time I had managed to stop his fictitious rental allowance, and had deducted from his salary a valid current month's rent on his lodgings. But, alas, in making adjustments for his arrears of rent and refund of nonexistent rental allowances, I had obviously used the wrong control slips. Thus, I unfortunately succeeded in taking a colossal amount of rental arrears from his salary and reducing his net paycheque to a pittance.

Regretfully, since in all of us there is a hidden socialist, I voided the Governor's pay slip and manually produced an accurate one on my office typewriter. I then made all the other adjustments to the system which were needed to set the records straight and ensure that the Governor's bank would, for the first time in three months, receive an appropriate deposit on his behalf. Clearly, I had reached the end of my tether and this scant victory served only to emphasize how bleak my chances for next month had become.

Manfully, I faced the truth and, with a heavy heart, I now went to see the chief accountant, as I prepared to burn, or cross, my last bridge. Quietly, but firmly, I presented my compliments and told him I had now lost all vestiges of control – through his misnamed control slips – over my portion of the payroll. I confessed my inability to rise to the challenge of computerized accounting, and asked to be transferred to a more mundane position. Morosely, he agreed we had a problem and ended our interview by saying he would consider my request.

Fortunately, since I didn't want to be sent to the bush, I was not alone in my inability to cope with our new system as, one by one; all the other payroll clerks in our department announced their failure to handle progress. Accordingly, after about a week's deliberation, and probably with the Governor's hearty support, our far-sighted chief accountant decided to abandon this great leap forward and return to our old unimaginative payroll system.

This was easier said than done, and for weeks we all had to work overtime, as we struggled to get our payroll ledger sheets back into shape and to trash the trash in the payroll control bins, which were themselves then trashed on the dung heap of history. Shortly thereafter, the chief accountant quietly joined all other sinners in the bush, as the payroll department sank back once more into the languor from which it had been so rudely awakened.

4. Passages

The British Colonial Civil Service was, in my jaundiced view, one of the world's most enlightened employers, with probably the best conditions of service I have ever encountered. In particular, I refer to the incredibly generous amounts of overseas leave we all enjoyed. For surely the major need of all conscientious employees worldwide is to spend as little time as is feasible at work and as much time as feasible at play.

Yet even though our service excelled all others in play time, it also had many other outstanding attributes. Most notable amongst these was an absolute requirement that all recruitment take place, just like the military, at the junior officer rank and, in addition, all officers had to receive as wide a variety of job experiences as possible, thereby ensuring a deep breadth of experience throughout the Service.

However, to the unwary, these enlightened practices could be dangerous and I well remember running afoul of the aforementioned Chief Establishment Officer on this very aspect of the Service. My *faux pas* occurred one afternoon when he stopped by my office with a simple request. It was hot and I was tired and uncooperative. I foolishly told him his request would be difficult to fulfill, and I would try to have it completed by noon the next day.

Bad mistake, for he sweetly smiled at me and said, 'Young man, 20 years ago I did your job, and if you find my request so difficult, I will happily show you how to do what I want.' Foiled, I assured him this would not be necessary and, one hour later, I hurried over to his office with the report he needed. Thus, I painlessly learned a great truth, for in a Service where everyone starts at the bottom, and frequent transfers are the norm, one needs to allow for the possibility of the boss knowing the score, even though, as we all know so well, that is a rarity.

Anyway, to get back to my story, this frequent transfer rule caught up with me some two months after our payroll frenzy, and I was sent to work in Passages, a small two-man section where overseas travel for the entire Service was handled. Fortunately, my new job was still in the headquarters of the Ministry of Finance, and I happily moved my Carlton cigarettes just a few offices down our main corridor from Payroll to Passages. I silently thanked God for once again sparing me from life in the bush. Equally gratifying was the fact that this job was the most interesting, and unusual, of my entire colonial career.

In the early 1960s the Passages Department, as the name implies, dealt almost exclusively with passages by sea, to Europe and back. It was, in reality, a government travel agency and, due to the very restricted number of commercial travel agencies in central Africa, it handled the travel arrangements for almost everyone going on overseas leave. Indeed, even if an officer made his bookings through a regular travel agency, they still had to be verified, approved and paid for through the Passages office.

Nevertheless, as previously mentioned, this section was small, having only two employees. I was the clerk, and my boss was Tom MacIntosh, a tall, slim, 35-year-old, balding, dour Scotsman, who served as the accountant; together we ruled the waves. It must, of course, be emphasized that in 1960, there was no such thing as a computer reservation system for foreign travel. No sir, we were not yet computerized, and since our telephones crackled and popped on long distance calls, making it difficult to conduct business, we did the bulk of our work by mail, as we booked, confirmed, paid for or canceled, the entire overseas travel of Northern Rhodesia's finest.

Thus, anyone wanting to make reservations for Europe had to begin the process at least a year in advance so that, after voluminous correspondence, berths could be confirmed and paid for about six months before departure date. It really was a far cry from today's instant computerized reservation systems. To my mind, they are one of the few real success stories of the computer age, and a boon to international travel.

Yet even without the marvel of modern telecommunications, we somehow got the job done, as we blissfully devoted ourselves to ensuring that our colleagues traveled according to their station in life. Naturally, this was all meticulously spelled out in our beloved Colonial Regulations – which seemed to be a virtual combination of the Magna Carta and the American Constitution – and determined each officer's entitlement based on his rank. Consequently, our officers were neatly segregated by status as they journeyed to and from Europe on a Union Castle liner, in a berth determined by their rank.

Normally, this meant Capetown, South Africa to Southampton, England, and return. Plus, as noted previously, first-class rail fare from Northern Rhodesia to Capetown and back. Thus, we had in Passages voluminous deck plans for all the Union Castle liners, as well as a complete schedule of all that shipping line's sailings for the foreseeable future. If an officer going on leave came to see us a year or so before the big event, we could, together, pick out appropriate berths on appropriate ships and, with luck, finalize travel arrangements in two or three months.

However, this seldom happened, because the berths we requested were usually unavailable, and the whole process had to begin again, with a fresh exchange of letters between our office and the Union Castle reservation centre in Capetown, South Africa. Yet sooner or later, sometimes after months of proposal and counterproposal, we always managed to get our customers in some kind of a cabin, on some kind of a boat, going somewhere. And, thank God, rail reservations were easier to book, since they did not provide for a specific berth, but merely for a seat on the train.

But these were the easy bookings, since passage to Europe by Union Castle liner was much too tame for our second and third tour officers, who thanks once more to Colonial Regulations, could tour the world at will. Our Bible clearly stated that any officer could apply the cash equivalent of his and his family's rail and sea entitlement to any conceivable booking he could imagine, providing only that at least three months of his vacation was spent, for health reasons, in a temperate climate. Of course, if an officer was overly imaginative, then he was required to send a cheque for all of his excess travel expenses to Passages, before we paid for his odyssey.

So, let the games begin. Our folks really hit the road running on this one. The most adventurous, if they could afford it, booked passage from Durban South Africa, to Durban South Africa, on the cruise ship Southern Cross. As its name suggests, it toured the southern seas, with the southern stars to guide it. Thoughtfully, this exotic luxury liner provided a six-month round-the-world cruise, with stops in Tahiti, Australia, New Zealand and even London, as it tried to comfort the poor, long-suffering, colonial martyrs.

I never made this trip but if the British Empire had lasted 10 years longer, I would certainly have considered it. Granted, it cost considerably more than one's entitlement, but, on the other hand, it provided room and board for the entire six months of the once-in-a-lifetime experience. Plus, since we were all on leave with full pay, I probably would have broken even by applying my salary during the cruise, to the cost of the cruise, which is, after all, a pleasant way to spend the taxpayer's money.

The Southern Cross was beyond the means of most junior officers but it was only one in a whole string of options available to Northern Rhodesia's migrating herds. In particular, many of my more mundane colleagues, and I, opted for a six-week voyage on a British India cargo liner from Beira in Mozambique, to London. This was the long way to Europe, following the east coast of Africa to the Red Sea and the Suez Canal, before crossing the Mediterranean to reach the north Atlantic.

Of course these working-class cruises were not overly opulent, but then the price was right, and they certainly offered an interesting variety of ports of call. Normally, but not always, these ships would stop at Dar-Es-Salaam in Tanganyika, the island of Zanzibar, Mombassa in Kenya, Aden in Yemen, Suez and Port Said in Egypt, Marseille in France, Barcelona in Spain, and finally Gibraltar, as they slowly headed towards England.

The world was our oyster. No idea seemed to be beyond the imagination of our wandering flock. They came up with the most unlikely of destinations, such as the Seychelles and Madagascar in the Indian Ocean. One colleague went to the United States and had a fabulous time, even though he lived on Greyhound buses for most of his two-month tour. Our officers spread out across the globe like locusts, and happily I helped them devour it by booking their tickets. I quickly became a first-class ticket agent with a tremendous store of knowledge about the world's faraway places, with strange-sounding names calling, calling to me.

It was the advent of air travel which really allowed my customers to take wing. When the airlines first began to replace the shipping companies as the main carriers of intercontinental travelers, they had a very attractive method of calculating airfares. It was based primarily on mileage, and allowed an almost unlimited number of stopovers.

For example, if one wanted to fly from Lusaka to London, the basic airfare would be based on the mileage between these two cities by the normal route. However, one could make this flight in as many stages as one wished. Multiple stopovers were permitted, provided only that each new destination was closer to London than its predecessor. In addition, stages could be booked open-dated, so that one didn't have to decide up front how long to stay in any one location.

Now obviously, when you did this, you had to go to the relevant airport, when you'd seen enough of Khartoum, and exchange your open-dated ticket for one on a specific plane on a specific day. But it was worth it, because even when one's circuitous route exceeded the norm for the trip, the excess fare charged was usually quite minimal, and I never saw one over 25 percent.

Those were the days when men were men and the airlines were as flexible as chewing gum. Certainly this was, in my opinion, the golden age of travel, and I well remember Mr. MacIntosh standing up with a ticket which reached, in its multiple parts, from his shoulder, to his feet. Unfortunately, my colonial career was too brief and I never had the opportunity to really milk this option. Still, I gave it my best shot, and, although that is another story, I did once make the following flights at 10 percent over basic:

FROM	TO
Entebbe	Nairobi, Kenya
Nairobi	Addis Ababa, Ethiopia
Addis Ababa	Asmara, Eritrea
Asmara	Beirut, Lebanon
Beirut	Damascus, Syria
Damascus	Amman, Jordan
Amman	Tel Aviv, Israel
Tel Aviv	Athens, Greece
Athens	Rome, Italy
Rome	London, England
London	New York, U.S.A.
New York	Louisville, U.S.A.

That, I would submit, is a fairly adventurous trip, and surely not bad for a little old country boy from Lancashire, back in the good old days when packaged flights and conducted tours were only just beginning to destroy the reason for visiting out-of-the-way places. Well, as they say, all good things must come to an end, and after about nine months in Passages, I was transferred to Internal Security. Yet I could not complain, since I had really enjoyed the experience of being a travel agent in such a remote part of the world. Indeed, to this day, I still feel a sense of *déjà vu* whenever I visit a travel agent and sometimes I even feel that I know more about travel than my travel agent, which surely is a preposterous thought.

5. Boot Polish

Once again my guardian angel performed without blemish, keeping me in Lusaka and away from the dreaded bush. Mercifully, Internal Security was situated on the second floor of the Ministry of Finance, and so, without delay, I quickly moved my cigarettes to their new location. It was also very nice to be working in a department with such an important-sounding name and, although I never found out exactly what we did, we must have done it well, since no one ever complained. Plus, I was obviously on my way to the top, for now I had an office on the second floor of a three-floor building. One down, one to go. Perhaps tomorrow a knighthood!

In the meantime, I decided to tread carefully in this new department, which was apparently very prestigious and had a much larger staff than Passages. Whereas previously, we had been but two, with one boss, my new home had a staff of three, with two bosses. Naturally I was, as always, the clerk. Paul Bokenham, a tall, rangy, hyperactive South African of about 40, was the senior accountant, and Pat Burgess, a tall, slender, distinguished-looking Englishman of about 50, was our senior finance officer.

Never before had I been exposed to so much rank, and it was

therefore with much fear and trepidation that I moved into an office centrally located right between the grandiose offices of these two very senior civil servants. How wise I was to worry, since I soon discovered that I was working for two of the more interesting lunatics in the Northern Rhodesian Service.

The first inkling I had of their unique work habits occurred about a week after I joined this duo and, inadvertently, took part in one of their intriguing little customs. It all began, quite innocently, when Mr. Burgess came into my office early one morning and solemnly asked me to call Mr. Bokenham on the telephone. 'What for?' I politely replied, having nothing I needed to say to our colleague. 'For nothing, just talk to him,' Boss No. 1 answered, before leaving my office. Like a good junior clerk, I called Mr. Bokenham and asked him if he thought it would rain today. Now admittedly, that was a pretty dumb question to ask in the middle of the dry season but it was the best I could do on such short notice.

Understandably, Boss No. 2 was not amused and told me so in no uncertain language before hanging up his phone. However, the resulting silence was soon broken when, to my surprise, through the partition which separated our two offices, I heard an explosion of inelegant Afrikaans. Shortly thereafter, a somewhat blackened Mr. Bokenham burst into my office like a leading member of a local Zulu impi.

Hastily I tried to remind Mr. Bokenham that we were both on the same side. He speedily rejected this argument by pointing out that anyone who put black boot polish into the earpiece of his phone was automatically an enemy. Nonplused, I inquired as to why he believed I was responsible for his black ear. He replied that I was the one who called him with a damn fool question.

'If you hadn't called, I wouldn't have picked up the phone and stuck a boot-polished earpiece into my ear,' he explained, as he prepared to throw me through my window. Wisely, I refrained from further discussion and, after rising from my chair, I concentrated on keeping my desk between us.

Silently we played ring around the desk, until Mr. Burgess came back into the room, and politely asked me if I intended to play with Mr. Bokenham for the rest of the morning. 'Not if you will tell him you made me call him,' I pleaded, and immediately the scales fell from Mr. Bokenham's eyes as he realized who was really behind his facial adornment. For a moment or two, he stared angrily at Mr. Burgess, trying to decide if he would rather kill our boss, or keep his job. Finally he decided to keep the job, said something disgusting in Afrikaans, and rushed off to the bathroom to attempt to depolish his ear.

Thoughtfully I regarded my cherubic boss, and said accusingly, 'you could have got me killed.' Coolly he replied, 'Yes, I suppose so, but it would have been worth it.' Then, as I began to see the funny side of what I hoped was not a typical workday, we both began laughing until the tears streamed down our cheeks. Slowly our laughter subsided and thoughtfully I stared at the dangerous lunatic for whom I now worked. Nonchalantly, as if sensing my thoughts, he smiled a friendly smile and, as he turned to leave my office, he said, 'thank you for your cooperation, I'm sure you will do just fine in Internal Security.'

Unfortunately I was not worried about doing just fine. I was more worried about surviving Mr. Bokenham. But I need not have worried, for about a week later someone mysteriously boot polished Mr. Burgess' telephone, and with both Mr. Bokenham and I gleefully sitting in his office, Mr. Burgess elegantly decorated his own right ear when he took an important call from the Minister of Finance.

With honour satisfied, Mr. Bokenham no longer looked vengefully in my direction, and Mr. Burgess decided that since we had a pervert in our midst, he would declare the phone system off limits to all practical jokers. Consequently, for a day or two, Internal Security relaxed, although, as befits a prudent man, I always examined my phone for boot polish before I risked using it.

6. Get Thee Behind Me Satan

Just to set the record straight, and before I begin this next story, let me categorically state that I am not a professional criminal. I have never considered nipping down to the corner grocery store for a little inoffensive armed robbery. Yet on one occasion during my year in Internal Security I did, for a week or two, seriously consider a life of crime.

Perhaps the reason was the obvious one – opportunity. Because I, and only I, had the means to rob every government safe in the colony, whenever I chose. Perhaps, in addition, I was also tempted by the rapid approach of home rule for Northern Rhodesia and the sense, among the white community, of apathy, despair, chaos and anger which overlaid the transition of power, from the known to the unknown. Or yet again, perhaps it was just a feeling that all the whites had: since we were going to finish up in South Africa anyway, why not leave with a golden handshake?

Nevertheless, whatever my rationale, I really did spend several sleepless nights, with two or three of my closest friends, planning and considering the colonial heist of the century. For me it would have been easy, since I had the little black book and the keys to the kingdom. This treasure trove was kept in a small combination safe, built into the wall of my office. I alone knew the combination, since I had personally set it, on the day I assumed my responsibilities in Internal Security. In addition, because of the importance of my little black book and keys, I soon got in the habit of changing my safe's combination on a monthly basis.

So what did this book and those keys have which made them so valuable? Nothing much, except that between them they provided access to every government safe in the colony, in the most elementary manner. You see, my book listed, in alphabetical order, the name and random code number of all our safes, and my keys gave entry to a nearby vault, whose walls contained several rows of progressively numbered hooks from which, in many cases, there dangled a key. And, you've guessed it, the random code number in the book, corresponded to the relevantly numbered hook in the vault, on which that particular safe's duplicate key dangled. Thus, if an entry in my Bible read, 'Solwezi boma – 247,' then key number 247 in the vault would open the Solwezi boma safe.

Hence, I really did possess the keys to the kingdom and it was my job to solve the problem when anyone, God forbid, lost his key. Therefore, to continue the above example, if the District Commissioner in Solwezi lost the key to his safe, his only recourse was to mount an armed guard in front of the safe and call me with the good news. I would then immediately retrieve his duplicate key from my vault and dispatch the government locksmith post haste to Solwezi. Once there, this skilled craftsman should, after opening the safe, have no trouble altering its lock and cutting two new keys. Then, to complete the circle, he would give one new key to the District Commissioner and bring the other one back to Lusaka, for safekeeping in my vault.

Now that was how the system was meant to work. But once, as I intimated, I nearly opted for a variation and became a thief, by using one of my duplicate keys to rob one of Her Majesty's safes. This novel approach to my job, occurred to me when I realized how easily I could 'borrow,' just for the weekend, the duplicate key to any safe in the country but, more importantly, to any safe not close to Lusaka. If I intended to stay out of jail, I had to be above suspicion in any robbery I instigated, which meant I had to rob a boma far from home. Therefore my plan called for two like-minded friends to join in the venture and visit my distant target early on the applicable Sunday morning, while I stayed in Lusaka to work on my alibi.

If we hit a large urban boma like Ndola, our haul would come close to a quarter of a million pounds, which to us in those far-gone days, was a very considerable sum of money. However, since we were educated criminals, my plan then called for them to bury the loot in a safe place and, after giving me back my key, resume their role as pillars of society. Finally, when we all trooped into work the following day, I had only to return my newly washed key to the vault, and I too was in the clear.

Would my heist have worked? Who knows? I never did it, and I never found out. Still, it was an intriguing idea, and I don't see how I could have been blamed for a robbery in Ndola, provided I was able to prove I never left Lusaka. Also, don't forget that the District

Commissioner in Ndola, who had the original key to his safe, was going to have some interesting questions to answer on Monday morning, when he came to work and found his safe open and empty. Indeed, he would obviously have been the prime suspect and it was my British reluctance to get an innocent man in trouble which played a large part in my decision to stay poor.

But it would have been nice to have been able, hopefully, some five years or so after the heist, to have dug up my share of the loot and taken, for beginners, a six-month cruise on the Southern Cross. Yet it never happened, and all I am left with is the memory of spending several sleepless nights, when I really thought I was going to become a criminal. So why did I stay clean? Maybe I was scared, but I like to pretend it was because I know right from wrong, even though, on this occasion, I came awfully close to choosing wrong

7. My Annual Interviews

Perhaps the one thing I really regret about my life in Africa is that it was so short; it lasted for only seven brief years. Clearly I should have been born 50 years earlier, when life in the British Colonial Service was really interesting, and I could have had a full 30-year career.

However, I had more than most and so I cannot complain too loudly. Plus, in my first three years, my annual interview was such a disaster that I never dreamt of having a future in the Colonial Service, since my yearly evaluations seemed to be far from encouraging and did not bode well for the future. My problems began, ominously, towards the end of my first year of service, when my boss informed me that he would not be doing, as was the norm, my annual evaluation. Instead, Mr. Lewis, our august Permanent Secretary, who sat at God's right hand, would see me.

On the appointed day, like a lamb led to the slaughter, I was ushered into Mr. Lewis' sanctum – and slaughtered. He began mildly enough, by listing my physical shortcomings, and then grew more serious, as he doubted my mental stability. In short, he found me wanting and asked for more.

Next year, same scene. Again, Mr. Lewis stoked my fire, and again he demanded improvements, although this time he did allow as to how I was hovering on the fringe of the human race. Discouraged, I vowed to keep trying, and wondered why none of my friends made this annual pilgrimage to the third floor. Was I really that bad? Ken Bayman and Peter Van Eden never went to see the Permanent Secretary. They just had a nice cup of coffee with their boss and were told to keep up the good work. Lucky them. When we compared notes, they made matters worse by condescendingly agreeing with Mr. Lewis' appraisal of my performance.

Year three was a mirror image of my previous disasters but, this time, I was not prepared to suffer in silence and, at the end of my interview, I had the following conversation with my tormentor: -

Me:	'Excuse me sir, can I say something?'
Mr. Lewis:	'Certainly.'
Me:	'Well sir, I don't understand why every year I am reviewed by you, while none of my friends go through this annual roast. If I'm really that bad, why don't you just send me back to England?'
Mr. Lewis:	'Good Lord. You really don't understand, do you?'
Me:	'I'm afraid I do sir, which is why I'm depressed.'
Mr. Lewis:	'Young man, why do you think I interview you? Don't you know I have 500 officers in this ministry and I only interview about 12 a year?'
Me:	'I suppose 488 of them are doing better than I.'
Mr. Lewis:	'Good Lord. You couldn't be more mistaken. Why should I waste my time interviewing officers who are doing their best and can't do any better? You have been earmarked as a superior prospect and I intend to do everything I can to develop your potential. With a little luck you may have my job one day but only if I push you hard while you're still young. I certainly wouldn't waste my time with you if I didn't believe you have what it takes to reach the top. If I've been too harsh, I'm sorry. Actually, you have performed outstandingly in all your posts but I want you always to strive to improve! Understood?'
Me:	'Yes sir. Thank you sir.'
Mr. Lewis:	'My pleasure. See you next year.'
Me:	'I look forward to it, sir.'

And so I did. But I never told Ken and Pete what Mr. Lewis had said, partly because I'm not sure if they would have believed me, but also because, even then, I knew that my career was going nowhere. Already the winds of change were beginning to strengthen in Northern Rhodesia, and however much promise I showed, I showed 30 years too late. That was the sweet irony of Mr. Lewis' rather interesting managerial style, since the future was not ours to command. Thus, while I had my reservations about his motivational methods, I did respect his intentions, and was glad to know that I would, in another world, at another time, have enjoyed a full career, in the British Colonial Service.

Strangely enough, by way of a postscript to this story, I received a rather nice letter from the British government about two years before my 55th birthday. It was then some 20 years since I had left the service. To my amazement, the letter said that the British government had now decided it owed a debt of gratitude to those colonial officers whose careers had been nipped in the bud. Therefore, the letter said, they would increase my minimal pension from a pittance to a respectable sum, as soon as I reached the colonial retirement age of

55. Suspiciously, I wrote back and asked if they were serious. They replied that they were, and sure enough, when I turned 55, they started to send me the nicest monthly reminder of what might have been, if my country had not gone away.

8. Privacy

I will conclude this brief overview of life in the British Colonial Civil Service with a few words about our annually published Staff List which, in many ways, epitomized the Service's *modus operandi*. This 400–500 page book was given to all officers yearly, and also to all new arrivals. It was a complete Who's Who of the Service and listed, in alphabetical order, everything anyone would ever want to know about every officer in the Service, from the Governor to the most junior clerk.

The list contained the date of an officer's birth, the educational qualifications he possessed, graduation dates, the date he entered the Service, his rank, his pay scale and his current salary. Plus, if an officer was married, the list included his wife's name, her date of birth, the date of their marriage and, if they had children, their names, sex and date of birth.

In short, the Staff List revealed all. As a new recruit, I spent many titillating hours reading my colleagues' biographies. Unfortunately, like a topless beach, it soon became humdrum, and then I only used it to brief myself on the background and relative importance of anyone with whom I had contact. Thus, I knew who I had to call 'sir' and who not to slap on the back, or send packing when they asked for stamps.

To be fair to me, I must add that I had not yet received my Staff List when I trimmed Mr. Nicholson down to size nor, quite obviously, could one always consult the Staff List before opening a conversation. Nevertheless, many times, after talking to someone on the telephone, I would wonder exactly who he was, and then a brief glance in my trusty encyclopedia would tell me the dates of birth for all of his children.

Yet our Staff List was more than a gossipy magazine, since it proved emphatically that we had few secrets within the Service, and no one was paid too much or too little. If you had a valid question, it could often provide the answer. Best of all, it always conveyed the message that the Service dealt openly and fairly with all of its staff.

This enlightened attitude was also reflected in our system of 'Thirds,' whereby a copy of all of the outgoing correspondence produced by a department was filed in the Thirds File. The file was circulated weekly throughout the department, to keep everyone informed about everyone else's activities.

There were, of course, some real advantages to doing this, since occasionally we would spot an error in a colleague's actions, and sometimes we would discover that two of us had hold of the same stick. But again, the best part was the feeling of belonging to a team, and that goes to the heart of what I have tried to express in these brief glimpses of how the Empire was run. Hopefully, I have also managed to convey a more human side of the British Colonial Service which, with all its faults, struggled valiantly to make central Africa a credit to the Crown.

Chapter 6

An Innocent Abroad

1. Caretaker Deluxe

I have tried, in the last two chapters, to paint a picture of my town and of the work-a-day world in which I laboured, with some success, to become a good white African. But now it is time to forget these serious matters, and return once more to my private life, which usually seemed to teeter on the edge of disaster. Indeed, during much of my life I have been blessed – or cursed – with a guardian angel who seems determined that I should not have a mundane existence.

However, on balance, the fates have been kind. This was especially true when, soon after Martin left for Livingstone, Mr. Lewis, the Permanent Secretary, invited me to babysit his splendid accommodation, during the seven and a half months of his upcoming long leave. My good fortune was, as Mr. Lewis confirmed, no accident, but came about through the good offices of Bill Taylor, a member of the Permanent Secretary's inner circle, and the gentleman whose house Bill Curphy and I had recently babysat.

Apparently, for so I was told, Mr. Taylor had been so pleased with the way in which his house had been preserved that he had recommended my services to his boss with considerable enthusiasm. Happily I accepted this bolt from the blue, and arranged to relinquish my one-bedroom flat in exchange for the tenancy of the four-bedroom house of the Number Two man in the Ministry of Finance.

This time I had really hit the jackpot and when, some three to four weeks later, I moved into my new pad, I was immediately deluged with offers from, alas, all my male friends who wished to move up in the world. Chief amongst these was my old friend, Peter Van Eden, who wanted to move out of his parents' home, which was way out of town, and into something a little closer to his women and work.

Delighted by this opportunity to perchance gather the crumbs, or women, that fell from the master's table, I accepted his offer and, within a week, he had become a suburbanite. The two remaining bedrooms were soon filled, one by my good friend, Maurice Hawkins, and the other by his good friend, Michael Voysey.

Although Pete and I had never met him, he soon proved to be a most welcome addition to our family.

Maurice and I went back a long way, because he was one of the first people I met in the government rest house. By then, Maurice was already a senior resident of this hostel, having lived there for more than a year, and he kindly did all that he could to make me feel welcome in such strange surroundings.

He was of medium height and build, with straight brown hair neatly brushed back from his face. By birth, he was English, from Somerset I believe, and, when our friendship began, must have been in his middle 20's. He was a federal civil servant and, as long as I knew him, he worked as a meteorologist at our prestigious international airport, which was only about a mile down the road from the rest house.

When we first met, Maurice was still in his pre-driving days, despite the fact that he was already in his second year in the colony. He continued his ambulatory ways for a further 18 months before fatigue took its toll and he bought an old Volkswagen Beetle. During the whole of this period, he was, of course, forced to remain in the government rest house, since it alone was within walking distance of his job. His frequent promenades must have been quite exhilarating, especially in the rains and, because he was a shift worker, most stimulating in the middle of the night.

Yet there was a method to his madness and a dream in his heart. Maurice craved a Mercedes Benz, and spent almost three years as a hiker and miser in order to turn this dream into reality. So why did he eventually break down and buy an old Beetle? I don't really know, except that three years in the government rest house, with some light exercise to boot, would have made even Scrooge consider such a modest purchase a necessity.

Anyway, by coincidence, he bought the car some two months before I got Mr. Lewis' house. Therefore, when I showed him my new home, he happily pronounced himself able and willing to move out of the government rest house and into the aristocracy. But he held steadfast to his dream and about three months later it became a reality. Maurice sold his V.W., took a month's vacation and flew off to West Germany where he purchased a beautiful diesel-engined Mercedes Benz.

He then brought it back by boat to Capetown and drove home to Lusaka in triumph. His perseverance had paid off in spades and even his novel approach to buying a car was, in fact, quite common in our society. Due to a quirk in our law, one could buy a new car overseas, thereby avoiding the sales tax, and then, by bringing it back to Northern Rhodesia as a used vehicle, one could also avoid the import duty. This was the cheapest way to buy a luxury car and, naturally, that was the path Maurice chose to follow to his place in the sun.

So finally, after three years of scrimping and saving, he had his

Mercedes and it was paid for in cash. He had done, by remaining true to his vision, what he set out to do and that is a most uncommon achievement. In addition, Mr. Lewis would certainly have been pleased to find a brand new Mercedes parked in his driveway, since the neighborhood definitely needed a tad more elegance. Yet unfortunately, as with all silver linings, this one had a cloud. Maurice's Mercedes idled, as do all diesel powered cars, like several drunken sailors in a bar-room brawl. Consequently, for the next few months, I was often awakened in the middle of the night by the most awful racket as Maurice either came home late or went to work early.

Nevertheless, he was a true gentleman and I really enjoyed the time we spent together in Mr. Lewis' house. However, like most of my friends, Maurice was destined to experience the great outdoors and, shortly before I moved on to my next caretaker's slot, he was posted by the federal government to the far side of the moon. In his case, the sadist in charge of his life chose Lilongwe Federal Airport in Nyasaland, which was definitely not a centre of western culture.

Fortunately, as I have previously said, we colonials were made of stern stuff and, early one morning, Maurice and his sturdy steed cheerfully clanked their way out of my life, as he headed for the outer limits of the known world. Naturally, I never heard from him again but, since I do believe that Lilongwe does have a paved road, I expect that he went for an occasional spin, in what may be the only Mercedes Benz in his new hometown.

Michael Voysey, the fourth member of my new family, was the only newcomer to my circle of friends. He was, like Maurice, a meteorologist at Lusaka International Airport but, unlike Maurice, had only recently arrived in Lusaka from Bulawayo in Southern Rhodesia, where he had previously been stationed. At the time we first met, he was about 25 years old, tall, wiry, bespectacled and dark haired. By birth, he too was English and came from Southampton in the southernmost part of my country. Indeed, his hometown was the same Southampton from which I had set sail for South Africa, so many centuries before.

My new friend was not a recent arrival in Africa, having worked at the federal airport in Bulawayo for the past two years, but he was new to Lusaka, and anxious to sever his connections with the government rest house. Therefore, since he already owned a car, he had already suggested to Maurice that they should team up and apply for a government apartment. Hence, when Maurice decided instead to move in with me, he logically proposed bringing Michael along as our fourth wheel. I'm glad I agreed, for Mike Voysey rapidly became one of my closest friends, and it was his wedding to Eve Williams that I subsequently tried to destroy.

But, in those early days of my friendship with Mike, Eve was still living in Bulawayo, where the two of them had met and fallen in love. However, she soon moved to Lusaka to be near her fiancé, and immediately thereafter took a job as a teacher in one of our federal schools. Eve, when she burst into our lives, was a vivacious, good-looking, dark-haired, highly excitable, 23-year-old-woman. She was of medium height and build, by heritage she was Welsh, although she had been with her parents and two sisters, in Southern Rhodesia for many years.

She was a truly delightful young lady, and for the next 18 months I enjoyed a very close friendship with both Eve and Michael, until we all returned to England on leave and went our separate ways. I last saw them in London and Southampton, by arrangement, and after that our paths diverged. Still, it had been fun, and I will always be grateful for the memories of those days, which were, without doubt, amongst the happiest of my life.

Thankfully the future is not ours to foresee, and back in Lusaka, in those idyllic days, the four of us settled down to a life of domestic tranquility, the envy of all our friends. We were perfectly matched to run a home.

Peter, who had once lived on a farm, was put in charge of the yardwork and, with the garden boy as his helper, kept our lawns in mint condition. He also planted tomatoes and other vegetables, which meant we often had fresh produce for dinner.

Maurice, who in addition to having a delicate taste in automobiles, was also a fastidious dresser, took care of the interior of our house and, under his careful tutelage, our houseboy kept our home spotless.

Michael, in his only known perversion, enjoyed grocery shopping. Therefore, with liberal input from our cook, he kept our pantry well stocked and developed an extremely close relationship with several of our Indian storekeepers. As an accountant, I kept our books and paid the utility bills. I also paid the staff their weekly allowances and monthly salaries. But my main task, in conflict with the cook, was the planning, or debating, of our evening meal. This was my specialty and, as best I could, I tried to ensure that we ate as befits those on whose empire the sun is not supposed to set.

All in all, it worked magnificently and, once each month, we would gather together for a final accounting of the previous month's activities. At that time, each of us carefully presented our total expenditures for the month, and the grand total, divided by four, was what we each owed. Cheques were then written by those who had spent too little and given to those who had spent too much. It was simple and we never argued over money which, in most families, is a common cause of strain.

Indeed, we hardly argued at all and each of us bought what we wanted, including liquor and cigarettes, and the tab was always split four ways, which may seem strange until you remember that even though Maurice didn't smoke, he always drank more than his fair share of milk. 'Keep it simple' was our motto and it beat the hell out of the system employed by two other friends of mine, who each had separate shelves in the refrigerator, on which they jealously stored their own sacrosanct food. Needless to say, these two friends soon split up, while we four went on from strength to strength.

We also were blessed with the finest of help, because Mr. Lewis' entire staff – cook, houseboy and garden boy had elected to stay on at the house and work for me, even though Mr. Lewis had already paid them in advance for all the months of his leave. Thus, these three gentlemen drew double pay, since I also paid them what Mr. Lewis had paid them, during the whole time I lived in his house.

This was a most unusual situation, because usually an officer's servants would take the opportunity to go back to their rural village and lord it over their relatives. However, for some reason they did not choose to do this and remained in Lusaka to supervise our home. Consequently, I enjoyed the services of a highly qualified staff, who knew the household's routine, while they, quite naturally, enjoyed having their incomes doubled.

Clearly, it was a real win-win situation, but then I'm easy to please and, as long as everything was perfect, I had no complaints. Indeed, I lived in such luxury in Mr. Lewis' home that I even began to question the need to ever get married, since a wife seemed like an unnecessary expense and a possible inconvenience. In truth, I had stumbled into the perfect setup for a bachelor in Africa and, luckily, I was able to prolong my caretaker's career during the rest of my first tour in Northern Rhodesia.

It was a good life, they were good times and, in 1961 and 1962, I was blessed with a higher standard of living than any I had previously known, or have since been privileged to experience. If that was darkest Africa, then someone forgot to turn out the lights and I rapidly forgot how to clean a pair of shoes. Truly, my cup was more than half full and I was wise enough to know this, as I sat with a gin and tonic on my elegant stoop at sundowner time, patiently waiting for the soft tinkle of the little bell which formally announced that dinner was served. Certainly those were the days when I came closest to having it all and I shall always be grateful for having known such luxury and luck.

2. Afternoon Tea

Of course luxury can itself be dull, unless it is enlivened with a little flair, and I can honestly say that the afternoon teas which I supervised were, to say the least, imaginative. My premise was this: the more unusual the sandwich I offered, the more memorable would be the result. Accordingly, between 4 and 5 p.m. daily, the cook and I attempted to tickle my friends' palates with a unique blend of flavors.

One of my better creations featured sardines and strawberry jam. This odd combination produced a really delicious sandwich and quite whetted my appetite for further culinary adventures. Each day I served a new delight. My repertoire soon grew to include bananas and marmalade on toast, sliced egg topped with pineapple jam, ice cream sprinkled with diced onions, and even a fruit cake, in which bacon had been delicately substituted for the fruit.

Nothing was too outlandish for me to try and I can, without boasting, say that my three friends deeply appreciated my efforts. Sometimes they were so overcome at tea time that they wept, with joy I assume, as they sampled my gourmet selections. Unfortunately, our guests were sometimes more staid, and would firmly reject my snacks as they warily sipped their tea. But then, as we all know, even Michelangelo had his critics, and I have always felt sorry for those in which the joy of the unknown has yet to flower.

Actually, if you come right down to it, most of our preferences in food is the result of where we live. For example, no one in Africa ate catfish, which we considered unclean, while in America, it is considered to be something of a delicacy. Similarly, before coming to the U.S., I would never have dreamt of eating turnip greens, since my mother didn't raise me to be a cow. Nor do I fancy frog's legs or chocolate-coated grasshoppers and, even in my own culture, the idea of lamb with mint jelly, or turkey with cranberry jelly, was a little off-putting.

Hence, I soon came to the surprising conclusion that there are no strange food combinations, but only new recipes, which may only be new within the narrow confines of one's own experience. Therefore, I am not sure if sardines and strawberry jam is an original contribution of mine to the evolution of good taste. Hopefully it is, and, since there is already a Welsh rarebit, perhaps we could call this the Northern Rhodesian rarebit, which seems like an appropriately mysterious name.

Certainly, in more ways than one, my horizons were widened by our afternoon teas. I learned much about tolerance and also discovered that almost any new mix of foods is palatable, provided your mind is as open as your mouth. In addition, I think we all learned again that, with certain obvious exceptions, only a bigot rejects a new experience before sampling its flavor. Thus, what started out as an attempt to entertain my friends, finished up as an exercise in human behaviour.

3. If You've Seen One Bridge

Perhaps an unkind reaction to my culinary feats would be to suggest that I was at my wit's end for entertainment. Certainly, central Africa is not overendowed with places to visit and things to do, which is why we often took day trips to see our two bridges. The nearest of these, the Kafue River bridge, was about 50 miles from Lusaka and was a nice, simple road bridge, over a nice, simple river. The bridge itself had an interesting history, having been originally built during World War II as a temporary replacement for a more artistic structure which, until it was bombed by the Germans, had graciously spanned the river Thames in downtown London.

Naturally, when the war had been won, this inelegant temporary bridge had been dismantled, and a more suitable permanent replacement erected in its place. Shortly thereafter, the British Government thoughtfully shipped their temporary bridge off to Africa and had it installed as the permanent bridge across the Kafue river, in Northern Rhodesia.

Consequently, I am extremely confident when I say that the Kafue river, at the place where our bridge passed over it, is exactly the same width as the river Thames in London. If it hadn't been, we would have been forced to alter the width of our river to fit our bridge, and that, I was reliably told, would have been a tad inconvenient. But at least our bridge had a history, and how many bridges have spanned major rivers on two different continents? Not many, I'm sure, and, for want of a better reason, we now had a valid excuse for our pilgrimage to Kafue.

What did we do when we got there? Well, we parked our cars, and walked across the bridge to the other side. Then we walked back across the bridge to our cars, and went home, exhausted with happiness. Could we have fished? I don't know. I do know that African rivers are not good news and have several permanent drawbacks. The first is, of course, crocodiles, who seem to ignore the bait on the pole and, in a reversal of roles, try to dine on any fisherman found loitering on the river's bank. The second is hippopotamus, who also go in for role reversal by attempting to eat any pleasure boat foolish enough to go trolling on their private preserve. And that is exactly what happened to Pat Burgess, my boss at work, one Sunday afternoon, when he tried to go cruising down the river. Luckily, he survived, but he lost a very expensive boat and most of his tan.

Yet these first two dangers pale beside the third, the scourge of disease. For unfortunately, over most of Africa, Bilharzia, a terrible, usually fatal, wasting disease is endemic. This disease comes, I believe, in the form of a parasite carried by water-borne snails, and attacks the intestines of those with whom it makes contact. It truly is bad news, and very common in the African population, who have no choice but to use river water. The message was clear: stay away from the river; it is a dangerous and unhealthy place and best admired from a distance. Accordingly, on our trips to see the Kafue river bridge, that is exactly what we did, and then we went home to plan our next adventure.

I never had a bad experience with an African river but I sure remember reading about one, in our local newspaper. It was 1960, and this drama began when a group of African women went down to the local river to wash clothes. They were attacked by a large crocodile, which seized one of the women. Panic ensued, and most of the villagers fled in terror as they sounded the alarm. In response, a passing white police officer rushed to the scene and tried to rescue the unfortunate lady. The crocodile now turned on him and bit off his leg. Then, in a fitting climax to this horrible drama, a second incredible act of courage took place when one of the other African washer women, went back into the water and dragged the injured policeman to the river's bank.

Finally, when it was all over, the first lady was dead, the white policeman and the second African lady had survived (although he was badly mauled) and the crocodile had disappeared. A few months later, in recognition of their bravery, the two heroes of this story were awarded the George Cross, Britain's highest civilian medal for gallantry. In addition, in a more practical vein, the African lady was also awarded a brand new 10-speed bicycle, in order, I assume, to more diligently flee from crocodiles.

Clearly, our rivers had bite. To admire them from the safety of their bridges was wise, especially if one wanted to grow old intact or live long enough to visit the Churundu bridge.

As far as we were concerned, this was the mother of all bridges. It spanned the Zambezi river at a non-existent spot in the road called, naturally, Churundu. This wonder (the bridge, not the wide spot) lay about 75 miles past Kafue on the Salisbury road, and was one of the prettiest suspension bridges in Africa, perhaps in the world. In some ways, it had a superficial resemblance to the Golden Gate Bridge in San Francisco, although Churundu was considerably smaller. Even so, its single span was most impressive, as it soared some 150 feet above the mighty Zambezi, in a half mile leap, from shore to shore. It had the distinction of being the only road bridge across the Zambezi, from the Victoria Falls to the Indian Ocean, a distance of at least 800 miles.

This bridge was formally known as the Otto Beit Bridge, although I don't know who that Afrikaans gentleman was. I also don't know when the bridge was built, or anything else about it, except that it stood on the border between the two Rhodesias, since the Zambezi River was the official demarcation line between the two countries. However, back in the 1960s, when the ill-fated Federation of Rhodesia and Nyasaland still flourished, there were no border crossings or custom posts at the bridge, because both Rhodesias were part of the same happy family, and peacefully waiting for all hell to break loose.

So, what did we do when we got to Churundu? Well, obviously, we again parked our cars, and walked to the other side. Still, it was a much longer walk this time, with a dizzying view over the guardrail, a much bigger river, a much lonelier place and more flies. Yet in essence it was little different than tripping the light fantastic across the Kafue. Nonetheless, it must have been worth it, since we went there quite often. Of course, there was the added pleasure of being able to stamp one's foot on the far side of the bridge and say, 'It really broadens the mind to visit foreign countries, don't you think?'

Unfortunately, there was nothing there to see, and no one to speak to, which made us feel more like fools than tourists. Hence, we faced the inevitable and, still having fun, retraced our steps across the Zambezi. Then we went back to our cars and once more went home, exhausted with the joie de vivre for surely a trip to Churundu was the perfect way to have a nice day.

4. Let's Go To The Movies

In the early 1960s, Lusaka was a great place to visit, but not a nice place to live for anyone who was a sincere Charlton Heston fan. This dichotomy, quite naturally, was a very significant drawback to our town's ambience, and came about because, to its everlasting shame, Lusaka did not possess a cinemascope screen. Thus, we were all deprived of the opportunity to see the great man in those wonderful Hollywood cinemascope epics which so enthralled the more civilized world.

One can't have everything in life and I was consoled by the thought of my next trip to the Churundu bridge. However, for some strange reason, my enlightened attitude did not sit well with Peter Van Eden who, perhaps because he was younger than I, yearned to see a cinemascope film, and brooded constantly over life's inequities. Finally, when Ben Hur was released, Peter's passion reached its zenith, and he firmly resolved that, whatever the cost, we would not let Ben Hur's chariots pass us by. But what could we do? There didn't seem to be a solution until Peter, appropriately, decided that if the mountain would not come to Mohammed, then Mohammed must go to the mountain.

Cautiously, I pointed out that he had the wrong religion for Charlton Heston, but Peter had the bit between his teeth and was impervious to doubt. Therefore, with true religious zeal, he hastened to our sole travel agent and, within a week, was the proud possessor of two circle seats in a cinema that was currently showing Ben Hur. Happily, he showed me these tickets and politely waited for my adulation. 'Where is the cinema?' I asked with a sinking heart. 'Salisbury, Southern Rhodesia,' he casually replied. 'When are we going?' I wearily queried. 'This coming Saturday night,' was the answer, as he continued to wait for my praise. 'That's nice,' I admitted, facing reality and a 700-mile drive, since our destination was at least 350 miles from Lusaka.

Bright and early on the next Saturday morning, Peter and I left for

Salisbury in his car – since it was his idea. Once again we passed over the bridges at Kafue and Churundu, but this time we kept going, and by 4 p.m., we were in the parking lot of the grandest cinema in Salisbury. For two hours we wandered the streets of that delightful city, which I had never previously visited, and after a nice meal in the theatre's restaurant, we went to the evening performance of Ben Hur. It was great, it was wonderful, the first cinemascope film that either of us had ever seen and, in particular, the chariot race really took our breath away. Enthralled, we sat on the edges of our seats until, about 11 p.m., the movie ended and, in a daze, we returned to Pete's car.

Now all that remained of our odyssey was to retrace our path to Lusaka, and eventually, after nodding to our faithful bridges, we finally arrived home at about 9 a.m. Sunday, just in time for morning prayers at Lusaka cathedral. Admittedly, it had been a fairly long drive to go to a movie, and most of our friends thought we were crazy, but we had been well rewarded for our efforts. In addition, not too many people can boast, or confess, that they once drove 700 miles to go see a film in a foreign country. Yet, that is what we did and we were proud of ourselves for not tamely accepting exclusion from the cinemascope age.

5. What I Did With My Summer Vacation

If anyone else was to tell me a tale equivalent to the one I am about to relate – as I attempt to explain the true nature of my first two-week vacation in Africa – then there's no way I would believe them. Sure, I'm familiar with plenty of similar stories, but these were always Hollywood movies, usually starring Doris Day and Rock Hudson. That kind of thing never happens to real people in real life. Not true; it does.

To really appreciate the irony of this story, you have to understand that colonial Africa shared at least one facet with the Wild West of the American frontier – single white women were in very short supply. Companies did not, in those days, recruit young ladies and pack them off to Africa. Adventurers seeking to start a new life in the unspoiled wilderness of Africa were almost always men. South Africans moving north were usually male. Women did not come to Northern Rhodesia unless they came with their husbands and then they often regretted it.

Africa can be a harsh, isolated and boring place – not for a visit, but for daily living. There was no entertainment, no electricity, often no stores in most of our smaller townships, and usually they were also without the services of a qualified physician. A visit to the dentist could take a week and include a 1,000-mile drive over dirt roads.

I have really racked my brain and I cannot recollect meeting any single white women during the years I spent in Kasama or Solwezi, when my turn eventually came to live in the bush. Kasama, a veritable metropolis, had a white population of about 500 but no girls to date. Solwezi was much smaller, with a white population of about 75 and definitely no eligible white ladies. If you were single and white, and were posted to a rural boma, then you definitely needed to bring a lot of books. You were certainly going to have a wonderful opportunity to develop your mind.

It was also a well-known fact that two years was the longest a bachelor could safely be stationed in a rural boma. After that, he gradually became 'bush happy' and had to be brought out in a strait jacket before he went native. Yet even in the cities, along the line of rail, conditions were only marginally better, and eligible ladies were still not abundant.

Indeed, the competition for the favours of any available women, with a life expectancy greater than one week, was truly fierce, and usually in vain. Thus, for the few hunters amongst our fair sex, Northern Rhodesia must, in those predatory days, have been the next best thing to dying and going to Heaven. As for myself, it is sufficient to say that single white women were more of a memory than a reality.

Anyway, having painted my background, I will now return to my story, which begins when my three friends and I had been in Mr. Lewis' house for about two months, and I was finally eligible for my first spot of local leave. After careful consideration, I decided to drive down to the coast in Portuguese East Africa, or Mozambique, to use its other name, and spend a week on the beach at Beira, sunning and swimming in the Indian Ocean. It sounded delightful, and after a little persuasion, I was fortunately able to convince Maurice to come with me.

We made our arrangements, had our leaves approved, and looked forward to our adventure. But of course, one week before our leave began, Murphy's Law reared its ugly head. Maurice's leave was canceled, when one of the other meteorologists at the airport fell sick. I was, naturally, very disappointed, but decided I'd rather go alone than postpone the trip.

A couple of days later, the telephone rang at work and the local travel agent asked me if, as the grapevine said, I really was driving alone to Beira the following week. Somewhat surprised, I confirmed his rumour. He then went on to explain his predicament, which revolved around a customer who was sailing from Beira to England, on a British India passenger ship, due to leave Beira in three weeks. However, this client was afraid to fly and he had no other way of getting her from Lusaka to Beira. 'How about if you take her?' he asked. When I hesitated he added, by way of inducement, that she would pay all the gas from Lusaka to Beira. Finally, he suggested that the three of us meet at a local tavern the following evening, and kick around the idea. Foolishly I agreed.

Boy was I lucky, or so I thought, when, early the next evening over drinks, I was introduced to a lovely and charming young lady and willingly agreed to give her a ride to Beira. We set off four days later. The first day, we drove across Northern Rhodesia, through the Zambezi Valley, over the Zambezi River, across Southern Rhodesia and into Salisbury, its capital, as I retraced the path Peter and I had followed just a few weeks earlier.

En route, I learned why Helen was going back to England. Apparently, she had come out to marry a Peter Osterhassen. Something had gone wrong, the marriage had been called off, and Helen was one bitter young lady. She regaled me endlessly with the faults of men in general, and Peter Osterhassen in particular. It was not an amusing discourse, but, not wishing to give offense, I politely listened. I diplomatically refrained from mentioning that, although I didn't know the gentleman well, I knew him by sight, as his younger sister was a good friend of mine.

Understandably, by the time we got to Salisbury, I was totally exhausted in body and spirit and wished only for the blissful oblivion of sleep, in a nice quiet bed in a nice quiet hotel. Yet this simple need soon proved to be an impossible dream, because I now discovered that we had arrived in town on the biggest holiday weekend of the year in Southern Rhodesia. This was their Rhodes and Founders Day holiday, which was, or so it seemed, the equivalent of combining George Washington's birthday with July the Fourth.

Consequently, although Salisbury was a fairly large modern city, with a white population of about 80,000 and many fine hotels, it had no room at the inn. All of its hotels were full, except, just like in the movies, for one single-bedded room which we finally found after a two-hour search. 'I'll take it,' Helen said, relieved that the problem had been solved. Sadly I concurred; I am a gentleman, I have had a gentleman's education, I am a servant of the Queen, and I proudly wear a white uniform. Plus, of course, this was 1960, and our mores were far less practical, albeit more civilized. Morosely, I arranged to pick her up in the morning and disappeared into the darkness.

That night I slept in a side street. Well, actually, I didn't sleep, and for two excellent reasons. First, my British Ford Consol was too small to lie down in and second, this was July, which, in the Southern Hemisphere, is right in the middle of winter. July is the equivalent of December in Europe or America. And although all of Southern Rhodesia is in the tropics, most of the country is more than 5,000 feet above sea level. In winter, the days are mild, while the nights are cool – mid-40's Fahrenheit– and I definitely hadn't come prepared to sleep in the car. I certainly had no blankets. I almost froze that night.

Early the next morning, I presented myself at Helen's hotel. She looked refreshed. She said I looked tired and thoughtfully bought me a nice breakfast in the hotel restaurant. It looked like a nice hotel; wish I could have stayed there. We then left for Umtali, which is a small town on the southern edge of Southern Rhodesia, right on the

Mozambique border. More recently, it was the scene of a horrible atrocity, when several missionaries were murdered during the struggle for independence prior to the creation of Zimbabwe. But when we arrived, it was a peaceful little town nestled in the foothills of the surrounding highlands.

Umtali is around 250 miles from Salisbury and the drive took us about five hours. For some inexplicable reason I had difficulty staying awake while I drove but Helen helped. Luckily, she still had not exhausted her fury at her ex-fiancé, and selflessly entertained me with an endless diatribe against him.

Just before we reached Umtali, the road snaked its way up and over Christmas Pass, which must have been almost 7,000 feet above sea level. The summit was quite cool, in spite of the warmth of the late afternoon sun. There was a small campground and I noted a few hardy souls bravely setting up camp for the night in the comparative luxury of their camping caravans. A nearby marker said that the pass was called Christmas Pass because the first white settlers in that region passed over the pass on Christmas Day, in the early 1890's, and then founded Umtali in the valley below.

I couldn't believe it; I was two for two. Umtali was a total replay of Salisbury. We tried every hotel in town and finally the last one had one room, with a single bed. Helen took it ('see you in the morning,' was her parting shot.) Guess where I spent the night? That's right, the campground at Christmas Pass. It had a great view of the sunset and at least I could lie down at the side of the car.

In all truth, it really wasn't too bad. There was a large supply of firewood, so I was able to light a fire to keep warm and some compassionate camper in one of the caravans lent me a blanket. Luxury. The problem was, every time I went to sleep, the fire died down and the bitter cold soon woke me up. Then, I would refresh the fire and try to get back to sleep, before it was time to repeat the cycle. Still, it was better than the previous night, and there was also the added advantage of being able to fully appreciate the dawn from the perfect viewpoint of Christmas Pass.

Wistfully, I tried to look on the bright side, and, in my new found role as an ascetic, I almost came to believe that this was an ideal vacation. Cheap too, since my hotel costs were nil, and Helen had bought all the gas. So far, I had spent less than 10 pounds. At this rate, I had enough money to stay on vacation for about two years, but, on the other hand, I was afraid the routine I was falling into would kill me long before my money ran out.

Once again Helen bought my breakfast and once more I admired her accommodations. She also looked terrific, although she didn't say anything about how I looked. I think she had a sensitive soul and didn't want to disturb my feelings. We then drove across Mozambique to Beira, about 200 miles, which took us the better part of four hours. We didn't talk much – I kept all the windows open and one arm outside the car, hoping that the rush of wind would keep me awake. It did and we fortunately made it to our destination without wrecking the car.

Beira is, or was, the second largest town in Mozambique. Its main function was as a port. Much of Southern Rhodesia overseas trade passed through Beira. It also had miles of golden beach on the Indian Ocean, and a promenade with a row of beach front resort hotels. The town itself is quite old with a distinctly Portuguese flavor, and I would guess it probably had a white population of about 50,000.

I absolutely refused to believe it. I was now three for three. This was no longer a bad dream; it was a full-blown nightmare. If this was a movie, it was a horror movie, for it was now three days since I had been to bed, and I could hardly keep my eyes open, as we desperately sought two rooms. Once more, for the third consecutive time, every hotel was full except the last one, which again had one room available.

Two things saved me. First of all, this room had a double bed and secondly, but most importantly, we were now, mercifully, in Mozambique. I had moved from the prim and proper environs of a British culture to the more reasonable attitudes of a Latin-based Portuguese culture. However, when the desk clerk in this final hotel miraculously came up with one vacant room, I immediately begged him to see if he could find a second empty room. He couldn't, and our subsequent conversation went as follows:

> Desk Clerk: (formally) 'No sir, one room is all we have. But it has a double bed.'
>
> Me: (in a whisper) 'But, we're not married.'
>
> Desk Clerk: (slowly and with great solemnity) 'Enjoy your good fortune.'
>
> Me: (as the light began to shine) 'Thank you, I will take the room, and we will be staying one week.'
>
> Desk Clerk: (with studied indifference) 'Thank you sir.'

Calmly I went outside and told Helen I had taken the last room in Beira. 'Where will you stay?' she asked. Gently, for I am a compassionate man, I gave her the good news, that as soon as I had unpacked the car, I was going to bed and I wasn't getting up until tomorrow. 'Where can I stay?' she demanded. It was a good question, and I gave it serious consideration, before I detailed her three choices: She could sleep on the beach, she could sleep in my car in the hotel parking lot, or she was welcome to sleep in the double bed with me.

Not surprisingly, she greeted this triple decker with dismay, and replied that she certainly couldn't do any of those three things. Sadly I agreed she had a problem and encouraged her to pray for a solution. Then, after casually mentioning that I wouldn't lock the door to our room, I contentedly went to my repose while she retired to the hotel verandah, to pensively gaze at the miles of golden sand, and the beautiful blue waters of the Indian Ocean. A few minutes later I wearily climbed into bed, and joyfully slept the blissful sleep of the just, for a full 12 hours.

A punch in the ribs woke me at about 7 the next morning, and I soon came to realize that the tranquil part of my vacation was now over, and the truly hazardous part was about to begin. 'He's here,' Helen told me in consternation. 'Who's here?' I queried, as I struggled to collect my wits . 'Peter,' Helen replied with some exasperation, since clearly her ex-fiancé's presence in Beira should have been perfectly obvious to anyone with half a grain of sense.

Now I was wide awake. 'Are you sure?' I asked, for in desperate circumstances, hope springs eternal. 'Of course I'm sure,' she replied, before going on to explain that she had spotted him on the promenade yesterday evening, as he apparently went from hotel to hotel, checking to see if she was registered in any of them. She was sure he hadn't spotted her, and had got back to our room to hide, as fast as she could. Belatedly, she then proceeded to explain, that he had once threatened to come to Beira, and stop her from leaving on the boat for England.

Previously, she had thought it was just an idle threat, but now she had come to realize he was serious. But he was thankfully doomed to failure because, as she triumphantly announced 'He can't find us as long as we stay in our room, since this room is luckily registered in your name.' Horrified, I gazed at her in despair and sarcastically pointed out that we were also lucky to have a room at the front of the hotel. We might occasionally be able to peep through the curtains and see the beach. I then reluctantly got up, dressed, called room service, ordered breakfast and settled down to enjoy my vacation.

It really is strange how things transpire, I morosely mused. At first I couldn't find a room to get into, and now I had found one, I couldn't get out of it. Plaintively, I tried for one last ray of hope. 'When exactly does your boat sail?' I asked. 'Today next week,' I was told.

This too shall pass, I reflected, as I gazed at this young lady about whom I knew so little. In fact, I suddenly realized with a start, I didn't even know her last name, or where she was from in England, or how old she was, or what she did for a living. Sadly I acknowledged that, even though she was only of medium height, weight and build, she was, nevertheless, rapidly becoming a heavyweight in my otherwise peaceful life.

The next seven days passed relatively painlessly, I must admit. After careful consideration I reached the logical conclusion that since Helen had come with me on such short notice, Peter had no reason to suspect that we were shacked up together. Therefore, why should I hide? He wasn't looking for me, I hoped. So, throwing caution to the winds, I ventured out on the beach and went swimming in the Indian Ocean.

The water was nice and warm, and I enjoyed myself immensely as

I washed my cares away before adjourning to the beach to soak up the sun. It was such a nice day, and the warmth was a very welcome relief from the interior of southern Africa, which, as I previously noted, is quite cool in winter, because of its much higher elevation. The coast, being at sea level, is always a lot warmer. Indeed, in summer, it is stinking hot.

Anyway, I spent a nice leisurely and solitary week in Beira, and developed a very nice tan, while Helen spent her days in peaceful contemplation of the furniture in our room. From time to time I saw Peter in the distance, but I always gave him a wide berth. I may lack a refined sense of caution but I am not totally suicidal. It may also have been my imagination, but to me he looked bigger than I remembered him – much bigger. Furthermore, I soon found out that he was staying in a hotel just a block or so down the beach from ours.

This useful piece of information was craftily discovered one afternoon when I discreetly followed him down the promenade and saw him turn into the hotel lobby and pick up his key from reception. Strangely enough, I remember wondering if he had encountered as much trouble as me in finding a room. Probably not, since he had probably been prudent, and had reserved a room in advance. What strange and pointless things we often wonder when we are trying to avoid reality. Certainly I was trying to avoid Peter, whose brand of reality I had no wish to encounter.

At last, a break in the clouds, because one morning towards the end of the week, there was no Peter on the promenade. Could it possibly be true? Miraculously it was, since furtive and discreet inquiries at his hotel soon confirmed that he had checked out and left Beira. Evidently, Peter had not known the actual date, nor ship, on which Helen was leaving for England and so, with his mission stymied, he had reluctantly returned to Lusaka, after abandoning his fruitless search. Two days later, I drove Helen to the docks, wished her *bon voyage*, and waved goodbye as she sailed off into the sunset.

I should have been ecstatic, but by lunch the next day I was lonely; I missed her. It was too quiet. How odd to miss turmoil, yet now, after it was all over, the day seemed kind of gray, and I genuinely hoped that she had a very pleasant voyage back to England.

The following morning, with spirits renewed by a good night's sleep, I happily checked out of our honeymoon hotel – after generously tipping the desk clerk – and slowly began the long journey home to Lusaka. Contentedly, I went back the way I had come, and naturally I had no trouble getting hotels, since this was not a holiday weekend. I even stayed one night in Umtali, and stopped for a few minutes at my beloved Christmas Pass, which still had a further role to play in my wanderings. Then, when Salisbury was reached, I luxuriously spent the last night of my vacation in a very nice hotel, as I prepared to return to everyday life.

Back in Lusaka, I skillfully evaded going into too much detail, when my friends casually asked, 'Have a nice time?' Wisely and discreetly, I kept a low profile, and always answered this type of question, with an equally casual 'Lovely, thank you.' When all was said and done, there really wasn't anything else to say, was there?

6. A Quiet Weekend At The Zoo

Having just endured a two-week vacation, I was in desperate need of some rest and relaxation. Consequently, being of unsound mind, I happily accepted the Deans' invitation to accompany them to the Kafue non-hunting area, some two or three weeks after my fiasco in Beira. This, for me, would be my first genuine trip into the African bush, and I was excited at the prospect of finally seeing the African zoo. Prudently, we made careful plans for this weekend adventure by buying a game-spotting book and a pair of binoculars, before setting off in my car one Friday evening at about 5 o'clock, to go tame the wild.

We were all true tenderfeet because, unfortunately, there is very little game left in Africa. One can easily go for years without ever seeing an animal by chance. Of course, this is not always so, as an acquaintance of mine once discovered when he came hurtling around a bend in a country road, and collided head-on with an ambling bull elephant. Luckily, neither the elephant nor my friend were injured, since both were far too thick skinned. But, regrettably, the considerably more sensitive automobile was demolished. However, such encounters were rare and, in general, Africa is no longer the Africa of old.

The Kafue non-hunting area was not a game park, but was more like a national forest, in which hunting is forbidden and animals flourish. It was only about 75 miles from Lusaka, being just past our famous bridge, and some 25 miles down a winding track, which paralleled the river until the refuge was reached. Thus, we had no trouble getting to our destination by 7:30 p.m., and, just as the light began to fade, we hurriedly chose the perfect campsite. Naturally, as befits our tenderfoot status, we had no tents, and therefore we cleverly strung our mosquito nets from the lower branches of a large riverside tree under whose shade we had prudently elected to camp. We then enjoyed a brief supper, before adjourning to our sleeping bags beneath the stars, and within the safe protection of our flimsy mosquito nets.

It was a beautiful night and, after a few moments of listening to the occasional cough, grunt and howl, I drifted off to sleep. About an hour later, I was abruptly awakened by a loud thud. Quickly I shone my torch around the encroaching darkness, but no eyes reflected back to greet me. Puzzled, I went back to sleep and a little while later, the same thing happened again. Loud thud, no explanation. All in all, it must have happened three or four times during the night, but I never discovered the cause.

Next morning, quite early, I awoke to the smell of frying bacon and steaming coffee, which came from the driftwood fire where Sally was quietly preparing breakfast. Contentedly, I lay on the ground and watched the mist rising from the river, as the early morning sun poked its head above the horizon. This was living, this was what life in the bush was all about, and I continued to relax in my sleeping bag for at least five more minutes, until the Deans, pausing on their way out of camp, casually informed me that a stampede was heading our way.

Like a fly caught in a spider's web, I struggled with my mosquito net until eventually I broke free and, in my best underpants, joined the Deans in headlong flight from our camp. Fortunately, we were not pursued, since the family of invading bush pigs stopped to examine our camp before ambling off in another direction.

At last, I had seen my first wild animals which, as pigs, had spurned our bacon and done little more than disturb our peace. Gratefully, we crept back to our camp and, after I had got dressed, we ate our breakfast before getting ready for our first game viewing trip. But, just as we were preparing to leave, I suddenly remembered the thuds in the night, and asked the Deans if they too had heard any strange noises. They said they had, but, like me, had not been able to solve the puzzle. Soberly we considered the problem, until I turned my eyes to the heavens for guidance and, received the answer. There, above my head, was the firm evidence we had sought, and the obvious proof that we had camped under a tree which grew bombs.

This tree was a death trap, since it was festooned with two-foot-long, hard-shelled, torpedo-shaped pods, which dangled precariously from many of its branches, with only a long slender stalk hindering their lethal mission. Occasionally, as if to emphasize the point, one of these five or six-pound pods would break free of its stalk, and come hurtling down to the ground below. Several of these seed pods, for that is what I guessed they were, littered our campsite and, since some of them could easily have fallen from 60 feet or more, would have done considerable damage if they had scored a direct hit on their sleeping victims.

Relieved to have survived the night without a fractured skull, we prudently shifted our camp to a more benign tree and went in search of wild animals. These, we soon discovered, did not in general co-operate with tourists. Instead, they preferred to lie up in the shade of trees, and were often difficult to spot. But we had our successes as we drove around the little dirt tracks which criss-crossed the reserve. We also had the distinct privilege of being the only visitors to this non-hunting area that weekend. Of course in 1960, Northern Rhodesia was not a tourist destination, nor had package tours concentrated hordes of wild tourists in tame game reserves. Thus we toured a wilderness area as its sole intruders, and were blessed with a fleeting vision of African wildlife in its natural undisturbed setting.

Game viewing is definitely an acquired art. Sometimes all you see is a faint shadow against a bush, or the tips of a pair of horns just visible above the elephant grass. Accordingly, we drove extremely slowly and endlessly scanned the undergrowth for signs of game. From time to time, one of us would spot something and then we would slowly halt and train our binoculars on the possible sighting. Often, we would get out of my car to get a better view, but usually when we did this, the animals would retreat. For some strange reason, they did not seem to be intimidated by a car, which they appeared to treat as just another animal, but when human beings got out of the car, that was another story and the animals usually scattered.

To begin with, we saw the more common types of antelope. Then we struck pay dirt; I spotted a flash of white beneath a distant tree. Quickly I ground to a halt and trained my glasses on the suspect spot. We were in luck. The white I had seen was the front chest of a large male lion who lay at rest in the shade of a tree. Eagerly I scanned the nearby ground, and soon picked up about six or seven other adult lions, all of whom appeared to be taking a siesta. At last I was a real white African! I had spotted my first pride of lions and I desperately wanted a photograph to record my achievement.

I invited Dixie to take my camera and trot over to the lions for a photo fest, while I stayed with Sally in the car to make sure nothing went wrong. He rejected this lucid proposal and suggested I drive across the intervening bush for a little social chitchat. Thwarted, I agreed and, after ensuring that all windows were closed and all doors locked, we slowly bounced across 200 yards of uneven ground to the lion's tree. Our inelegant approach was watched with lazy disdain. I crept ever closer, until eventually I eased to a halt some five yards from the pride and switched off the engine.

In the ensuing silence, we spent the next 30 minutes photographing and watching them at play. Finally, the well-known curiosity of all cats took over, and they decided to investigate this strange blue beast. One by one, like Sunday shoppers, they wandered over to my car, sniffed our tyres and idly peered in through the windows.

It was just like being in a zoo, with two slight variations: one, this was a hundred times scarier than any zoo I had ever visited, and two, we were the ones in the cage. For about 500 years, or so it seemed, those lions inspected my car, while we sat inside trying not to think about the comparative thinness of the sheet metal which shielded us from our friends. In the end, since we refused to come out and play, they returned to their tree and, resisting Dixie's suggestion to give them a toot on the horn, I gingerly restarted my engine and made an orderly retreat to the comparative safety of the nearby dirt track.

A few more miles and we came across a small herd of impala peacefully grazing in an open meadow, neatly bisected by our narrow path's route. Enthralled, I stopped, and for the next several minutes we quietly watched from the edge of the clearing, as about 70 of these graceful animals contentedly browsed for lunch. Suddenly, as so often happens, something spooked them, and the whole herd fled towards the safety of some nearby bush. Fortunately, their line of retreat traversed the meadow and lay directly across the narrow trail we were following. Thus we had a ringside seat as each animal, in its turn, chose not to run over the track, but to leap above it, as if it had been a retaining wall.

The overall effect of this African ballet was compellingly beautiful, as a living rainbow of impala cascaded across the trail in an unforgettable display of wildlife in motion. It was, for a magical moment or two, a private glimpse of paradise, and then the scene changed as the last gazelle disappeared from view. Stunned, I turned to my game viewing book, which confirmed my eyes by telling me that the impala was Africa's finest jumper, and could easily top 10 feet in height and 30 feet in width in a single leap. Certainly we too could now attest to this wonderful animal's leaping ability, since we had just seen (and never would forget) a most extraordinary example of its prowess.

During the rest of the afternoon we systematically covered every track. We saw plenty of game, but mostly in ones or twos, because the days of Africa's thundering herds were long since gone. As the light began to fade, we drifted back to our camp and enjoyed a leisurely supper before taking to our sleeping bags under the spreading branches of what we hoped was a non-combative tree.

On Sunday morning I woke early to the sounds of a school of hippos playing in the nearby river. Entranced, I watched their antics and decided to measure the length of time a hippo could stay underwater without breathing. Cautiously, I stood on the river's bank watching a hippo until it submerged, and then, wristwatch in hand; I stared at the same spot in the river, as I timed the interval before it burst back into view, to snort in another lungful of air. I discovered that, on average, a hippo stays submerged for about five minutes, and when I consulted my trusty 'Animals of Rhodesia,' it quickly verified my findings. Content with my status as an emerging zoologist, I went to breakfast, where we all gave thanks for having been privileged to see Africa, while it was still Africa.

Our plans for our final morning in the reserve were simple: find elephants. We could not go back to Lusaka without seeing an elephant. Some things are just not done in polite society, and this was one of them. For more than an hour, we toured the reserve, scanning the bush. Finally our patience was rewarded when Dixie spotted a lone bull elephant at the entrance to a narrow ravine, some 100 hundred yards from the track we were following, off to our left-hand side.

I parked my car on the verge of the track and we all got out to admire the distant elephant, which thoughtlessly soon disappeared back up the ravine. Sally was satisfied, but Dixie and I were not. We wanted a good, close-up view of our elephant and, if possible, a couple of frameable photographs. Accordingly, cameras in hand, two lunatics gleefully set off up the ravine in search of the quarry.

The going was rough, but this was an insignificant hindrance, since our search was quite brief and eminently successful. Indeed, we only had to go a scant 200 yards up the ravine before contact was re-established with our elephant. However, this glad event was slightly marred when the elephant, from a distance of about 50 yards, burst into view as it came charging back down the ravine with murder in its eyes.

My initial reaction to this charge was intense sympathy for Dixie, because I was in tiptop shape and Dixie was not. Consequently, being fleeter of foot, I was going to leave Dixie to be trampled underfoot as I fled back to our car. Like lightning, I whirled on my heels, and set off down the gully at a speed Linford Christie would have envied. Yet my erstwhile companion was already 10 yards ahead of me, and continued to widen the gap as his spindly little legs pumped with enthusiasm for staying alive. Sadly, I realized that I was the tail-end Charlie, and took stock of my position which, in my considered opinion, did not look good.

Strangely enough, I was immediately consumed by a tremendous burst of anger. I was a highly educated, sophisticated, cultured, civilized man and I was about to be stomped to death by a dumb brute of an animal. Not only was that unfair, it was also improper. I deserved more out of life than to be squashed like some insignificant beetle. But, as calmer thoughts re-entered my head, I knew I had only a moment or two left to save my life, since in the soft sandy soil of this ravine, I could not hope to outrun the devil on my tail.

It is said that when you are near death, your whole life flashes before you. Well, in my case, this did not happen. Each moment seemed to last a thousand years, and I had all the time in the world to think and plan. Suddenly, I remembered how all the great white hunter books I had ever read, had emphasized how deeply all wild animals fear man. Without exception, all of these books said that if you stood and stared down a wild animal, it would retreat. So, with nothing to lose, since my life was already forfeit, I skidded to a halt and spun around to face Armageddon.

He was a beautiful sight. He would have made a wonderful photograph as he came hurtling down the ravine like a runaway loco-motive. Unfortunately, just as I had surmised, my 50 yard lead had now shrunk to 25, and death was approaching posthaste. But old man Lewenstein had been right, and thanks be to God for good liter-ature, which broadens the mind and saves lives. Truly, those wonderful great white hunters had told it like it is, for as soon as I turned to face his charge, my foot-stomping friend also applied his brakes and slithered to a halt about 10 yards in front of my vantage point.

In mortal fear, I stood and stared him down, while he, in frenzied anger, stomped, trumpeted and flapped his ears until, after several lifetimes, he began to gradually take a few backward steps. At last, to my everlasting relief, he slowly turned around, with a last defiant earth-shaking trumpet of rage, and then he nervously retreated back up the ravine and out of my sight.

It was quiet standing in that gully. The sky was very blue, the trees were very lovely. Even the few blades of grass were very green. I stood there for maybe five minutes, considering the unbelievable fact that I was not about to die and wondering what to do with the rest of my life. Eventually, I turned around and, with one last fearful glance behind me, to confirm the absence of death; I nonchalantly strolled down the ravine and back to my car.

The Deans, naturally, were glad to see me, since they had not relished the thought of going back up the ravine to recover my pieces. Sally gave me a big hug and then began to cry. Dixie gave me a big grin and then went back to throwing up his breakfast, which was apparently his most pressing engagement at that particular point in time. Diffidently, I asked Sally if she had any aspirin since I appeared to have developed a headache. Sally said she didn't have any. Oh well, no day is perfect and once Dixie took a break from his activities, we all climbed into my car, where we sat in silence for some considerable time.

At length, after our hearts had ceased pounding, we regained our composure and, after a brief discussion, came to the enlightened conclusion that this place was definitely not your normal zoo. Moreover, as Sally firmly reminded us, Dixie and I had been extremely lucky, and it was a miracle no one had been killed. Chastened, I started the engine and drove back to camp, since it was now time to pack and go home. As we drove, I complimented Dixie on his burst of speed and inquired as to whether he intended to run back to Lusaka, or was willing to waste time by returning to civilization in my car. Dixie allowed as how he would ride, and inquired as to whether I intended to make a habit of staring down elephants. I said I didn't care if I never saw another elephant for the rest of my life, and on that happy note, we reached camp.

Quickly we packed our gear into my car, all the while casting furtive glances at a suddenly ominous bush, and some 45 minutes later, began the 75-mile drive back to the comparative safety of civilization. We had been lucky and we had learned a valuable lesson. Africa is not a zoo. Wild animals are not to be trifled with, and must be viewed with caution, if you wish to outlive the experience.

Miraculously, I had managed to survive my introduction to African wildlife, and subsequently went on to enjoy many other game-viewing trips, but I never again felt comfortable with elephants.

Not even in the circus. To me, the elephant will always remain the most dangerous of Africa's big game.

From that day forward, I have always been uneasy at the zoo, where even under the best of conditions, the animals do not roam freely, but are caged in mind as well as body. Nevertheless, I do reluctantly admit the need to have zoos, particularly when they help to preserve an endangered species and also, I suppose, as a viable way to teach home folks about the wonders of nature. But whenever I go to a zoo, I see again in my mind's eye that wonderful rainbow of leaping impala, and I mourn once more for the loss of freedom, which all animals in captivity are doomed to endure.

Chapter 7

More Uplifting Experiences

1 . Who's Going To Do The Dishes?

Having barely survived my first taste of life in the bush, I was in no particular hurry to again leave asphalt behind. However, that is what I reluctantly did about two weeks after my elephant-baiting stunt, when Peter Van Eden suggested we take a two-day trip. He wanted to go sunbathing in the Kariba Gorge of the Zambezi River. This seemingly odd proposal was, in fact, quite sound, since at the time it was late winter in Northern Rhodesia, where temperatures stayed mainly in the mid-60s, except in the Kariba Gorge, some 2,000 feet lower than Lusaka and, hopefully, some 20 therapeutic degrees warmer.

Hence, early on the following Saturday morning, we set off in my car with suntan oil and deck chairs in tow. We were bound for one of central Africa's most isolated areas, which stretch for about 30 miles along the border of Southern and Northern Rhodesia. It is, I assume, the product of several eons of wear and tear by the Zambezi River, and we had decided to enter its domain by a small inter-village track, which left the main road some 30 miles before Churundu was reached. Then, if our ordinance survey map was reliable, we intended to follow this rural route for about 25 miles, until it dead ended on the banks of the Zambezi River.

The total distance, from home to river, was around 125 miles and, for once, everything went about as smoothly as travel on African roads will permit. Predictably, this rural track was more like a bicycle path, and we probably averaged no more than 10 miles per hour, as we slowly bounced our way towards the banks of the mighty Zambezi.

In due course, just before noon, we shuddered to our destination. Soon after, we set up our deck chairs and began to work on our tans under the welcome gaze of a warm tropical sun. This was truly the life of Reilly, especially since for lunch and dinner we had a plethora of cold food lovingly prepared by Mr. Lewis' faithful staff. Consequently, we spent the rest of the day as gentlemen should, with the help of a 12-pack of beer, before contentedly retiring to our sleeping bags that night under a warm tropical moon.

Both of us slept well, but on Sunday morning when we awoke, we were immediately faced with an awesome problem: who was going to cook breakfast and, even worse, who was going to do the dirty dishes afterwards? Peter pointed out that he had never done either task, and so I prudently elected to cook breakfast if he did the dishes, which seemed to me to be the less dangerous chore. He willingly agreed that I looked like a better cook, whatever that meant, and so I fixed eggs, bacon, fried bread and toast, of a quality which even Moses would have applauded.

After eating his fill, Peter morosely eyed the greasy plates, while I settled down to my place in the sun. Eventually, facing the inevitable, he gathered up the pots, pans and dishes, and disappeared down a faint trail which paralleled the river bank. Puzzled, I watched him go, and then spent a pleasant two hours reading the central African version of Time magazine. Finally, just when I had begun to worry that the crocodiles may have eaten some of Mr. Lewis' dishes, Peter returned to camp in the company of a scantily clad native, who bore in a wickerwork basket on his head, our sparklingly clean breakfast utensils. In amazement, I watched as the native unloaded our pots, pans and dishes and, after receiving a pack of cigarettes from Peter, happily left our camp smoking a Peter Stuyvesant cigarette.

Cautiously, I smiled at Peter and then started the following conversation:

Me: 'I saw it. But I don't believe it.'
Peter: 'What?'
Me: 'That native.'
Peter: 'What about him?'
Me: 'Who was he and why was he carrying our dishes?'
Peter: 'Because he washed them.'
Me: 'Why did he wash them?'
Peter: 'Because they were dirty, why else?'
Me: 'Forgive me, I was being foolish. But tell me, where did you find him?'
Peter: 'About two miles downriver from here.'
Me: 'Two miles – what were you doing two miles down the river?'
Peter: 'Looking for someone to wash the dishes. Thank God I found that fisherman, or I could have been gone all day.'
Me: 'Yes, it was a stroke of luck. But what did you say to him?
Peter: 'I offered him a pack of cigarettes if he washed my dishes in the river, and he gladly accepted.'
Me: 'He spoke English?'
Peter: 'Of course not, but you know I speak Bemba.'
Me: 'Lucky you, else you may have ended up washing the dishes yourself.'
Peter: 'No, I don't think so. I would have found some way of telling him what I needed.'
Me: 'So why did he have to come all the way back here?'

Peter: 'To carry the dishes. Anyway, I didn't have a full pack of ciga-
        rettes with me.'
Me: 'You've had a real exhausting morning.'
Peter: 'No sweat, it was fair. You cooked breakfast.'

For a moment or two, I considered extending the conversation and
then I realized that since both Peter and the tribesman were having a
nice day, it would be churlish of me to proceed. I therefore smiled
vacantly at Peter, who acknowledged this mark of approval by thankfully settling down in his deck chair to enjoy some well-earned
relaxation. However, this story does have a point: Peter never seriously
considered doing the chore himself, as long as there was a snowball in
hell's chance of finding an African to do it.

This philosophy was almost universally held by the white South
African community. They seemed to consider that manual labor was
a black African prerogative and unhealthy for whites. Thus, Peter
was not being cruel or unkind when he went in search of a houseboy to do his dishes, but was merely living out his culture's customs
and was prepared to pay handsomely for the help he needed.
Similarly, most of my friends did not have electric vacuum cleaners
or washing machines and dryers, or any other labor-saving device.
Instead, they had mops, brooms, dustpans and African elbow grease
to clean their homes. Their wash was also done the traditional way,
with the bathtub being used as a washtub, while the sun did its best
as a dryer.

Perhaps, since a culture's humour is said to reflect its mores, I can
best sum up this aspect of South African society, by recounting a
popular joke.

Once upon a time, two American tourists were sitting in a London bar
having a few drinks, when one asked the other if he thought sex was
work or pleasure. The second tourist thought for a few moments and
then replied, 'Pleasure.'

Unfortunately, this was not the answer the first tourist wished to
hear, since she firmly maintained that sex was undoubtedly work.

The debate grew heated and soon spread to involve the rest of the
bar's patrons.

For an hour or more, the argument waged fierce but no decision was
reached. Half the drinkers voted for sex as work, and half thought it
was pleasure.

Finally, the bartender called for order in the house, and proposed
that the dispute should be decided by asking the next patron to enter
the bar to determine the issue by giving a final tie-breaking opinion on
this lofty matter. Luckily, everyone accepted this proposal, thus avoiding a riot, and all eyes turned expectantly to the door.

A few minutes later, innocent of what momentous burden he was
due to assume, a young white South African breezed into the bar and
ordered a beer. Gravely, the bartender explained the situation and
gravely the South African considered it as he slowly drank his ale. At

last, when his glass was empty, he turned to the bartender and, with a cheerful smile, confidently announced that sex was pleasure.

His decision, naturally, was hotly debated by the assembled throng, until the bartender again called for silence, and asked the young South African to justify his answer. 'That's easy,' he said. 'You see, in South Africa, the blacks do all the work, so, since we whites do our own sex, it must be pleasure.'

Clearly, as I said before, a culture's humour, or lack of it, reflects the values it holds most dear and, for good or for evil, most South Africans had a very clear picture of how the Garden of Eden should be run. Probably, as current history seems to confirm, they were wrong, although it is certainly not my intention to pontificate on other people's points of view, but rather to explain what life was really like in central Africa, just before the winds of change blew the door off its hinges.

Peter, blissfully ignorant of my wide-ranging thoughts, continued to soak up the sun until, by mid-afternoon, it was time to go home. As we eased our way back towards civilization we soon came upon an old man limping along the track in the same direction as we. I slowed to a halt, and Peter asked the old man where he was going. At length, after some linguistic acrobatics, Peter decided that the old man was going to a village some 10 miles up the trail, and we promptly offered him a ride.

Reluctantly he climbed into the back seat. Still holding the door jamb with one hand, he used his free hand to slam the door shut on the other hand's fingers. Pandemonium then ensued, as this extremely dexterous feat was heatedly debated, in Bemba, between Peter and the villager, who luckily was not seriously injured, but was seriously perturbed.

Eventually, with calm restored, we resumed our crawl up the gorge, but now with one very apprehensive villager wide eyed in the middle of my car's back seat. This was, in all probability, the first time he had ever been in a car, perhaps one of the few times he had ever seen a car since, the Kariba Gorge is an extremely remote and inaccessible place.

'Can you believe how far I have come?' I silently thought. My mind wandered back to my own first ride in a car and to the splendour of those winking cat's eyes which marked the nighttime path from Preston to Chorley. Certainly I could sympathise with my passenger. I wondered what he was making of his first ride, and what kind of tale he would tell in the village that night.

Most likely he would be a big hero. At least I hoped so, and I continued to ruminate in this vein. About an hour later, we arrived at the barely discernible turnoff from our track, which led to his village. Solemnly, we all went through the traditional hand-clapping ritual of a formal goodbye, before I slowly drove off and left him standing by the side of the trail, watching my sky-blue bird until we disappeared around a bend in the road.

Three or four hours later, we were back in civilization, with a nice suntan to flaunt before our friends and no unhappy stories to relate. It had been a pleasant, quiet, relaxing weekend and, as I climbed into my comfortable bed after a late-night shower, my mind returned to that little old man who, somewhere out there, must also be preparing himself for sleep. In miles, we were quite close but in lives, we were a million miles apart, and like two ships that passed in the night, neither of us would ever understand the other's world.

2. Kariba, The Dam

The name Kariba is an African word and it means, 'Where the waters have been trapped.' It is, like so many native names, a beautifully descriptive term. It perfectly catches the spirit of that pristine lonely place, and the 30 miles of captive river within its grasp. Happily, at the spot which Peter and I had chosen to enter this wilderness, it was still a remnant of old Africa at its finest and untouched by modern man. Yet, that was not the case a scant 10 miles further upstream, where the gorge dramatically narrows to a mere 2,000 feet in width, and 20th-century civilization has given Kariba a whole new meaning.

For there, amazingly, towers the incredible Kariba Dam, which man in his infinite wisdom had chosen to build in this remote location, as a monument to progress and the realization of a dream. The work on this mammoth project, one of the greatest feats of industrial

Kariba Dam under construction on the Zambezi River in 1959

engineering ever undertaken, was begun about three years before I came to Africa and, for the first year or two, the bulk of the time was spent in making the site accessible and livable.

To begin with, hundreds of miles of good-quality dirt roads had to be built, to link both sides of the Zambezi at Kariba, to the Lusaka-Salisbury highway. Then, on the Southern Rhodesian side of the river, an entire town was built on a hill overlooking the site of the dam. This town was reputed to be quite impressive, with a clubhouse, Roman Catholic Church and several hundred houses, all for the bene-fit of the many workers who came to work on the project. In due course, the main contract for the dam was awarded to an Italian company, who began their work sometime in 1957.

However, the Zambezi did not surrender quietly and, for the first two years of the dam's construction, the river, during the rains, exceeded all previous flood levels as it attempted to foil its new enemy. But its efforts were rebuffed and, by the end of 1959, with great fanfare and pride, the project was nearing completion. It was, by all accounts, a wonder to behold and, for someone as incurably curious as I, a mandatory excursion.

Therefore, about a month after my visit to Kariba the gorge, Maurice and I, in his Mercedes, went for a day trip to Kariba the dam. It was about 150 miles from Lusaka. Our route was much the same as the one Peter and I had followed, except that we did not take any village trails. By noon we had reached our destination.

The dam itself was very impressive. It was over 400 feet high in the middle, and arched for more than 2,000 feet across this narrow-est point of the Kariba gorge. In all, it contained over 1,350,000 cubic yards of concrete, which was a lot, and had made it one of the world's premier dams. If nothing goes wrong (bite your tongue, Mr. Murphy) it will eventually produce enough electricity to satisfy most of the needs of both Rhodesias, and greatly enhance their industrial development.

Equally impressive was the gigantic Lake Kariba, which is one of the largest man-made lakes in the world. It stretched for over 175 miles above the dam, and had a maximum width of almost 30 miles. As a result, this 2,000 square-mile lake was a story in itself, and mandated the resettlement of 50,000 natives, whose villages were drowned by the rising waters of the new inland sea. In addition, the Southern Rhodesian government launched Operation Noah, which rescued an enormous number of wild animals from the lethal grasp of this latter-day flood.

In those early days, when Maurice and I first visited Kariba, there was only one power plant (although now there are two) and it was on the Southern Rhodesian side of the river. It too was on a gigantic scale, and had been hollowed out of the southern wall of the gorge. The entire plant was underground and the chamber containing it was said to be large enough to hold St. Paul's Cathedral. Indeed, everything about Kariba was massive and a tremendous testament to man's ability to harness, or destroy, nature.

Patently, this wasn't your typical African village and, for several hours we toured the site, in awe at its pyramid-like splendour. We walked across the dam, took snapshots, admired the town and stared at the lake, as we tried to behave like a pair of city slicker tourists. Actually, although in my day central Africa was not a vacation resort, we were not the only gapers. In point of fact, there were some 20 to 30 other tourists doing the rounds of this new attraction which, after all, was quite a change from a bridge.

Yet, for all the awesome achievements which Kariba displayed, I came away with a sense of sadness for the lost majesty of the trapped Zambezi, whose flood was now but a dismal trickle. Its grandeur was gone, a poignant victim of progress. The lake was only half full, and the barest minimum of water allowable under international law was being permitted to flow downriver, through a single sewer-sized pipe at the base of the dam.

What a tragedy it was to see that mighty river tamely flowing through a concrete pipe in a concrete wall, as it struggled to resume its journey to Mozambique and the sea. Sadly I walked down the access steps leading to the river's only outlet from prison, and quickly took a picture of the Zambezi in chains. Then, as anticipated, I was forced to retreat from this sorrowful sight by an angry African police-man, who did not approve of trespassing dreamers.

Maurice too, seemed to sense the mixed blessings of progress, and it was in a quiet mood that we returned to his Mercedes and drove home to Lusaka, whose lights would, someday, be powered by Kariba's electricity. Thus, I knew full well that civilization had to be maintained, and I was also truly impressed with man's achievements, in one of the most inaccessible places I ever saw. Even so, I still didn't enjoy seeing the Zambezi in a pipe, and I don't like the idea of a million cubic feet of concrete in the wilds of Africa.

Anyway, in an attempt to look on the bright side, assuming of course there is a bright side to concrete (which I doubt) I cheerfully admit the virtues of Kariba to the Chilanga Cement Company. This small, locally-owned firm on the outskirts of Lusaka really hit it big when it became the sole purveyor of concrete for the entire Kariba undertaking. In all probability, this was one of the largest concrete orders ever issued. During the next few years, a steady stream of giant trucks rumbled over steadily deteriorating dirt roads, with an endless supply of the lifeblood of the Kariba dam.

Imagine, if you can, the reaction in that small establishment when they got an order for enough ready mix to pave the moon. Luckily, they spent their new wealth soundly and, in later years, I became a proud member of the Chilanga Cement Company Country Club, where no expense had been spared in building an international-qual-ity golf course.

But that is another story for another book and does not concern the marvels of our new dam which, in one notable aspect, did its utmost to be a credit to the Zambezi by thoughtfully featuring its own Victoria Falls. This cascade was entirely man-made, since the Italian engineers had boldly placed their sluice gates in the centre of the dam, about 300 feet above the downstream river bed.

In total, there were six of these gates, which would, hopefully, be used to regulate the waters of Lake Kariba, once the lake had reached its intended capacity. Now obviously these sluices could not be tested until the lake rose to their level, but eventually, about a year after Maurice and I made our trip to Kariba, the lake reached a level well above the bottom of these gates, and high enough to unveil their splendour.

Accordingly, an announcement was given to the press, that on such and such a day, at such and such a time, the sluice gates would be opened, one by one, to test their mettle. Plus, on the following day, the gates would be opened, two by two, to double the scope of the test. Fortunately the announcement was carried in our local newspaper and, as soon as I saw it, I immediately secured the two days of local leave needed if I intended to be a part of that historic spectacle. This time, I went alone, since no one else seemed interested and, on arrival, booked into a small fishing camp which had sprung up on the Southern Rhodesian side of the dam, just below the small town of Kariba. Then I went to sit on a wall, right next to the town's church, ideally situated for seeing the show.

In retrospect, I could not have chosen a better vantage point, since my perch was about half a mile from the dam, and about 500 feet above it. Consequently, I had a panoramic view when, precisely on schedule at 6 p.m., the leftmost gate of the dam was opened. It was spectacular. It transformed the dam into a thing of consummate beauty. A tremendous volume of water poured through the open sluice and, with a thunderous roar, arched into the river bed far below the dam. Further, just like the Victoria Falls, a large cloud of spray rose up to partially obscure the view and, where the rays of the setting sun pierced the spray, the homage to Victoria continued, as a beautiful rainbow soared above the falling waters.

Truly, we now had a dam worthy of the Zambezi, and a credit to the Queen. Spellbound and in awe, I sat alone on that wall until long after dark, as one by one, each of the six gates was opened for about 30 minutes of magic. Of course, once the sun had set, my view was somewhat obscured but, luckily, there was a full moon to give the display an ethereal quality, and always, as with Victoria, one could listen to the mighty sounds of the Kariba falls. Finally, when the last sluice closed, I went back to the fishing camp, had a fish dinner, and went to bed in my little tent with much more respect for this new Kariba.

The following day, precisely at 3 p.m. as promised, the spectacle was repeated, two sluices at a time, and was obviously more impressive. Again, I sat on my wall, this time with a smattering of fellow tourists, and took pictures of this new African wonder with its cloud of spray and encircling rainbow. Later, I went down to the dam itself and felt it tremble under the rush of its own avalanche of water. I even stood directly above one of the open sluices and gazed down for 100 feet or more, to the top of that dark green wall of water which burst forth from beneath my feet.

At last, the show was over and, after doffing my cap to the artistic vision of Italian architects, I happily returned to the fishing camp for a late-afternoon cruise on the lake. The next morning, I went home, proud to have been among the first to see the full glory of the Kariba dam.

Unfortunately, this story has a mundane ending, since I have recently read that those waterfall sluices had a negative impact on the river bed below the dam, and had soon begun to undermine the very foundations on which they were built. This poetic end to the Kariba dam was, understandably, not judged appropriate, and a less joyous way has been found to discharge excess water from the lake.

But, for a brief time, Kariba was more about magic than concrete. I have seen a dam which produced its own rainbow, in a dazzling display by a river set free of its chains. By chance, or perhaps by choice, I never again went back to Kariba, and so I am glad my last visit to the dam was such a beautiful experience.

3. Fishing

Even now, after all these years, the pain I endured when my car was stolen remains fresh in my mind. Nevertheless, I still remain convinced that serious crime in Northern Rhodesia in the early 1960s was almost non-existent – at least in the white society. In fact, with one notable exception, I cannot recall any crimes of violence, nor can I remember a bank robbery or anyone being held up at gunpoint and robbed. We were a very peaceful, orderly and safe society, with little resemblance to modern day cultures. Perhaps it is true that there was more crime in the native society but I never heard about it, and certainly it never affected me or my circle of friends.

However, there was one exception to the crime-free scene I have just described and that exception was fishing. This peculiar crime was endemic throughout Northern Rhodesia. It forced the prudent to guard against fishermen when taking off clothes, because, if you didn't, within the wink of an eye, they would be gone.

Fishing, to elaborate, was truly a most highly refined native custom, whereby the fisherman crouched in the bushes outside your home and, if a window was open, tried to delicately part you from your treasured possessions. Normally, they did this by means of a flexible bamboo pole, which all experienced anglers carried, and gently inserted through open windows to skillfully hook the treasures inside.

At times, this constant problem could be fiendishly funny, and I well remember Michael Voysey's account of a fishing experience, which culminated when he woke up in the middle of the night, shivering in his underpants. Apparently, he had foolishly committed the unpardonable sin and left his bedroom window open. This challenge had obviously attracted the neighborhood's best fly fisherman, who skillfully fished Michael's blanket and sheet without disturbing our slumbering hero. Eventually, in the coldest part of the night, Michael shivered himself awake and found, to his surprise, that he had only his pillow for company. Thus, he learned to sleep with the window closed, or his bedclothes tied down.

Actually, there were only two ways to fight fishing. The first, as I have said, was to keep the windows closed, because even if you had a fly screen, this could easily be removed or cut open. The second was to keep everything in a drawer and away from a direct fishable line to a window, since the unwary often, quite literally, lost their shirts and pants, when these were foolishly draped on a chair, beneath an open window. Of course, if you chose the second solution, which I did, you instantly became an extraordinarily tidy person and always slept with a firm grip on your blanket.

In hindsight, I don't think that I ever lost more than an occasional pair of socks but, as was the case with Michael, many of my friends had the distinct pleasure of waking up to a spartanly furnished bedchamber. Yet even if fishing was a constant torment, grand larceny was thankfully not, since, for some inexplicable reason, perhaps a sporting instinct, our native friends did not appear to go in for burglary or breaking and entry. Hence, I never heard of anyone coming home to find their house ransacked and half their furniture gone. But if you left your windows open and clothes lying around, your wardrobe would soon find its way to the nearest village. Still, nobody's perfect, and life was basically calm until, in 1961 or 1962, we unfortunately had our only totally unforgivable crime.

This outrage occurred near Kitwe, and began when a group of Africans, returning from a political rally, attacked a white woman and her daughter, who happened to pass their way in the family's Volkswagen Beetle. The mob stopped the car, shattered the windshield, poured gasoline onto its passengers, and happily tossed a lighted match into the vehicle. They then calmly watched as the bonfire engulfed these two innocent victims, and then retired to their homes.

The reaction to this, the only horrendous crime in all my years in Africa, was fierce. National boundaries were not respected and, within a matter of weeks, the guilty persons had been tracked to the Belgian Congo and arrested. A few days later, with scant regard for the niceties of extradition, these criminals were brought back to Kitwe, summarily tried for murder and, I believe, hung.

Thank God the horrible fate suffered by that young mother and child was never repeated. Indeed, the horrors of the Mau Mau in Kenya were never exported to Northern Rhodesia, which remained a quiet backwater of civilization on a turbulent continent. Nevertheless, that one terrible outrage sent a shiver of apprehension down our spines, since we were only 70,000 whites in a country of four million blacks. But, luckily, politicians of all colours and creeds joined together in condemning this horrendous crime and managed to keep the lid on our country. Thus, with one horrific exception, we never had to worry about our safety, but only about our clothes and the casting techniques of our neighbours.

4. Crocodiles Don't Like Open Water

Shortly before we left Mr. Lewis' house, I took a second two-week vacation, and, together with the Deans, went to visit Sally's uncle. According to Sally, he was a freelance trader who lived with his wife, in a palatial home on the shores of Lake Nyasa in Nyasaland. This house was apparently unique; it was supposed to have the only lawn on the shores of the lake, and was centrally located in the middle of nowhere, with at least a hundred miles of virgin bush between it and civilization. But Sally, who had once visited her uncle as a child, was sure she could find this isolated treasure and so, after an exchange of letters with her uncle, she led us forth, like Moses, into the wilderness.

Our route that first morning led us up the great east road for some 150 miles of empty dirt highway, until we came to the Luwingu River and, more importantly, the Luwingu River Bridge. Rapturously, we gazed at this new addition to our collection of bridges seen, and then, after photographing this wonder, we ate our picnic lunch.

An hour or so later, when the bridge began to pale, we continued for another 150 miles of nothing until, in the early evening, we came to Fort Jameson, the capital of the Eastern province, where we spent the night in the government rest house. Once again, we were using my car since, as always, the Dean's transportation was unreliable. Anyway, since it was their uncle we were going to visit, fair play dictated we do it in my car, if that makes sense. In addition, we needed a bigger car than their Volkswagen Beetle because this time, we had my goddaughter with us, which was the reason why the back of my car was overflowing with nappies.

The following morning, we awoke to the sound of rain. This was bad news but, with fingers crossed, we carried on and by mid-afternoon, we had slipped and slithered our way across 100 miles of wilderness until we reached Lilongwe, the nearest town to the fabled lawn. Luckily, the rest of the day was much more stimulating as, for at least nine hours, we followed a succession of dead end trails, to a variety of non-existent uncles.

Doggedly we sloshed our way through more than 200 miles of mud, and probably visited every native village in that part of Africa, as Sally continued to proudly proclaim she knew where she was. Finally, just before midnight and just before I ran out of gas, the law of averages came to our rescue. Suddenly, to our relief, my headlights dramatically framed a beautiful home in the darkness ahead. We had arrived and soon we were ensconced in nice warm beds in a nice safe house, which is infinitely better than touring the bush in the dark.

Bright and early next morning, at breakfast, I talked briefly with Sally's uncle, and asked him if it was safe to swim in the lake. 'Of course,' he replied. 'Crocodiles don't like open water.' Satisfied by this oracle's wisdom, I left him still seated at the table and went on a tour of his house. It was magnificent. It reminded me of the house in the film 'Elephant Walk' and, in particular, of the scene in the movie where a group of party guests ride bicycles up and down the planter's home.

This house, too, could easily have accommodated a bicycle or two and, if I could have found one, I would dearly have loved to try a few laps around my host's lounge. Yet I did not pursue the matter, since it seemed inelegant, and contented myself with admiring the wonderful view of Lake Nyasa from the enormous veranda on the front of the house.

Fortunately, it looked as if it was going to be a beautiful day, since the rain had passed. As soon as the Deans had finished breakfast, we all went outside to inspect our surroundings. Clearly this was Africa at its Hollywood best, with a lawn that was just as Sally had described it, and stretched for some 25 yards from the house to a seawall, which separated it from the white sandy beach of the adjacent lake.

In the middle of the lawn was a picnic table and some chairs and, for an hour or more, we sat in the sun, content to admire tranquility. To our right, in the centre of the seawall, a flight of steps led down to the beach and, in the shallow waters at the lake's edge, two family servants were doing this household's daily wash. On the beach was a dugout canoe, and an African fisherman patiently repairing his net. All was well with the world, and God was in Nyasaland.

Blissfully I savoured that perfect view, as I studied the calm, and clear azure blue waters of the lake before me. It really was quite irresistible, and so, when our breakfasts had settled, we all decided to go for a swim. Obviously it had to be safe, since my host had said so and anyway, there were two washerwomen in the lake to prove his point. We therefore put on our swimsuits and spent the rest of the day cavorting in the tropical warm waters of this African paradise.

Dixie and I swam until we were exhausted, and then we spent a couple of hours falling out of the dugout canoe. Truly, this was the most unstable craft I have ever seen and the slightest error of judgment would tip us both in the water. But we persevered and, eventually, we were smugly paddling to and fro like lifelong Nyasa fishermen. In the meantime, Sally and her daughter spent most of the day playing in the shallows and, in the late afternoon, Dixie and I joined them on the beach where we all built sandcastles.

It was just like Blackpool, except that we had a private beach, and it wasn't snowing. Life doesn't get any better than that, and it was a day to be treasured in one's memories. At long last, just before dusk, we returned to our rooms, tired but content and, after showering, joined Sally's uncle and his wife on the veranda for sundowners.

We sat and sipped our drinks as the peaceful loneliness of that idyllic spot seeped into our bones. I think, in some strange way, it was the isolation of this house which gave it such a special charm. One felt Africa, and knew one was as close to nature as it was possible to be, without giving up one's gin and tonic. In due course, when my glass needed replenishing, our gracious host limped over to the bar and performed his duties. He then limped back to my chair and gave me my drink.

Strangely enough, this was the first time I had seen him walk, and therefore I was somewhat surprised to see that he had quite a severe handicap. Bluntly, being more curious than genteel, I impolitely asked him if he had recently hurt his leg. 'Oh no,' he replied. 'It's an old wound that is bothering me more than usual today.' This answer intrigued me, so I pressed on and asked him how he had been wounded. 'I was unlucky.' He said. 'I got bitten by a crocodile when I went for a swim.'

By now I was really interested and, remembering his advice about clear and sheltered water, I probed him about which river he had been foolish enough to swim in, when he was attacked. 'Oh no,' he explained, 'I wasn't attacked in a river, I was attacked in the lake, just a few yards out from those steps, which lead down to the beach.'

Stunned, I stared at the lemon in my drink, as this Garden of Eden turned into a nightmare and then, as calmly as possible, I sympathized with my tormentor on his misfortune. Dixie, meanwhile, was staring at Sally with an accusing look, and Sally was staring at her uncle in horror. Logically, there didn't seem to be any point to recapping our morning's conversation about crocodiles and open water, since it appeared as if Sally's uncle had found the exception which proves the rule. Nevertheless, I determined never again to believe anyone who lived that far from civilization.

Shortly thereafter, dinner was served, and we all trooped into the dining room for a wonderful, if slightly unusual meal. The food itself was scrumptious, but because there was no grocery store within a hundred miles, it was all local and fresh. We had fish from the lake and chicken from the local village. There were also plenty of mush-rooms, which Sally's uncle delighted in, plus avocados, mangoes, bananas, yams and other tropical fruit and vegetables, which he grew in his kitchen garden or orchard.

Conversely, there was no bread since they had run out of flour, and no beef, milk, butter or cheese, since they had neither beef nor dairy cattle. Similarly, there was no bacon and eggs for breakfast, due to a dearth of pigs and a shortage of hens. Basically, they ate what they raised, grew or caught, which made for some very interesting menus. Even so, that dinner was delightful and, thankfully, they appeared to have an adequate supply of beer and hard liquor.

The next morning, after a mushroom and avocado breakfast, the Deans and I rendezvoused on the beach and stared in distaste at a suddenly malevolent lake. Wordlessly, we all went back into the house, found some magazines to read, and spent the rest of the day lazily thumbing through their pages, in the hopefully safe confines of a lounge chair on the lawn. Not for us, the joys of trawling for crocodiles, because we had suddenly lost our resolve to pursue the simple idyllic pleasures of life on the brink of eternity.

Yet still, before our eyes, those same two African ladies did their laundry, in either ignorance, fear, gallantry or indifference. But we were unimpressed. Wild horses would not have got us back into that water, although it was probably comparatively safe. However, we were not comparative swimmers, and, in future, decided to give as wide a berth to Africa's lakes as we already gave to its rivers.

Thus, for the next few days, we sunned and read most of the world's great literature until, all too soon, it was time to head back to Lusaka. Just before we left, I asked Sally's uncle if he had any African woodcarvings for sale. 'Sure,' he replied. He took me to a storeroom where he had hundreds of beautifully carved ebony figures, most intricately inlaid with ivory. It was the finest display of African carving I ever saw, and I bought a considerable quantity to take back home.

We then said our farewells to our gracious hosts and, after Sally had kissed them goodbye, we began the long drive back to Lusaka. This time, we had no trouble reaching Lilongwe, since Sally's uncle had given her detailed instructions for making the trip in less than nine hours. Consequently, the drive back to the main highway was uneventful and gave us all an opportunity to reflect on a time well spent.

But, on that occasion, I wisely took back more than memories, and I still have a display case full of beautiful African carvings, including one of a leopard in which the spots are inlaid in ivory. Sometimes when I dust my curios I pause to remember, and sadly reflect on the uncertain future, which faced those two charming pioneers, when their Nyasaland became someone else's Malawi.

5. Playing Chicken

From Lilongwe we headed for Zomba the capital of Nyasaland. This small, two store town, was about 150 miles to our south and 100 miles from Tete, in Mozambique, where the Portuguese had a ferry across the Zambezi. After that we would have a 200-mile drive through some very rough country to Salisbury and then back to Lusaka. Definitely we were taking the long way home, but we hoped it would prove interesting. It did.

The drive to Zomba was uneventful and we spent a lazy hour touring its few streets before deciding to visit the Zomba plateau. This little-known beauty spot is one of those unusual places that give a special charm to the magic of central Africa. It soars above the surrounding plain and dominates Zomba in much the same way as the better-known Table Mountain frowns down upon Capetown on the South African coast. Its charm is enhanced by its isolation, and by the cooler climate and lush vegetation that is to be found on the summit a good 2,000 feet above the hot and dusty plain below.

There was only one road to the top of the plateau and it gave us the most unusual driving experience that I ever encountered in all my years in central Africa. This road was not really a road at all, but was only a narrow track which snaked its way up the precipitous cliff face in a long succession of hairpin curves and don't-look-now overhangs.

Like all such roads, it is a wonderful experience to talk about and no fun to drive. Prudent drivers, in most other parts of the world, traverse such roads with caution. But this is central Africa, and the prudent driver attacks this road as if his very life depends upon reaching the top or bottom, within some pre-determined window of opportunity.

The reason for this seemingly rash approach is simple: It does. In order to survive, you have to be off this road, in less than your allotted time. Or risk a head on collision with traffic careening in the opposite direction. This stark reality is succinctly explained at the foot of the plateau, where a large notice board informs all passers-by that they are about to enter an alternating one-way street.

For the first 15 minutes of each hour ascending traffic may proceed. Conversely, during the third quarter of each hour, descending traffic will be permitted to leave the summit. The instructions concluded by reminding the contestants that it would be wise to complete your drive to the plateau's crest by half past the hour, at the very latest.

Adjacent to that time bomb of a notice board is the starter's clock. It is stark in its simplicity and only boasts a minute hand. In this world, minutes are precious, hours are irrelevant. The clock, at the bottom of the climb, is coloured green in the top right hand quarter of its face, while the rest of the face is coloured red. The moving finger signifies green for go and red for no go. Talk about a wheel of fortune, this is a real one. The prizes on this wheel can last forever.

Anyone foolish enough to try the ascent, providing that God travels in the passenger seat, will eventually encounter the clock at the top of the road. This clock is coloured green in the bottom left-hand quarter, while the other three quarters are coloured red. It is, from a mathematical point of view, a perfect counterpoint to its mate at the foot of the trail.

Stunned, I stared in disbelief at that notice board, while cold chills of horror gripped my mind, as I re-read the rules of the joust. Just then a large truck zoomed by as it completed its descent of the road at breakneck speed. It was not a reassuring sight and prompted me to discuss with the Deans several questions that deeply perturbed me: one, what happened if you broke down or had a flat tyre? Two, what happened when a vehicle arrived whose driver, especially a native driver, didn't read English? Three, could one really trust everyone to go by the book and not to cheat? Four, and most important, were the two clocks precisely synchronized?

But of course they had no answers, which only increased our apprehension as we pondered the imponderable. Either we were going or we weren't and so, when the minute hand reached the green, I drove up the nine or ten miles of the road, and we all spent a pleasant afternoon exploring the unique habitat of the Zomba Plateau. It really is a fascinating place to visit and I wished we could have stayed longer. But, not wanting to try my hand at jousting in the dark, we prudently left in the early evening, just as the sun was beginning to set.

As I drove down the trail, I discovered that it helped considerably if I concentrated my mind on the simple pleasures of an African sunset, and ignored the full implications of what I was doing. For the umpteenth time it occurred to me that the white man in Africa must adapt to a different philosophy of life, or come out of his tree, as the South Africans were fond of saying. You cannot measure by a Western rule. Nor can you greet each new situation with a comparison with how it would be handled in Europe or America. 'Different strokes for different folks' seemed to apply. Unfortunately, I also felt that another platitude – where ignorance is bliss, 'tis folly to be wise – was equally relevant. Happily, I concluded this soliloquy in our hotel bar later that evening, with a few too many drinks, which I felt I deserved.

6. The Ferry At Tete

Early the next morning we left Zomba for Tete, secure in the belief that this trip had no more rude surprises in store. How little did we know, and how innocently we motored into Tete some three hours later.

Mozambique, at that time, was about as developed as the Garden of Eden on Day One of creation. There were no road bridges over the Zambezi and only one rail bridge, which I believe, has since been destroyed in the civil war that broke out after independence from Portugal was achieved in 1970. Consequently, the Zambezi ferry at Tete has, or had, for I doubt if it still operates, the distinction of being the only means by which cars and trucks could cross the Zambezi, in the whole of Mozambique, unless they went by rail.

Given this paucity of choice, we arrived in Tete that afternoon with the firm idea of enjoying a relaxing sail upon the lower Zambezi, which had now attained a width of several miles as it neared the end of its 1,600 mile journey to the Indian Ocean. However, our hopes were quickly dashed when we reached the river and watched in horror as a large truck miraculously boarded the ferry.

Sadly, we sat in my car, carefully debating the wisdom of turning back and retracing our steps, in order to avoid this opportunity to cruise on the majestic Zambezi. Our decision didn't come easy, and may have been influenced by my reluctance to be foiled, for the very first time, on an African road. But in all probability it was our combined stupidity, or the thought of a thousand-mile detour, that finally kept us from admitting defeat. In any event, we eventually overcame our desire to flee the challenge ahead and decided to proceed as planned.

Our problem was not with the ferry; indeed, it was a very nice ferry, and I would have been more than happy to sail on such a ship, providing of course, that I could find some non-gymnastic way for my car to board it. Unfortunately this did not seem likely, since no one had bothered to think of a sane way of driving a car from the shore to the deck of the ferry, or, assuming stage One was successful, of returning your vehicle to dry land. There was no landing dock or jetty on the river's bank. There was no mechanical ramp on the front of the ship, waiting to be raised or lowered as needed, as surely there must be, on all the ferries in heaven.

Apparently, the Portuguese operators of this ferry saw no need to provide luxuries and frills, as they contentedly moored their boat about 10 feet out from the river's bank, and thoughtfully left a yawning abyss between the ferry and its passengers. This minor problem had been casually bridged by two 12-inch planks, which lay invitingly between the rampless deck of the ferry and the steep jagged edge of the river's bank.

Unsure of what to do next, but in no hurry to make a decision, we disconsolately spent the next half hour sitting in my car and silently cursing the romance of Africa. My mood was not helped when I watched another fairly large Portuguese truck safely make the trip from shore to ship, with one of its double rear wheels on the plank, while the other rode air.

Now, obviously, I was not going to have the same comforting margin of error as that just displayed by the semi-airborne truck, since my car, like most cars, had single rear wheels. Regrettably this meant, that if I were to drive my car as poorly as the truck had been driven, then my car, unlike the truck, had only a 50-50 chance of riding the plank. Tete did not look like the kind of place which would have the equipment necessary to fish my car out of the river. It looked more like the kind of place that may not notice if I sank.

Finally, I decided to give it a try, and the Deans got out of my car to watch from a safe distance. I dutifully followed the Portuguese hand signals of a member of the ferry's crew, who seemed to be in charge of shepherding recalcitrant vehicles into the warm bosom of his vessel. All went well until I had almost reached the river's edge, when my nerves failed me and I ground to a halt. I got out of my car thoroughly terrified, because I had just discovered that the drive over the planks was blind. My car was a sports model with a long hood, which meant that I lost sight of the planks I was aiming at long before they were reached by the car's front wheels.

For the first time in my life, I was either too chicken, or too wise, to give it a go. I knew in my soul that I was not prepared to bet my car, and possibly my life, on the hand signals of someone who didn't even speak English. If I was going to drive over those planks, I had to line it up. No foreigner, however experienced he may be, was going to shepherd me aboard that ferry.

Luckily, just as I was about to give up in despair, inspiration came. I knew how to do it: Self-reliance was the answer. First, I gauged the remaining distance from my front wheels to the edge of the planks. Then, I gingerly drove my car forward until I felt the front wheels touch the planks. Now, I stopped the car, got out and, with Dixie's help, carefully positioned the rails to match my car's proposed trajectory. Next, I ensured that each plank was wedged against its tyre, and confirmed that both my front wheels were positioned in the absolute centre of their piece of timber. Finally, I went behind the car and made certain that each row of rear wheel, front wheel and plank, was beautifully aligned in a perfectly straight line.

Satisfied that I had solved the problem, I got back into my car and bravely drove forward for at least three feet, before stopping to re-evaluate the situation. Once more, I got out of the car and examined the lay of the land, to determine if all was still on track. It was, and I could no longer delay the moment of truth. I got back in the car, gripped the wheel firmly to keep it true, said a prayer, and gently eased my way aboard the ferry. A piece of cake; nothing to it; why had I taken so long? I was neurotic. I was also very relieved to be on the ferry and not in the water. The Deans, quite literally, walked the plank and then we all settled down to enjoy the ride across the river.

When we reached our destination on the opposite bank of the Zambezi, I coolly faced the unavoidable truth, that if it goes up, it must come down. I also prayed for the grace to do it slowly and safely, as I calmly noted the ease with which the Portuguese planking system had made the transition to our new moorings. But, with my experience, I had no fear of this old friend, although the Deans still exercised caution by walking ashore. I felt that I had become an expert on the strange ways of people who spoke a foreign tongue. It was therefore with a casual air of boredom, that I followed the desultory hand signals of a crew member, when my turn came to drive the planks and leave his ship. It was easy, especially after I closed my eyes.

Happiness is seeing the Zambezi River in your rear-view mirror and I even had time to brood as we uneventfully completed our homeward journey, content that the ferry at Tete was history. Now why, I wondered, did such an unreasonable situation exist? A few more planks, a pound or two of nails, a little time, and presto, they'd have built a couple of decent ramps. It shouldn't cost much, and the work wouldn't take more than a day or two, at most. Why not make a simple improvement, which had to enhance the quality of life, of everyone who used that ferry?

Surely no one could find fault with such an obvious step forward. Puzzled, I kept searching for a reason why no brave soul had bothered to build adequate ramps, and eventually I came to a simple conclusion, which I still believe to be one of Africa's saddest truths.

The answer, frankly, is indifference. Nobody cares enough to find a better way. It isn't the climate, it isn't the lack of natural resources, or education, which keeps most African countries in such dire straits. For though it is true, that conditions in Africa are harsh, it is still indifference that covers the continent like a blanket and snuffs out the faintest spark of progress.

Therefore I firmly believe that more foreign aid, or more trade, would not significantly benefit this part of the world until its people alter their basic approach to life and accept the possibility that some new ideas may be good ideas. If this does not happen, even though the ferry at Tete runs till the end of time, it will still continue to load and unload vehicles in much the same way that it had handled mine.

Given such a level of contentment with the *status quo*, then logically, the driver of any car unlucky enough to go swimming, must automatically be responsible for the accident, thereby freeing the unfazed ferry operator from blame, and allowing the farce to continue. This inflexible philosophy seems to be fairly common throughout the Third World, and may help to explain why the citizens of most underdeveloped lands, tend to resist change, in spite of the benefits it may offer at a minimal cost in time, money, or effort.

Perhaps I am wrong and over simplify. But at least I learned one valuable lesson, and concluded my musing with a vow that in future I would plan all trips to carefully avoid all ferries. Wisely, I tried to keep this pledge, which meant that a walk around my yard was about as far as I ever went. However, I noticed that my hair didn't get any greyer and sometimes I even thought that I looked a little younger.

7. Moving On

Almost before we knew it, the time had come to welcome Mr. Lewis back from his leave and move out of his house. Now came the flip side of being a caretaker, as we each tried to decide where to go next. For Maurice the answer was easy, since his posting to Lilongwe – the tourist Mecca I had just visited – coincided with the end of our sojourn in comfort. Accordingly, he packed his few belongings into the back seat of his Mercedes and drove off, out of our lives and into the wild African yonder.

Peter also made the big move, by doing something he had been threatening to do for more than a year: joining the Rhodesian army as a second lieutenant. Hence, he too loaded his meager possessions into his car and left for Bulawayo, the home base of the Rhodesian army. It was, in all truth, one of the saddest days in my life, when I waved him goodbye, since we had shared so many memorable experiences. But once again the moving finger wrote, and a friend moved on.

Ironically, we were to meet just one more time, some two years later, and in rather dramatic circumstances, during the upheaval in the Belgian Congo, which followed that country's chaotic transition from a colony to an independent republic named Zaire. At the time, I was stationed in Solwezi, close to the border of the old Congolese province of Katanga. It had, under the leadership of Moise Tchombe, recently declared its independence from the new republic, and was now in full-scale rebellion against the rest of the erstwhile Congo. To make matters worse, if that was possible, this conflict had also drawn the enthusiastic participation of the United Nations, who had sent an army to Zaire to keep the peace, by conquering the Katangese.

Africa was beginning to boil, and unfortunately, with impeccable timing, I now had a ringside seat to a major conflagration. It threatened at any moment to engulf Northern Rhodesia, as the fighting drew ever closer to our ill-defined border with Katanga. Consequently, the Rhodesian army had been dispatched to Solwezi to protect our citizens, if needed, from the Ethiopian troops of the United Nations' command. It was a tense situation and, for several days, the incredible concept of going to war with the United Nations was a very real prospect for the tiny garrison at Solwezi. Naturally, as I've already noted, I was strategically poised in the middle of this cauldron of trouble and so, too, was Peter Van Eden and his platoon of infantry.

Of course, I had no idea he was also in Solwezi until, in the most amazing meeting of my life, he came strolling into my office one afternoon, toting his automatic rifle, and looking for Frank Bennett. We shook hands, and then spent an hour reminiscing about the good old days in a long vanished civilization. At last, as the light began to fail, he went back to his dugout and I went home to my little country house, which inexplicably was now a prominent feature on a potential battlefield. In all honesty, there really is no way to describe one's feelings at the prospect of going to war with the rest of the world – kind of like Iraq's recent experiment – especially when you're convinced that you are going to lose.

Yet that was how fate had dealt our cards, and Peter and I were prepared to die for our cause, in that lonely outpost of the white man's Africa. Thankfully, nothing dramatic ever happened. The Ethiopians stopped their advance about three miles short of our lines, and the peace of Solwezi was not disturbed.

In due course, a month or so later, when all danger had passed, Peter stopped by my office to say goodbye, and then climbed into his truck as his regiment prepared to return to Bulawayo.

Soberly, I watched his convoy slowly grind its way out of our village in a cloud of dust, and suddenly I knew I never would see him again. And so it was, as the winds of change continued to blow through Africa with ever-increasing ferocity. In my case, the wind blew to America, but for Peter it blew into the worst of all nightmares: civil war against the nationalist guerrillas of Southern Rhodesia, as that tragic land struggled through its death throes towards the birth of Zimbabwe. I often wonder what happened to him and where he is today, and my mind sometimes returns to the last time I saw my carefree friend, in his camouflage fatigues and combat boots.

But, let us now return to Lusaka in the more tranquil waning months of a memorable 1960, and to the imminent return of the formidable Mr. Lewis, about to reclaim his own.

With two of our number gone, it only remained for Michael and me to move out of our home and on to our next adventure. Michael, as befits a bespoken man, decided on a low-key approach, going to live with a young couple he knew, but I had more grandiose plans. Accordingly, once I had returned Mr. Lewis' keys and servants to his tender care, I went back to my beloved government rest house, and began an aggressive campaign for the affections of a young lady I had fallen in love with at the cinema the previous month.

Like a kaleidoscope, the patterns of our lives had changed dramatically in the last few weeks, as we four musketeers diverged to follow our stars. We were now in three different countries. One was off to war, while one was off to love, which may be the more dangerous game. Nevertheless, it had all been fun, and if the idea of life is to celebrate life, then it had all been a resounding success.

Chapter 8

Girls

1. Getting Serious

Many romantic moons ago, when I was a teenager, my father spoke to me of serious things and so, some 40 years later, I will devote this chapter to the subject of girls, a very serious subject in colonial Africa. There was, as I have already explained, a dearth of eligible young ladies in Northern Rhodesia in the early 1960s, and the competition for their favours was correspondingly fierce. Thus, since I am by nature a shrinking violet, this discourse will sadly be somewhat brief and will be confined to a few anecdotes about four of the most charming ladies I ever knew. One was Scottish, one was English, one was Rhodesian and one was South African. Hence, I can claim to be free of ethnic bias, and a credit to my father, by my ability to concentrate on the serious things of life.

2. Janet Higgins

Occasionally, with luck, we all find a friend like Janet, although this charming young lady was never a girlfriend of mine, in the narrowly accepted way in which we usually define this term. However, in a broader and perhaps more meaningful way, she was one of the best and closest girl friends I ever was privileged to know. Luckily, for me, we met soon after I arrived in Northern Rhodesia, at the end of 1958. At the time, and for the two years of our friendship, she was living in the government rest house. She was a small, stocky Scottish girl from Glasgow, with long brown hair which, when not tied in a bun, reached down almost to her waist. By profession, she was an executive secretary and, as such, had been sent to the colony to assist the Chief Establishment Officer with his duties.

Her laugh was infectious, her good humour legendary and her ability to consume vast quantities of whiskey without passing out was quite astounding. She was, perhaps, about 30 years old when we first met, and rapidly assumed the position of the elder sister I never had, since, at that time, I was a very immature 23. Bill Curphy and Peter Van Eden

were equally under her spell, and often the four of us would sit in
Janet's room in the rest house, drinking Scotch whiskey until Janet,
sober as a judge, called it a night by rolling our bodies out of her room.

For us, the thought of going to a party without Janet was unthinkable and I can still see her long brown hair swirling in the breeze, as
she gaily danced away our cares and concerns. Her voice was soft and
mellow, and her brogue was very broad, which made her sound like
a female Bobby Burns. When she laughed, which was often, she filled
the whole room with her merriment, and our hearts with her joy. She
was a very dear friend of mine and I shall always be grateful for
having had the opportunity to spend so many delightful hours with
this very special woman.

In due course, as with most of my other friends, her first tour of
duty came to a close and, after one last stupendous party, she went
back to Europe for good, some two years after we first met. Once
again, a dear friend dropped out of my life and, once again, she
vanished without trace. But this time I did, in a roundabout way, get
a smidgen of information, when I subsequently talked to someone
who relayed a rumour that Janet had got married in Glasgow, and
settled down to the life of a middle-class housewife. If so, lucky
fellow. For my part, I'll never forget her and I hope that her life has
been fulfilling and rewarding.

3. Sonja Henning

The first time I saw Sonja Henning, she was engaged in a rather hectic
game of table tennis in the game room of the government rest house
in Lusaka. I had, at that time, just obtained my driving license and
was currently living with Martin Crosby in a small apartment adjacent to my *alma mater*. It was, as I recall, a rainy Saturday morning
in January or February of 1960, and I had idly wandered over to the
government hostel in a bored attempt to relieve what was, so far, a
very monotonous day. The rest house was depressingly deserted, the
lounge was empty, and I dejectedly headed for home, down the corridor which fronted the game room. As I passed this room, I glanced
forlornly inside, expecting to find it deserted, and was enchanted to
see two unknown females vigorously pounding a table tennis ball
back and forth.

This was a most unexpected development, which had all the hall-
marks of a sunny day and so, with an interest merely in the game, I
entered the room to watch the young ladies at play. They were both
quite good at table tennis and, for 10 or 15 minutes, ignored me as
they concentrated on their game. For my own part, I was content to
lean against a wall in my great white hunter pose, and wonder why
all the other men in the rest house had not become students of this
attractive sport.

Both girls were quite pretty, an unexpected bonus in my days in central Africa. One, in particular, was petite, with a good figure, long red hair and that clear alabaster-white skin which sometimes makes an English girl the envy of her South African peers. As a bonus, she had the bluest eyes I ever saw, and a very wide smile, which she flashed each time she scored a point. In short, she was worth watching, especially since it was raining, and I therefore settled down to study her form.

Eventually, the two ladies finished their game – the redhead won rather easily – and I politely introduced myself. A few delicate questions, a specialty of mine, elicited the information that they were both high school teachers from England, and had only been in the colony for two days. Now I understood why they had not been trampled by the ignoble crowd's maddened stampede, and I graciously offered to give them both a tour of the city in my humble chariot.

The second girl said no, she had to go and wash her hair. The redhead said maybe later, if I could beat her at table tennis. This I modestly agreed to attempt since, purely by chance, table tennis is the only game at which I excel, and I now had a perfect opportunity to preen my feathers before her admiring gaze. And thus began a delightful romance with Sonja Henning, a 23-year-old Londoner with a master's degree in mathematics, a superior intellect and a very warm personality.

She also had a temper to go with her red hair, and showed it, as she struggled mightily to win a game until, eventually, since I am a gentleman, she won one. We then went for a ride in my car and, when the sun began to shine in more ways than one, we finished up at our local swimming pool for a late afternoon swim, which gave me a further chance to appraise her bikini-clad figure. Our relationship, fortunately, continued to blossom and, during the next six months or so, we were fairly constant companions, until I fell in love, at first glance, with the woman of my dreams.

In retrospect, I really don't know why Sonja and I never became really serious about each other. I guess it was just one of those things where two people get romantically involved, even though both understand it will not last forever. Then again, I may just have been too foolish, another virtue of mine, to recognize the treasure I had.

Who knows? But we had fun, and did the round of our cinemas, nightclubs and restaurants, just as if we were living in Manchester. Truly, those were the good days, since we both had plenty of money and an elegant lifestyle, in which a bevy of servants catered to our every whim. It was, without doubt, a period in which I came close to having it all and, luckily, I was wise enough to know it and enjoy it.

Probably, we started to drift apart about four months after we met, when I moved out of my apartment, and into Mr. Lewis' house, while Sonja, at almost the same time, took an apartment of her own on the other side of town. Certainly it is true to say that we ceased to date as frequently as before, when we ceased to live as close to each other as we had in the past. Nonetheless, we always remained friends, and Sonja was the only one of my ex-girlfriends who came to my farewell party, in January of 1962, when I left Lusaka for my seven and a half months of overseas leave.

However, in addition to being a good friend, Sonja also taught me a stern lesson in human nature in the raw. To my chagrin, this illuminating cold shower was administered one memorable evening when, with the lights turned down low and passion on the rise, she blithely informed me that most of her friends thought I was gay. Now, in case anyone has not had this peculiar experience, let me assure you it is a guaranteed coolant for ardor.

Startled, I took refuge in the requisite cigarette and inquired as to whether or not she had come out of her tree. Happily, she assured me that she still had a firm grasp on a sturdy branch, and merely thought I would be amused to learn of my reputation. I was not. She then explained that since I had previously dated two of her friends, and had made no pass at either of them, they had concluded I was a homosexual!

'But what if I just wasn't turned on?' I protested. 'Ha!' she replied. 'No woman would ever accept so unflattering an explanation.' Come to think of it, that is probably true. 'Then will you speak up for me?' I pleaded. 'Perhaps,' she answered, before going on to point out the hazards to her own reputation, which a too vigorous defense of mine would potentially create.

Sadly, I agreed with her analysis and pondered the possibility of raping the two young ladies in question, in order to set the record straight. Regrettably, my loyalty to my Queen prevented any such drastic proof of my masculinity, and so I decided to try to grow hair on my chest, instead. Yet I never forgot that lesson, which proved how easily one can be falsely branded by those who jump to unfounded conclusions.

In truth, all I had done was take a couple of young ladies to a movie or two and, since I didn't get amorous, they had both deduced I was a man's man. Apparently, if one didn't attack everything in a skirt, one had to be a homosexual. Now that's a nice, simple logic and I determined, then and there, never to judge anyone until I was doubly sure double, that I had all the facts. And then, for good measure, I decided never to judge anyone anytime since, as the Good Book says, 'Judgment is mine, saith the Lord.'

Naturally, as is my wont, I eventually lost touch with Sonja, as the years rolled by, and so I really don't know what joys, or perils, her future held. Perhaps she too went back to England, or perhaps she bucked the trend and stayed in Africa. But, whatever she did, I wish her well, and I still remember the first time I saw her, with her flashing grin and long red hair, as she pounded a table tennis ball in a game room in Lusaka, so many, many years ago.

4. Wendy Pugin

Rationally, I do not believe in love at first sight since, to me, that is irrational. Therefore, when it happened to me, I refused to believe it, which is why my brain said, 'You fool,' while my stomach got sick, and my heart pounded with fierce enthusiasm. Quite obviously this was not a desirable set of symptoms, and should, most definitely, have been restricted to a Doris Day movie. Unfortunately, my problem was real and began, not inside the cinema, but outside, when I first saw and fell for a young woman who was sauntering down the street hand-in-hand with, you've guessed it, Peter Van Eden.

It really was weird – I saw, and she conquered. We never even spoke. Peter never even saw me. They were on the other side of a street in downtown Lusaka late one evening, and passed from my view moments after I saw them. All in all, I must have seen his companion for a full 20 seconds, at a distance of 50 feet, and I was in love. Truly, this was ridiculous, and I hurried home to wait for this temporary bout of insanity to pass.

But it did not, and later that week, I casually made my first move, by diffidently asking Peter the name of the goddess he had been escorting down the street when my world turned topsy-turvy. Maddeningly, he couldn't remember and therefore, very slowly, I worked him through his sex life for the past four or five days until finally he said, 'Oh, you must mean Wendy Pugin.'

'Who's Wendy?' I breathed, trying desperately to disguise my passionate interest, as Peter filled in the blanks, and nonchalantly told me that she had recently arrived in town from Livingstone, where she already had a fiancé whom she planned to marry in about six month's time. Great news, I don't think. 'So, she's not one of your girlfriends?' I probed. 'Hell no, I don't even like her very much,' he replied. And so I was free to abort her engagement, if I could only figure out some innocent way to meet this young lady.

Luckily, Peter proved to be a mine of information, since he had apparently scouted Wendy pretty thoroughly, before he lost interest. Consequently, I soon discovered that my target was 19 years old and worked for the Federal Internal Revenue Service, who had recently transferred her from Livingstone, her hometown, to Lusaka. Peter also said that she was currently living in our famous government rest house, which thereby became the centrepiece of my campaign.

Accordingly, the very next day after work, I went to see the manager of our hostel and, since this gentleman was a good friend of mine, I took him into my confidence. At first he doubted my sanity, but then, when I begged for his assistance, he became more sympathetic and agreed to help me zero in on my target, if I would only explain what I needed. 'Nothing much,' I said, 'I just need to move into a room next to hers.' 'What a good idea,' he enthusiastically responded but, alas, after checking his records, he gloomily reported that the two rooms adjoining hers were both occupied.

Undaunted, I arranged to move into another nearby room which, luckily, would be vacant in two week's time, when my lease on Mr. Lewis' home expired. Nevertheless, I expressly instructed my friend to make sure that if either of the two more strategically located rooms fell vacant during the next two weeks, it was to be immediately reserved for me. This, he readily agreed to do and, after giving him my work telephone number, I went home, secure in the knowledge that anyone who could stop elephants at a glance would surely have no trouble with Wendy Pugin.

Right on schedule, about 10 days later, my friend called to say that some undiscerning lout had moved out of one of the rooms next to Wendy's, and all was arranged for me to be the new tenant. Hence, I happily moved back into my old stomping ground the very next weekend and took to lurking behind the curtains of my room. Fortunately, Wendy was very regular in her habits and thus, purely by chance, I was able to bump into her at fairly regular intervals, on the verandah which fronted our rooms. Naturally, I did not rush in, but rather, for the first day or two, contented myself with a casual good morning and good evening. A few days later, I ventured a remark about the weather, always a safe subject for an Englishman, and, by the end of the first week, we had exchanged names.

So far, so good, and now it was time to increase the stakes. Therefore, on Monday of the following week, I invited her to share my table at breakfast, and we soon developed an easy, casual, informal and unsuspicious relationship. Everything was under control, I hoped, and I even had time to reflect on the woman of my dreams. She was, by birth, a Northern Rhodesian and came from a French Huguenot family which had been in southern Africa for almost 200 years. Her French ancestry showed in her looks, since Wendy was definitely much darker and more Latin looking than most of the young ladies I had previously known.

She was probably not classically beautiful, but her long black hair, brown eyes and dimpled smile combined to create a very attractive picture which, when added to her medium height and outstanding figure, created a very alluring image. Of course, since I was smitten, I may not be a good judge of Wendy's appeal but yet, it is fair to say that when she entered a room, most men's eyes automatically turned in her direction.

For a day or two, I was at a loss for my next move. Then Wendy came to my rescue by sadly announcing at breakfast one morning that the following day was her 20th birthday, and her fiancé would not (how sad) be here to share it with her. This was the opening I needed and so, with the help of my numerous friends in the rest house, I made my plans.

When Wendy walked into the lounge the next evening, she was

amazed to find it decorated with streamers and balloons as her new friends charmingly celebrated her birthday. She cried. It was really quite touching. We even had a birthday cake and everyone joined in the fun. The rest of the evening was spent dancing to the strains of the hostel's stereo system which, not surprisingly, performed impeccably under Janet's careful tutelage.

Thankfully, a good time was had by all, and it was almost midnight before Wendy and I strolled back to our respective adjacent hovels. Obviously, she didn't have to search far for the organizer of her impromptu party, since I was the only other person who had known that today was her birthday. As we said goodnight, she quietly asked me why I had done it. Ever the gentleman, I softly replied, 'To see you smile,' and triumphantly adjourned to my chamber.

During the next few weeks, our friendship slowly developed and we even went to the occasional movie – albeit on a purely Platonic basis – until finally I encountered a tremendous stroke of luck; although at the time I did not know it. This fortuitous event occurred when Wendy was talking to her mother on the telephone and casually mentioned that she had recently met a charmingly safe young Englishman, here in Lusaka.

Her mother was ecstatic, due, as I subsequently discovered, to a hearty loathing for Wendy's current fiancé, and immediately encouraged Wendy to broaden her relationship with this newfound knight in his shining armor. Naturally, she took her mother's advice, as all good girls are wont to do, and within another week, we had progressed to the fringe of a goodnight kiss.

Gradually our relationship developed and within a month, Wendy had to face the fact that she now had two boyfriends. Deliberately, I refrained from pressing the issue, since this was, in my opinion, one bridge she would have to cross alone. Finally, when her fiancé came to Lusaka for a weekend visit, she gave him his ring back and told him their romance was over.

It was a solemn moment, and when she told me she had done it, I felt genuine sorrow for this man I did not know, but whose life I had irrevocably altered. Yet, what else could I have done? Wendy was obviously meant to be mine. Besides, I was young, in love and victorious, and so, after sincerely congratulating her on her wisdom, I contentedly began to daydream about the joys of a Wendy-filled future.

Everything was coming up roses until my dream abruptly turned into a nightmare, some two weeks later, when I lent her my beautiful car for a weekend visit to Livingstone, and was sorely tormented in return. That was when my angel became a demolition-derby dervish, and considerably altered the basic outlines of my automobile. Sadly, I realized that Wendy came with a price tag and two cannot always live better than one. But she was unhurt and repentant, while my car was devastated but repairable, and thus, after a few rocky bumps, our romance resumed the even tenor of an African delight.

Love was our bond, and, during the next few months, we were nearly inseparable as we contentedly made the rounds of Lusaka's nightspots, or just stayed home and talked. Of course, it was also very convenient to have a girlfriend in the next room to one's own, since it required the absolute minimum of effort to pick her up for a date, and to subsequently take her back home. Indeed, it was almost like being married. There was something absurd about saying good-night to Wendy, as I unlocked the door to the room next door to hers.

Certainly, it was a unique situation. But then, about three months after I moved into the rest house, I acquired the home of our colony's Chief Establishment Officer for a seven and a half month stint. Amazingly, this officer was even more senior than Mr. Lewis and his home was correspondingly grander. He was also, you may remember, Janet's boss, and I expect her influence probably had something to do with my continued good fortune.

Nothing, apparently, now stood between me and Government House if I continued to find this kind of favor with the colony's top brass. They appeared to be passing me from one to the next, in a touching vote of confidence in my house-sitting skills. In addition, since the sun always shines on the just, my new home was only about half a mile from the government rest house, and thus, when I abandoned my faithful room, whose mission had been accomplished, I was still within easy striking distance of my sacred hunting ground.

Naturally, I enthusiastically savoured my return to the kind of accommodation I deserved, and Wendy was also suitably impressed by my newfound grandeur. For now we could sit on my verandah in

Victoria Falls, 1959

the evening over drinks, and she was a frequent visitor at my elegant table. Once again, I had three other roommates, two of whom were new to my circle, while one, Michael Voysey, was an old friend. Understandably, all three of these gentlemen speedily fell under Wendy's spell, and the five of us, plus Michael's fiancée Eve, spent many a delightful evening in my new home's sumptuous lounge. Truly, those were the good old days, but always, in the back of my mind was the realization that the colonial era was fast ebbing to its close in this my tropical paradise.

In fact, it was all slightly sad, but it was all so much fun while it lasted, and perhaps the finest time I ever had in Africa was during those few months in late 1960 and early 1961, when the sun shone down on my perfect world. Everything we did was fun, but best of all was that memorable occasion, when Wendy and I decided to celebrate the new year of 1961 in Livingstone, her hometown and the site of the world's most romantic waterfall.

Accordingly, we both took a week's vacation from work and, on the 28th of December, 1960, with me driving (I'm not a total fool) we slowly motored down to Livingstone. Once there, I delivered Wendy to her childhood home, where I was introduced to both her parents. They welcomed me most graciously, and thanked me for bringing their daughter home for the holidays. I then went on to Martin Crosby's house, where I had arranged to spend the next few nights and brush up on my bridge playing skills.

Martin, of course, was overjoyed to see me and had himself taken a few days leave, to introduce me to his present hometown. Consequently, bright and early the following morning, after Martin had been overwhelmed by his introduction to Wendy, the three of us ventured into paradise, as we tried to view the Victoria Falls from every conceivable vantage point, on both the Northern and Southern Rhodesian sides of the river.

Strangely enough, viewing the Victoria Falls is not quite as easy as it sounds, because these falls are not like the Niagara Falls, and there is no one place from which the whole falls can be seen at one time. This is because, at Victoria, the Zambezi has, over the ages, cut its way back through a succession of gorges, until it reached the line of the present falls. Thus, unlike Niagara, where one has an uninterrupted view of the falls from the downstream side of the river, the view of Victoria is restricted by the opposite wall of the gorge, into which the mighty river tumbles.

Therefore, in order to view the falls, one has to scramble across the wet and slippery rocks of this gorge's far side, until one reaches its downstream edge. Then, from this dangerous place, one can perilously peer out through the mist and rain which engulf it, and hopefully catch a glimpse of the wall of water which plummets down from the opposite edge of the gorge, a scant 100 yards beyond one's perch, across the abyss.

Just to stand there on that trembling rock and gaze at the endless cascade is truly an unbelievable experience. It stretches as far as one can see, left or right, and disappears from view into the mist beneath one's feet. The noise, of course, is unbelievable and it is impossible to communicate, except by hand gestures, but then, there really is no need for words in that primitive place at the centre of one of nature's great accomplishments.

It is also possible to stumble along the far side of this 400-feet-deep chasm until one comes to its centre, at a place appropriately called the Devil's Cauldron. For there, at the centre of the spectacle, and about half a mile from the start of the gorge in either Rhodesia, is the place where the Zambezi River has forced an exit from the Victoria Falls gorge, as it pursues its journey to Kariba and the sea.

Without doubt, this is the perfect spot for a holiday photo and I still have a snapshot of Martin looking elegant in the midst of creation. Behind him are the falls, while to his right stands the opening in the gorge which is no more than 100 yards wide, and majestically marks the boundary between the two Rhodesias. A little further downriver, the turbulent Zambezi enters the first of several much older gorges, Victoria Falls from eons ago. Eventually, after fighting its way through 10 miles of rapids, the still furious river triumphantly emerges from this wilderness and assumes a more tranquil aspect.

In my day, this wild, infinitely lonely place was still an almost completely unspoiled remnant of the Garden of Eden. It had no Maid of the Mist, no man-made vantage points, no souvenir shops, no ice cream vendors, no tours and virtually no tourists. Consequently, on that never-to-be-forgotten day when Wendy, Martin and I paid homage to its awesome majesty, we did not see another visitor, but were privileged to be alone with God and nature.

After sampling the gorge from both sides of the river, we soon discovered that the best view of the falls could be had from the two edges of the gorge, because from there, one can see across the falls for several hundred feet until the mist obscured the view. Plus, on further investigation, we also found out that on the Northern Rhodesian side of the falls, there was a steep trail which led down to the floor of the gorge and the base of the falls.

Naturally, this hazardous path was not to be missed, and so we slithered our way down some 400 feet of muddy slope until, unbelievably, we stood at the foot of the falls. Now we could gaze up at the wall of water which shimmered in the sunlight just a few yards to our right. Truly it was an utterly indescribable sensation to stand there in the midst of Heaven and watch, while the tropical sun pierced the curtain of water with a succession of beautiful rainbows which floated and danced before our eyes. Once, for a magical moment, we stood at the centre of a rainbow, and every way we turned, we could see all the colours of light encircling our awe-struck group.

Drenched, we finally clawed our way back out of the chasm into a more humdrum world. We felt humble, but also elated, as we retreated from the roar of the falls and beat of its spray. Most certainly, we had visited the home of the 'Smoke that Thunders' and, as we walked back to Martin's car through the two-mile thicket of the Victoria Falls rain forest, we could still hear the song of the falls and see its blanket of cloud.

The following evening, after going to a movie, Wendy and I had an extraordinary experience when we visited the Victoria Falls illuminations. This stellar event had recently been inaugurated, after much soul searching, by the government of Northern Rhodesia, as an experiment in progress. Clearly, no one wanted to commercialize the falls, but the idea had been broached that a single soft white spotlight, shining at night on the most accessible and visible stretch of the falls, might produce a pleasing effect.

Obviously not everyone agreed, but eventually, after much debate, a lone spotlight was installed on the top of the gorge and directly across from one of the main cataracts of the falls. Predictably, this new venture drew mixed reviews, with many people saying it interfered with nature. But in the main, it was deemed to be a worthwhile enhancement of the falls by night, and a wonderful aid to romance.

Thus, after seeing John Wayne in a particularly unromantic cowboy shootout, I was eager for a change of pace and Wendy and I drove down to the falls at about 11:30 that night. It was an eerie experience, walking through the rain forest in total pitch darkness, with the roar of the falls growing ever louder in our ears until, suddenly, we burst out of the gloom and onto the brink of the falls.

Immediately to our right, and stretching away into the darkness beyond, was an endless roaring cascade, while to our left was the far wall of the gorge with its solitary beam of light, which turned a small portion of the falls into a soft white wall of ethereal water. All else was utter darkness, just that one magical frame of dancing light, which shone amid the noise and spray, like a dream of perfection turned to reality.

Spellbound, we both stood there, quietly holding hands for the longest time until, by mutual consent, we reluctantly turned away from one of the most beautiful sights we would ever be privileged to see. Slowly, we retraced our steps through the rain forest and, drenched but overflowing with joy, we drove back to Livingstone and civilization. Again, thank God I was wise enough to realize how lucky I was to be able to see such sights, not as a member of a tour group, but as one of only two intruders into an almost pristine world. Whatever happened next, Africa had been worth it, and I went to bed that night a deeply contented man.

The next day was New Year's Eve and Wendy, Martin and I put on our glad rags and went to the Victoria Falls Hotel for the New Year shindig. By chance, or perhaps by design, this prestigious hotel, one of Africa's finest, was just across the river from Livingstone and was thus in Southern Rhodesia, although most of its clientele that night had come over from the more populous northern shore of the Zambezi. Happily, the party itself was first class and the three of us, together with some of Martin's other friends, wined, dined and danced with uncharacteristic abandon.

At midnight, we all stood in a circle and sang 'Auld Lang Syne.' At daybreak, since we danced till dawn, we all went out on the back verandah of the hotel to drink champagne, while we watched the sun rise on the first summer's morning of 1961. Once again, it was a lovely, romantic spot and, although one could only catch a glimpse of the falls some three miles distant, we could still hear their roar in the early morning hush. We also could see the clouds of spray which marked the location of the falls, and marvel when this crown slowly turned to pink as it began to reflect the first burst of sunlight from the awakening African horizon. It was good to be alive, and home in the Federation of Rhodesia and Nyasaland, even though, as always, I felt a twinge of regret at the prospects of what the future may hold.

Soon, as is the norm in the tropics, it was full day and, since our party clothes were beginning to feel sticky, we all gratefully climbed into Martin's car, for the short ride home to our respective beds, and blissful oblivion. Later, much later, after a good day's sleep, I went over to Wendy's parents' home for New Year's dinner and drinks. The following morning, we said goodbye to Martin – whom I never saw again – and contentedly returned to Lusaka, in love with each other and life itself.

For a little while longer, all went well. Then, slowly, inexorably, our relationship began to deteriorate. To this day, I don't completely know why, nor can I adequately explain it. Yet for some indeterminate reason, I could not see myself and Wendy in 10 years' time, and I was beginning to resent the incessant cloud of suitors which swarmed in her wake. It really was discouraging and sometimes, at a nightclub, I would scarcely get to dance with her as every Don Juan in town played 'excuse me' the moment we set foot on the dance floor, or hot-footed it to our table to invite my young lady to dance.

Apparently, what had attracted me attracted others, and it was exhausting always being on one's toes to ward off the competition. Quite often, I felt like Horatius guarding the entrance to Rome and, like him, I began to yearn to get off the bridge. Admittedly, for her part, Wendy did not encourage other suitors, yet I always felt uneasy, and took to watching my back.

But surely it was more than the desire for a quiet life which cooled my ardor, even though, as I previously said, I never really identified the source of my discontent. Perhaps I was just immature and not willing to settle down. Truly, who knows why we do what we do? Certainly, I seldom do and this time, with my heart about to break, I went ahead with my decision to end our relationship. However, I couldn't just tell her goodbye, since I knew that within a week, I would be crying for forgiveness. Thus, I had to do it in a way which would make reconciliation impossible, and boy, did I succeed in that endeavour!

How well I remember that fateful and appropriately rainy day in March of 1961, when Wendy called me at work to ask if I would come and pick her up at her office at 5 p.m., since her normal carpool ride had been canceled. Sadly, I seized this golden opportunity to end our relationship and morosely agreed to be her chauffeur, although I had no intention of fulfilling my pledge.

Shortly thereafter, at 4:30 p.m., I left work and drove home to the comfort of the house I was currently caretaking. It was still raining, which matched my mood and, after telling Mike Voysey to expect a visit from Wendy, I retreated to my room, to await the end of my dream. About two hours later, a somewhat bedraggled Wendy arrived at our house, and politely inquired of Michael if Frank was at home. Mike said I was and Wendy, who had just walked three miles in the rain in high-heeled shoes, limped into the lounge. She then declined Mike's offer to fetch me and, instead, burst unceremoniously into my room.

Our meeting was brief. Wendy asked me why I didn't come to get her, as we had arranged, and I replied, 'It was too much trouble.' She looked at me, as I lay on my bed until, after an interminable silence, she turned on her heel and, without limping, marched out of my life. As soon as she left my room, I sprang from my bed and raced to the window. Wendy, after declining Michael's offer of a ride, strode purposefully down our winding driveway, into the deepening dusk of that rainy evening when our romance died such an inglorious death.

I never did see her again, although for several weeks I daily picked up the telephone, intending to call and ask her forgiveness. But I never did. The break, as intended, had been too complete. It was truly over. A few months later, a mutual friend told me she had applied for, and been granted, a transfer back to her hometown of Livingstone. I guess she had no reason, perhaps no wish, to stay in Lusaka, and I hope she found happiness in her old backyard.

From time to time I still wonder what became of her, and so many of my other friends in the traumatic days which were soon to engulf their homeland. Like Peter Van Eden, she was an African, and had nowhere to retreat to when life in central Africa began to deteriorate. Hopefully, by now, she is a grandmother somewhere safe. Yet I will always remember her the way she was when we both stood in awe before the cascading splendour of the Victoria Falls, as seen in the beam of a single floodlight on a dark tropical night.

In the wake of my traumatic breakup with Wendy, I decided, as young men are often apt to do, that I would avoid the female trap like the plague. Consequently, I avoided serious involvement with another African lady for the better part of a month. However, this time I did not make the first moves, but was bowled over by the frontal assault of a charmingly frank Afrikaner who seemed to know precisely what she was doing, which was a distinctly new experience for me.

5. Dawn Oakum

Once again Peter Van Eden was the catalyst, even though his connection was tenuous, since I first met Dawn Oakum at a party given by Peter's younger sister, who unbeknownst to me had ulterior motives. But on this occasion, although I found Dawn to be very attractive and intriguing, I quite wisely refrained from making any overt moves in her direction. My hesitation was simply a matter of good taste, and prudence, since I, at the ripe old age of 25, had no intention of getting involved with a 16-year-old adolescent. I most definitely was not about to embark on a career as a cradle snatcher, nor did I relish the idea of leaving my girlfriend in the parking lot, while I slipped into a nightclub for a quick beer. No sir, there are some things a gentleman does not do, and having an underage girlfriend is certainly not considered a prudent investment.

Proudly, I conveyed this sentiment to Peter's sister the day after the party, when she called me at work to ask me what I thought of Dawn. I even expressed the additional view that I might be interested in Dawn's mother, but not, under any circumstances, in jailbait. Nevertheless, my response went unheeded, as Peter's sister coolly replied that 1) Dawn was 24; 2) Dawn was divorced; 3) Dawn had a five-year old son; 4) Dawn was a registered intensive care nurse and 5) I was not worthy of her efforts as a matchmaker. She then rang off after haughtily announcing she would tell Dawn I avoided high school juniors.

Stunned I tried to regroup, especially when, about an hour or so later, Dawn charmingly called me at work and invited me out for an ice cream, provided of course I could get permission to stay out until 6 p.m. Humbly I agreed to ask Mike Voysey to extend my curfew, and she said good, she would pick me up at home at 5 o'clock that afternoon, long before it went dark. Straight after work I quickly hurried home, and barely got there before Dawn arrived, in a very nice automobile.

Instantly, I recognized my mistake. She definitely didn't look like she was 16, but was obviously a very mature 14-year-old. Quietly, I introduced her to Michael who, judging from his expression, had her pegged as a precocious 12, and then I climbed into the passenger's seat of her car and left for an uplifting banana split.

Just to be on the safe side, I warned her that if we met anyone I knew, I would introduce her as my granddaughter, and on that charming note, our friendship began. Like Wendy, Dawn was an African by birth, although she was not a Rhodesian, but had been born and raised in South Africa. She was also as fair as Wendy had been dark, with pale blue eyes, pure white skin, a crooked smile and ash blonde hair which she wore straight and long in the Veronica Lake tradition.

Most striking of all was the aura of youth and innocence, which surrounded this tall, slender, willowy child, who was apparently only six months younger than me, since that was what her driving license amazingly confirmed. But then, I had led a hard life chasing elephants, and she had retired early as a housewife. Besides, I think blondes have an unfair advantage, since they always seem to look 10 years younger than they are, and thus I should not be surprised if Dawn, wherever she is, still manages to turn back the clock, as she continues to slough off the years.

Anyway, after ice cream, I grew bold and we went to a movie before Dawn took me home about 10 p.m. We then sat in her car in my driveway for a few moments and, after agreeing to go swimming the following Sunday with her son, we parted with the knowledge that this was going to be no ordinary relationship. Her story, which I got in bits and pieces over the next few weeks, was typical of most young ladies in her situation. She had been married early, at 18, to a fellow Afrikaner in her hometown in the Transvaal and had come with him to Kitwe on the Northern Rhodesian copperbelt, when he took a job in one of the copper mines.

A year or so later her son had been born, and then, since they needed the money, she had gone to work in the mine hospital and had, after much study, passed all her exams to become a registered nurse. Unfortunately, her job at the hospital was on a rotating shift and when she was on the night shift, her husband began to do some extra curricular activities to enliven his bed. One night, she came home from work early and found him in an awkward athletic position. His explanation that this was an excellent way to lose weight was not accepted. Soon thereafter, Dawn sued for divorce.

She then took her son, whose custody she had received along with her divorce and, some six months before we met, left Kitwe to start a new life in Lusaka. This, understandably, was not easy, because she had, at the time, very little money, no home and no job. However, when she got to Lusaka, she had a stroke of luck and was hired by one of our richest residents, a 60-year-old widower, who needed a qualified nurse companion to look after his 95-year-old mother.

Now obviously, in the circumstances, this was the perfect job for Dawn, since it gave her and her son a home, as well as a fairly substantial income. There was also the added advantage of working for a rich man, who maintained a large bevy of servants to do all of the real work, and therefore she did not have to do any of the drudgery normally associated with geriatric care. In fact, as future events may have borne out, I suspect that Dawn's main job was to bring a little feminine charm into an otherwise rather dull household.

Strangely enough, I never actually met Dawn's employer or his mother, although I often visited his comparatively palatial estate during the six or so months that Dawn and I were a twosome. Sometimes, when he was out of town on a business trip and the old lady had retired to bed for the night, which she did quite early, I would go around to his home to spend a quiet evening with Dawn, in sumptuous splendour. Occasionally, we would have a candlelight dinner in the formal dining room, where my host's highly trained staff catered to our every whim, as they cooked and served the most elegant of meals.

But usually, we would skip dinner and just take sandwiches and drinks out to the rear verandah, which overlooked a large private pool, where we loved to swim in the warm tropical darkness. It was so beautifully quiet and secluded in that pool late at night and often, as we swam, it was almost as if we had become the only people in our own very sheltered little world.

Once more, those were the good days and, once more, I was in love with a woman, with life and with Africa. It also was kind of ironic how different, and yet how similar, Dawn was from Wendy. Where Wendy was Latin, Dawn was Nordic. Where Wendy was more robust, Dawn was slender, almost fragile. Where Wendy was carefree, Dawn was quite serious. Yet both were completely African and had very little knowledge or interest in our western life.

Neither hungered for conspicuous consumption, and both were supremely content to live out the rest of their lives without ever seeing a genuine traffic jam. They were true children of Africa and did not complain about life's little discomforts. Of course, they also didn't cook, do dishes, clean or sew. But then, why should they? God had provided a house full of servants to handle such mundane matters. Certainly, they were creatures of the good life and I shall always be grateful that I, too, sampled its splendour.

Dawn was, in all truth, one of the nicest women I ever met, and I still remember how, on Saturday afternoons, she would faithfully come to our local soccer stadium to watch me play. I don't think she understood the game, yet she always cheered when I ran on the field and looked proud if I scored. She may, in fact, have been my only fan, since I was never a star, but only a vigorous chaser of an elusive round ball. Still, I had fun and, win or lose, it was always a thrill to look up into our stand and see her blondee head amid the loyal band of enthusiastic but undiscerning spectators who endured our efforts. Indeed, she was often the only bright spot in a succession of dull afternoons, on which my team endured yet seldom prevailed.

Eventually, as was the story of my life, our romance began to cool, as our dates became less frequent, and our meetings more awkward until, finally, without ever actually talking about it, we had our last date. Once again, I don't know why a romance ended. Perhaps I had bad breath, or perhaps all romances ultimately wither and die. That most certainly was the case with all of mine, in my first three years in Africa.

However, in retrospect, I think that in those idealistic days of my youth, I may have been looking for the perfect woman, and was never satisfied with a mere mortal. In addition, I also, in those days, had trouble with the idea of marrying a divorced woman, especially one with a child. No member of my family had ever been through a divorce. I was young, innocent, stupid, or perchance just 25, and always looking for the grass in the field next door.

In any event, whatever my motivation, my time in Lusaka was fast drawing to a close because, shortly after Dawn and I broke up, I left town on my own long leave, and when I returned to Africa, it was now my turn to do penance in the bush. Consequently, if for no other reason, I never did see or, except on one occasion, hear of Dawn again, as she vanished from my life without trace. Regrettably, the one time I did hear a rumour about what she did after Frank, I was saddened by what I was told.

According to a mutual friend, she married her employer about a year after we broke up, and thus became the genuine mistress of his estate and, I assume, financially secure forever. But I still have trouble with the concept of that April and November union, although I hope and pray she was, and is, supremely happy. Of course, whether or not they stayed in Lusaka after independence, I do not know. Nor do I know where they went if they left, although I would assume that they went back to South Africa, since he too was a South African. In any event they, like all of us, were most surely destined to live in interesting times, as our country crumbled and died, in our arms. Nevertheless, for a little while, Dawn and I shared something special, and built memories I will never forget.

6. What More Can I Say?

I have tried, in this chapter, to paint a portrait of the more intimate side of my life in colonial central Africa in the early 1960s. My purpose was not to boast of my conquests, but to introduce some very lovely ladies to my readers. If I have been successful, I may also have shown how similar our boy-meets-girl scenario was to that of the average European or North American couple.

Like them, we were ordinary people living ordinary lives, and doing ordinary things. Our hopes and dreams were quite normal, except that on occasion, the romance of Africa enabled us to paint with a more colourful brush. Probably, in addition, we were influenced by a feeling of impermanence, since all of us knew we were living in the latter days of the British Empire.

Thus, we tended to live more for today than for an uncertain tomorrow. Then again, we had money, cars, houses and servants, which meant that our standard of living was probably closer to the American dream than any to be found stateside. We had no pollution, no unemployment, no debts, no worries, no traffic jams and virtually no crime. Our lives were simple, even rustic, but not without elegance. And somehow it seemed easier to fall in love under a tropical moon, than in the cold, damp drizzle of a Lancashire mill town.

Chapter 9

Days Of Wine And Roses

1. My Rhodesian Ridgeback

No sooner had I strategically relocated to the government rest house in pursuit of Wendy, than the colony's Chief Establishment Officer, Tom Shaw, came to see me in my office. Naturally this was a great honour since the C.E.O. was, as the initials suggest, a very exalted official in our colony. Indeed, he was Number Two to the Governor and lived in the splendour befitting his rank. So obviously I was overjoyed when he announced that, on Mr. Lewis' recommendation, he was prepared to give me his house for the duration of his upcoming long leave, which was due to start in about three months time. That, fortunately, was just about perfect, a gift from the gods, since in three more months I would have either scored or struck out with Wendy.

Accordingly, as mentioned briefly in the preceding chapter, I once again left my *alma mater* for the life of a suburban squire. This time, I got an older four-bedroom house. It stood in its own grounds in a quiet backwater close to where I worked, and equally close, in case of emergency, to the government rest house. The house itself stood well back from the road, with a circular driveway in front and long winding corridors leading from the lounge and dining room to the various bedrooms, which were tucked away in the furthest reaches of this rambling home. It was quite pretty, with white stucco walls, both outside and inside, and a rather quaintly tiled red roof.

Regrettably I did not, on this occasion, inherit any servants, but had to hire my own. Yet I did inherit a large Rhodesian Ridgeback dog, which I had imprudently agreed to baby-sit while the Shaws were in Europe. Luckily, I was immediately joined in this new venture by my old friend Mike Voysey, who relished the opportunity to take up where we had left off when we moved out of Mr. Lewis' home. The other two rooms soon went to two new friends from the government rest house, who had recently arrived in Lusaka from previous postings with the federal government in Salisbury, Southern Rhodesia.

Both of these new housemates soon became close friends, and both, as ushers, would subsequently accompany me to Umtali when

Michael finally tied the knot. One of them, Peter Ferrett, was German by birth and had been adopted as a small child by a British military couple stationed in Germany.

By coincidence Peter was, like Wendy, an internal revenue officer and, to further the coincidence, worked in the same office as Wendy. He was, at the time we met, a tall, gangling, fresh-faced young man with tight, curly hair and a pleasant disposition, which helped make him a most agreeable companion.

My other new roommate, Tom Baxter, was even younger than Peter, being only 22, and had recently arrived in our Federation from Kenya, where he had been born, but had wisely left, as his homeland plunged into the full chaos of the Mau Mau uprising. In appearance, he was a short, slender blonde, and wore his hair in an unfashionable American-style crew cut. However, he had no other peculiarities and was cheerful and friendly. Plus, as an added bonus, he was fluent in Swahili and could easily converse with all of our servants at will. This was a great boon whenever I reached an impasse with our new cook, John.

Sometimes my limited Bemba failed me, and then, once Tom had casually explained my needs, I could but envy his easy familiarity with the natives, since it gave him so much more access into the African scene than I would ever enjoy. Yet on the other hand I did not covet his job since, like Michael, Tom worked at the nearby airport, where he slaved as a dreaded customs inspector, and manfully spent his days searching through suitcases for, I assume, the Holy Grail.

Happily, we were a compatible quartet and harmonized well from the beginning. Michael and I kept the same chores as we had at the Lewis', Peter got housework and Tom, since he was an African by birth, was placed in charge of the jungle which ringed our home. Everything was sweetness and light, except for my new dog, which resolutely refused to let me go to my bed alone.

This unwanted intrusion, and slight inconvenience, was subtly revealed to me on our first evening in the Shaw's house. Apparently, I was not the only one who intended to sleep in that room, because there, neatly spread out on top of the covers, and in the middle of the Shaw's king-size bed, was their king-size dog.

Morosely we regarded each other, both of us somewhat offended by the presence of the other. To me, there was a dog on my bed, while to him, there was an unwanted stranger in the room. Suddenly, with the benefit of hindsight, I began to question the wisdom of my flippant agreement to keep this hound and I began to wonder if perhaps there was room in Michael's bed for one of his dearest friends. Now in general, I must confess to being quite fond of dogs, but in my opinion the Rhodesian Ridgeback seems to be only vaguely related to this species and to possess most of the qualities of a particularly vicious wolf.

By extraction, this breed is native to Rhodesia – hence its name –

and has as its most distinguishing feature a ridge of hair running down the full length of its back, but lying in the opposite direction to the rest of its coat. At first, second, or subsequent glances, this peculiar effect looks quite ominous and, since these dogs are about the size of a Doberman, makes them seem extremely unfriendly. They were, I believe, originally bred to hunt lions, much like the British hunt foxes, and would happily tackle the occasional lion or two.

In short, these dogs were for real and I now had an opportunity to prove man's mastery over the savage beast, if I intended to sleep in my bed during the next few months. Consequently, for openers, I tried a few stern, 'get downs,' which only solicited a low rumbling growl in response. Next I tried pulling and pushing, which was rewarded with more vigorous growls and a fine view of some rear molars. Finally I tried subterfuge, by applying a superior intellect to the problem.

Casually, I switched off the light and, ignoring my companion, quietly slid beneath the covers, upon which he continued to recline. Then, when his even breathing convinced me he had been lulled to sleep, I strategically curled myself into a ball, with my feet in the middle of his back. With one ferocious lunge, I catapulted him from his position on top of my bed.

But this canine cannonball was no shrinking violet and he enthusiastically returned to the fray, while my more fortunate housemates, roused no doubt by the noise, began to gather in my bedroom doorway as the Shaw's dog and I bitterly fought for the high ground in the middle of my bed. Stunned, they observed his frantic efforts to regain his perch, and then, wisely displaying more prudence than I could afford, they quietly left us to enjoy our evening's entertainment, which ended in an armed truce when he reluctantly agreed to sleep at the bottom of my bed.

The following night the contest was resumed but, eventually, through a combination of sweet talk and violence, I persuaded him to sleep on a rug on the floor at the foot of my bed. Now I really felt like Beau Geste, and contentedly left my bedroom window open – to encourage the local fishermen to engage in a meaningful relationship. Yet best of all, I had clearly won this brute's affection and nightly he lay at my feet in our lounge as we sipped our after dinner drinks.

Once, when Peter raised his voice in an overly enthusiastic response to something I proposed, my dog protectively rose to his feet and snarled his disapproval. Peter went white, I quieted my champion and henceforth, everyone spoke in a hushed murmur when they addressed my kingly presence. It was all rather gratifying and I soon came to love that wonderful Rhodesian Ridgeback, which seemed to have adopted me as his master.

Much later, when the Shaws came back, they discovered to their horror that they no longer had a dog, since he now was mine in body and soul, even after I relinquished their house and moved in with the Baymans. Somehow my faithfully unfaithful dog found out where I worked, and began to appear daily, beneath my window at the Ministry of Finance, to plead for our love with mournful howls until I reluctantly went outside to comfort him. Joyously, he would greet my stern rebuke, and then would trustingly comply, as I sadly loaded him into my car for the short ride home to an embarrassed Mrs. Shaw.

At first nothing I did seemed to discourage him, but at long last, after almost two weeks, he got the message and I lost my dog. Nevertheless for several days thereafter, I often looked through my window at work, half hoping to see my friend loping across the lawn to greet his unworthy master. Yet obviously, I couldn't keep him; he had only been mine to caretake and I guess he finally readjusted to the new old occupants of the Shaw's master bedroom.

2. Physical Energy

It would probably be unrealistic to compare the architectural splendours of Lusaka to those of London, Paris or Rome. But we were not without significant landmarks and chief among these was our glorious statue of Physical Energy. This statue, by a famous sculptor, was a duplicate casting of an original work that stands in Hyde Park, in the centre of London. It depicts, in classical style, a semi-nude Grecian warrior astride a dramatically prancing horse, and was presented to the city as a memorial to the achievements of the colony's alleged founder, Cecil Rhodes.

Depending, of course, on one's point of view, as with Columbus, the statue was either a wonderful memorial to an outstanding pioneer, or merely an irritating eyesore. Still, even if one deemed it politically unsound, one had to admit that this vibrant work was spectacular and, to me, it presented an unavoidable challenge.

Naturally, as befits its subject, it was a very large statue, probably twice as big as life size, and stood on its 20-foot plinth in the middle of a large traffic circle which fronted the Ministry of Finance. Behind the statue, on the other side of the road, was the colony's High Court. In front of the statue, but again across the highway, was the recently completed Church of England cathedral. Thus, the island of green grass which boasted this work of art, was surrounded by Finance, Justice and Religion, and could truly be said to stand in one of the most prestigious spots our colony had to offer. Certainly this was the only thing we had that compared, however inadequately, with Trafalgar Square, and it was probably the busiest intersection in the city.

Twice each day I drove slowly past that man on a horse, on my way to and from work and, daily, I admired him thoughtfully from my office window which overlooked his island.

Eventually, I turned for advice to the only other raving idiot whose skills I admired, and Dixie Dean cried with joy as he enthusiastically agreed that my idea was quite crazy and totally unacceptable. Accordingly, we took our plan to Sally, Mike, Eve and Wendy, for this was during her tenure as my keeper, and they sadly agreed to join our venture, in the faint hope of keeping Dixie and me out of the city jail.

Three nights later, at about 1 a.m., the Dirty Six swung into action from our base in Mr. Shaw's innocent home, where I had now been living for about six weeks. To begin with, Dixie and I drove down to the government radio station in his car, less suspicious since he worked there, and 'borrowed' a truck, to which Dixie had thoughtfully 'borrowed' the keys. We then loaned to ourselves an extension ladder, which we quickly stored in the back of the truck and, with Stage One completed, Dixie drove the truck back to my house, while I followed discreetly behind in his car.

So far, so good. Now for Stage Two which required Dixie, Mike and I to go to the local ice cream parlour for their ice cream cone. Furtively, with Michael clutching his tool kit, the three of us climbed into the truck and Dixie drove us to the nearby store. Once there, like a finely drilled SWAT team, we raced with our ladder to the front of the store, which was adorned with a gigantic plastic ice cream cone. We leaned our ladder against the biscuit part of the cone and, while Michael and I steadied the ladder, Dixie scampered up it to detach the ice cream topping, with its requisite red cherry, from its more mundane base.

This was one of the more hazardous parts of our little scheme, since none of us had been able to come up with a convincing explanation for this little tableau if, perchance, the police should cruise by. Brazenly, I had decided if caught, to plead temporary insanity, which was obviously ridiculous, since there was patently nothing temporary about my condition. However, we were in luck and, after a few undisturbed minutes, Dixie unceremoniously dropped the cherry-laden scoop on my head, as he came scrambling down the ladder. Our prize, and our ladder were hurriedly loaded into the back of the truck and we gleefully made our escape from the scene of the crime.

Two down, two to go, and we now began to feel that a life of mealie meal porridge in the city jail could possibly be avoided. Slowly, we drove back to our house for a soothing cup of tea, since that is how the English always steady their nerves, and then, with Dixie driving the truck while the rest of us followed in my car, we headed out to improve the ambience of Physical Energy.

Craftily, we parked both vehicles in the gloom behind the High Court and, when we could see no telltale headlights in the darkness, the three ladies rushed our ice cream across the intervening lawn, to the protective shade of the statue's plinth. Subsequently, when the coast was again clear, we three men speedily bore the extension ladder in their wake, as we charged like demons from Hell across the wide open tundra of the traffic island.

In theory the rest of the project should have been easy, but in practice it proved almost impossible. The plan was simple: We merely had to place the ladder against the plinth, and I would trot up it with the cherried ice cream, which I would then strategically place between the horse's rear legs. No problem – the culmination of a wonderful evening of cultural relaxation – except that I couldn't do it. In the first place, the plinth was taller than I had bargained for, and our fully extended ladder was still two feet short of the base of the statue. But worse, I couldn't hold the three foot long scoop of ice cream in my hands and hold on to the ladder at the same time. I needed two pair of hands and that was the solution we finally latched on to, as teamwork carried the day.

Quite appropriately, the criminally astute brain behind this logically illogical idea, belonged to a woman, in this case Sally. With Wendy keeping watch for approaching vehicles, at which time we all froze into hopefully invisible immobility, Dixie and I dutifully mounted the ladder in romantic tandem. I went first, with my cherry above my head, while Dixie came second, one rung below me, and pinning us both to the ladder in a firm embrace. Gradually, with Michael and Eve steadying the ladder as we reached its higher elevations, we inched our way up to the base of the statue. Frequently we froze as we were warned of the approach of some late night reveler, but fortunately no one apparently saw anything unusual.

Perhaps, although I doubt it, we were not as clearly visible as we felt, which may well explain why no one spotted our strange ensemble or stopped to investigate Dixie and me, as we did our Abbot and Costello routine. But then again, I guess most people don't scan for vandals at 3 a.m., as they beat a bleary-eyed path to their homes and their suspiciously waiting wives, who surely would have rejected such a sighting as absurd.

Or maybe, Heaven be praised, our guardian angel was working the night shift, because, as I previously said, we were not disturbed and at last, with a suitable flourish, I triumphantly placed our scoop of ice cream beneath the horse's front legs, since that was where the cone fit best. Nevertheless, my dollop was still quite close to the exact spot where our prancing horse, could have chosen to relieve himself, and the overall effect conveyed, I hoped, a suitably cultured message.

Contentedly, we eased our way off the ladder and then, when the coast was clear, the six of us sprinted back to the High Court with Michael and Dixie triumphantly waving the ladder, as they led our strategic withdrawal. Three down, one to go. Quietly, we drove both vehicles back to my house where Michael and the ladies remained, while I, in Dixie's car, followed his taillights as he prudently returned our purloined truck to his sleeping workplace.

Nothing stirred as he quickly parked the truck in its allotted space and restored the ladder to its appointed spot. Finally, he climbed into his car and we drove back to our base, with the slightly unhappy feeling that comes when all the excitement is past. Yet I certainly had no wish to repeat the night's adventure, since the score was now a pristine four down and none to play which, with visible proof of our existence adorning our town, was probably more than we deserved.

A little while later, when Dixie and I had safely returned to my home, the enterprise drew to a close as the six of us happily shared a congratulatory pot of tea. I admonished the group on the wisdom of silence and the party broke up. The Deans took their leave and Michael and I drove our young ladies home to their well-deserved beds, before we too retired to our rooms, with the smug belief that the night had been well spent.

The following morning, after a good two hours sleep, I routinely made my way to work with all the innocence of a newborn lamb. It was a beautiful day and consequently, I was not disturbed by the extraordinary congestion that seemed to have occurred at the traffic circle which housed our gracious statue. Oh well, into every life a little rain must fall. Patiently, I eased my way to work, as I philosophically endured my first central African traffic jam which, in all likelihood, I had definitely caused.

For such had been my intention and, when I reached the traffic circle after a brief delay, my patience was most amply rewarded, with a sight that gladdened the cockles of my heart. Because there, praise be to God, was Physical Energy, in all its glory, mightily prancing above its cherry and dollop, as the morning rush hour traffic slowed to a crawl, before this poignant statement of an obscure point of view.

Happily I joined the procession which circled our tribute to Rhodes's vision, and valiantly, I tried to mimic the other jaded commuters as they resolutely refused to believe their eyes. Eventually, in high spirits, I reached the Ministry of Finance and, after parking my car, I quietly joined the bulk of its staff, which appeared to be having a picnic on its front lawn. Their reaction was, understandably, British, since most seemed to think it was a pretty poor show, and another obvious example of the decline in the standards of morality, which had naturally accompanied the advent of talking picture shows. I, quite properly, enthusiastically agreed and, fully aware of the risk involved, took several pictures of my handiwork, with the camera I had imprudently brought to work.

Modestly, I then retired to my office and condescendingly ignored the commotion outside, until the sounds of a siren heralded the approach of Lusaka's premier fire engine. Sadly I watched from my window, as the firemen toted a king-sized extension ladder over to the cause of the commotion and unceremoniously removed my adornment. But not without considerable difficulty, I was quietly pleased to observe.

They had almost as much trouble taking my cherry down, as

Dixie and I had encountered in raising it to its lofty perch. In the end, they just pitched it from its vantage point to the grass below and, as they loaded it into their truck before driving away, my 15 minutes of fame came to its close, with the re-establishment of a housebroken statue.

That evening, when I went home, I just happened to pass by the ice cream parlor, which had, I noted with surprise, already remounted its nouveau art on its cone, and was doing a thriving business from the curious who came to see the source of the outrage. We had, of course, never really doubted that our stage prop would soon be returned to its accustomed spot, since Lusaka was a small town, and our ice cream parlor probably had the only cherry on public display. Thus our fire department would not have been unduly burdened to identify the source of their trophy, which could then be restored to its rightful owners. still, it was nice to have this loose end tied up without delay and without further inconvenience to someone we had no wish to hurt.

Regrettably however, this enlightened attitude to community relations was not shared by the editor of our local newspaper who, in the next day's issue of the Lusaka Times, waxed eloquent on the various ways he would like to punish the vandals who had desecrated the pride of our city. His theme appeared to be that we lacked a sense of humour and were intent on hastening the end of civilized society in central Africa. He also expressed the hope that we would soon be apprehended by the police and brought to justice without further delay. In short, he was not amused and his editorial reflected his displeasure.

We also incurred the wrath of our local African nationalist politicians, who, being politically savvy, felt obliged to issue a statement strenuously denying their involvement in this criminal act. They even suggested, ingeniously, that this despicable deed had probably been done by some Europeans who wanted to stir up trouble between the races by blaming the blacks for the vandalism of the whites. Definitely, it seemed as if we were not popular with anyone and we wisely kept a low profile as we waited for the storm to pass.

Luckily the storm soon passed and our assault on the Empire was quickly forgotten. But not by us, and each morning as I drove to work, I always experienced the same slight thrill, as I passed the scene of our triumph over the sacred virtues of prudence and conformity. Yet perhaps I too was beginning to weaken, since I now decided to come closer to toeing the party line and thus, during the next few weeks, I contented myself with helping Mr. Burgess in his fetish for boot polishing other people's telephones. Nevertheless, it had been fun to visit the edge and I did not regret our taste for the absurd, even though I resolved never again to repeat our one brief foray into the dark side of life.

3. The Braggart

From time to time, we all encounter one of those obnoxious people who seem to know it all, and happily flout the rules with impunity. Often, they boast of their deeds with great bravado and usually, I take their spiel with a large grain of salt. But on one memorable occasion I did not, as I joyfully watched a braggart strut his stuff, before the last audience he would ever have chosen. This happy event occurred one evening, shortly after our dolloping caper, when Peter Ferrett and I dropped into a neighborhood bar for a quiet beer or seven.

Peter, you may remember, was a tax investigator and, as such, was not reputed to possess the milk of human kindness. However, this was probably a false rumour, since I had always found him to be a delightful companion and a barrel of fun, especially after a few drinks. On the night in question, the two of us were sitting at the bar with a few other regular patrons, when a robust middle-aged man with florid features strolled into the room and joined our group.

Immediately the mood changed, as he began to dominate the conversation, which eventually turned to the subject of income taxes and their bite on the working man. Our new leader quaffed his beer with relish and briskly took up this morbid subject with commanding authority. His message was clear – only a fool pays income tax – and he went on to elaborate at length on the artistic way in which he absented himself from the government's flock.

Everyone was enthralled and listened with rapt attention. Most had expressions of envy on their jowls, but Peter's face wore the dreamy, contented smile of a tax agent who has entered the Promised Land. He even went so far as to buy a beer for his newfound friend and, as the evening progressed, these two divergent souls rapidly cemented their friendship. Finally, just before we all decided to call it a night, Peter skillfully closed the trap by soberly exchanging names and telephone numbers with his hapless victim and smoothly promising to stay in touch.

True to his word, Peter honoured his pledge and, bright and early the next morning, with an address garnered from the telephone book, he politely wrote his new friend a nice letter of invitation – to an income tax audit. It was, said Peter, a moving moment in his career, topped only by the expression on the braggart's face when, in response to the summons, he entered Peter's office for the dreaded contest and instantly recognized his inquisitor.

Fortunately, Peter had a sense of humour and although he threw the book at his client, he did not press criminal charges. Still, even though this foolish man managed to avoid jail, his total tab for back taxes, interest and penalties, was probably substantial enough to lower the volume of his rhetoric for at least the next couple of weeks. Yet I doubt if he really, over the long haul, learned the lesson, since that type of person seldom benefits from life's more illuminating moments.

But I did, that's for sure and I never boast in bars about anything, not even about statues I have tried so thoughtfully to improve. Silence, I now firmly believe, is basically golden and can, on occasion, reach diamond proportions as it counters the demons of bureaucratic authority.

For example, this non-verbal approach was probably the only safe way to deal with my other good friend, Tom Baxter, in his official role as a customs inspector in the underworld of undergarments. There, in that erotic land, it was extremely unwise to tempt those who had the means to make you pay their price and Tom, in particular, was certainly not loathe to use his considerable powers of search to inconvenience anyone whose attitude he found offensive.

Thus, his dinner-time stories often contained an account of some self-important clown who had greeted a polite inquiry with an injudicious response and had, in return, been invited to enjoy the pleasures of a strip search. Indeed, I soon came to the ominous conclusion that every prominent citizen of our colony would eventually reveal all to Tom's lecherous eyes and therefore, since I am a prudish man, I began to treat all customs agents as if they were Rhodesian Ridgebacks, ready to attack if provoked.

Consequently, I have never been troubled at a border crossing, even though, on one occasion, I accompanied a young lady who encountered a French Tom. This unhappy event occurred when she responded to the 'anything to declare' question by brightly answering 'yes' as she flippantly revealed three cigarettes in a moldy old carton that had seen better days. Instantly, the French customs officer, an obvious disciple of Tom's, broke into a cheerful grin and politely invited her to step this way for the appropriate strip search.

Horrified, I sat on my suitcase and waited with growing impatience until, about an hour later, she made it through customs with her composure in tatters. If only she had asked, I could have told her to be nice to those who have the authority to make your life miserable. It may not be cute but, as Tom and Peter taught me, it is better to be prudent than naked or poor.

4. The Laws Of Chance

A long time ago, when I was quite young, a famous British politician expressed the view that serious automobile accidents happen, not because someone does something very foolish, but because 50,000 people do something slightly foolish – and one of them is very unlucky. Now perhaps, although it sounds rather dull, this traditional view of the Law of Chance, is the best explanation there is for the occasional extraordinary coincidence we all encounter at least once or twice in our lives.

Yet I still tend, as a romantic, to reject this mundane approach to unusual events, and search for an alternative answer to life's strange turns and twists. In particular, I am reminded of an experience I had in Lusaka. It occurred shortly after Peter's unplanned meeting with his unlucky client but was not, in my opinion, as easily explained by the rules of chance.

It all began at football – soccer – practice one winter afternoon in July of 1961, when a new recruit named Jack turned up to try out for our team. He was about my age, around 25 or 26, and was really quite a good player. After practice, we casually exchanged a few words and I discovered that he hailed from Bulawayo, Southern Rhodesia, although he would, for the next six months, be living in Lusaka, since he had recently taken a job in our town as a site engineer on a large building project.

Accordingly, he had brought his soccer togs and was hoping to make our team. Politely, I wished him luck and promptly forgot about this new acquaintance until the following Friday evening, when the team roster was posted for Sunday's game. To my surprise, I found out that the team now boasted two Bennetts. Both of them were listed as strikers – wide receivers – and to my further surprise, I soon determined that while I, as usual, was one, our new recruit was the other which was, in itself, quite a coincidence.

After the game, which we won, I asked him more about his background. 'Oh, I'm a Rhodesian, born and bred,' he replied. 'Then how about your father, is he a Rhodesian?' I probed. 'Oh, he's English,' he said. 'Where from?' I asked. 'A small village in Lancashire,' he responded. 'Which one?' I queried, in wonder. 'Oh, you'll never have heard of it,' he disparaged. 'Try me,' I suggested and he politely smiled before he softly answered – 'Eccleston.' Stunned, I sat in our dressing room and stared at him until finally I said, 'I hear you, but I don't believe you – because I too am a Bennett from Eccleston, and therefore we must be related!'

Just a few more queries and we had established the fact that we were half cousins, our fathers full cousins, while our grandfathers, naturally, were brothers. Indeed, the coincidences continued to grow since his grandfather, whom he had never met, was well known to me and I called him Uncle John. Truly, what a small world it surely is, even though we tend to think of it as being so large, and how on earth can one calculate the mathematical odds of meeting a totally unknown relative, purely by chance, on a soccer field in the middle of central Africa? Certainly, they must be enormous and right at the outer limits of random coincidence.

But the story is not yet done, for the very next day – the very next day – I received the most amazing letter from my father back in Chorley, some four miles from Eccleston. In this letter, my father mentioned that, although I did not know it, I did perhaps have relatives somewhere in Africa. He then went on to recount, in some detail, a previously secret story about how, long before I was born, a son of his Uncle John's had left home under a cloud and had vanished without trace, except for a persistent rumour which said he had gone to Africa. This cousin, my father went on to say, had been about as old as he was and therefore his children, if any, would probably be about my age. Finally, Dad concluded his letter by admitting that Africa was not a small continent but, who knows, maybe someday I would miraculously meet, in my African travels, another Bennett with roots in Eccleston.

Now in order to fully appreciate the significance of this letter, one must realize that never before, in my two and a half years in Northern Rhodesia, had my father alluded to my having relatives in Africa. So why did he suddenly write me a letter about them and why did it arrive exactly one day after I discovered my African cousin? Surely, I am not really expected to accept these further coincidences, on top of the previous coincidence, as just an extreme example of random chance, like winning the lottery?

I tend to agree with Burt Lancaster who once, as the moderator of a mysteries show, said that while he didn't understand all of the events in his show, he was convinced of the existence of alternative truths in the universe. Perhaps that's the answer – alternative truths – for I definitely believe there are many things we do not, as yet, understand. Probably, when we do, our new awareness will better explain, certainly much better than random chance, the string of coincidences I have just described.

Yet the story is still not quite done. There remains one last coincidence to relate which, surprisingly enough, occurred on the very same day as I wrote this section of my book. For on that day my wife, by coincidence, chose to visit the local Mormon library in Norfolk, Virginia, in order to trace our family's tree back to the Stone Age, which was something she had been meaning to do for years.

In due course, she returned with a copy of the entries she had found under Bennett and there, large as life, was an entry recording the birth of a child to my Uncle John on the 10th of August, 1914. Could it possibly be true, was this, by chance, the birth announcement of the son who went to Africa, or was I looking at the entry of his younger brother? Most probably the latter since my father was born in 1904, but once again, coincidence seemed to be flirting with the outer edge of reality.

During my upcoming long leave in England, I had another coincidental experience which, again, was almost too much to accept as a chance encounter. This time, the law of probability caught up with me in a small seaside hotel, where my parents and I had gone for a few days vacation. My mother, justifiably, was very proud of her globe-trotting son and eagerly told all the other guests about the distant land where I lived and worked. One morning at breakfast, we were joined by an elderly lady who had heard that I had recently come back from Northern Rhodesia, and wanted to know if, by chance, I knew her nephew who also lived in darkest Africa.

The odds, of course, were enormous but I patiently listened to her excited chatter before gently pointing out that Africa was a big place, in which her nephew could easily live without having me as a friend. 'Well, yes I know,' she replied, 'but I thought perhaps you may have met him.' Mother smiled benignly on us both and, with no avenue for escape, I reluctantly asked the old lady to tell me her nephew's name.

'Michael Voysey,' was her answer and once more, I felt the chill of alternative truths as I tried to cope with her impossible answer. At last, hardly able to believe my ears, I slowly said, 'Well actually, I do know him, in fact we lived together for over a year and I was his best man when he got married.' Unfazed, Michael's aunt gleefully said, 'You see, I knew you would know him,' and my mother enthusiastically agreed, that she too had known this apparent truth.

Startled, I regarded these two visitors from outer space with cautious eyes, as I pondered how either of them could feel so confident, about a one-in-one-hundred-million long shot. In fact, the more I thought about it, the more improbable it became, since Michael and I came from opposite ends of England, and had no mutual friends in that country. Thus, this coincidence had needed an aunt of his to travel to Wales at the same time as we did and, obviously, to stay in the same small hotel. Plus, for extra measure, she also had to be crazy enough to ask a foolish question of a complete stranger, who easily became the bigger fool when he confirmed her irrational assumption.

But surely there must come a point at which random chance is not a satisfactory answer for this kind of mystery, and then the thoughtful man will be forced to go further afield as he seeks to understand the unknown. Personally, I lean towards the belief that life is a book, with a pre-determined sequence of events, following an ordained pattern.

Accordingly, much of what we regard as chance is merely the pages of the book being turned as its plot unfolds. Therefore we are not leaves blowing in the wind but rather ships that steer their assigned course. Hence our coincidences become, in many instances, merely the reflection of our destiny. Perhaps not, although for me, life has had too much pattern in its uncertainties and this was especially true in those eventful days when I lived in central Africa.

5. Integration

Regrettably, I must admit that during the whole of my first year in Northern Rhodesia, segregation of the races was almost complete, across a fairly wide spectrum, and rigidly enforced by custom and taboo. Indeed, in the Ministry of Finance, the only black Africans were the tea boys who wheeled their trolleys from office to office, with the nectar of the gods. However, this was soon to change and within the next year, wholesale integration had become the order of the day. Consequently, the whites-only soccer league in which I played was merged with the blacks-only soccer league, some two or three weeks after my cousin joined our ranks.

Fortunately, this enormous social and political change was achieved without turmoil, by the simple expedient of assigning each white team five pre-selected black players from the black league. So now you can see why, on one momentous day, five black athletes turned up at our stadium and were reluctantly issued our hallowed blue and white togs. For a couple of weeks, we all practiced together as they learned our style and then, purely on merit, three of them were promoted to our first team.

The following Sunday, we played our first interracial game and it was a delightful, uplifting experience. Early in the game, I raced down the right wing of the field and, as was my wont, gently lofted the ball into the mouth of our opponent's goal. Usually this was a futile manoeuvre, since we were not a very good team and our opponents normally had no trouble in clearing their goal line. But not today, since fortune clearly favours the integrated, and, in a moment of supreme beauty, a blue and white shirt soared above the mêlée, as its wearer headed home a picture perfect goal.

Stunned, I trotted over to congratulate my new hero, and was met with a big smile as one of our new players laughingly said, 'Good ball, Bwana, well done.' That's funny, I thought, he doesn't look as black today as he did yesterday, indeed, he could almost pass for white. A little later in the game, we two repeated our performance, when I again centred the ball and he obligingly scored.

By now, I was beginning to get the message and I decided that the colour of a player's jersey is much more important than the colour of his skin. I also wholeheartedly endorsed the concept of a multi-racial league, since we appeared to have the best black players in town and, with their enthusiastic participation, we went on to have a most successful season.

Now I readily admit that playing sports together is not a panacea for racial harmony, but it is a good place to start, and it was the first visible evidence in Northern Rhodesia of the fundamental changes which were beginning to occur. It was also a valuable learning experience for me, since in years to come, I would play in many soccer matches in which I was the only white player on the field, and sometimes the only white person in the stadium. Yet I never felt lonely, because I always knew that my jersey established a special bond between me and the other 10 members of my team.

In Africa, the sportsman is king, particularly in South Africa, where rugby and cricket are almost state religions. Indeed, I truly doubt if we in the west realize how deeply the sports boycott of South Africa has hurt their man in the street. To him, living as he does, in an isolated corner of the world, there is nothing on Earth to compare to the joy of watching a touring English, Australian or New Zealand team being thrashed by the Springboks. This is what he lives for, and for 20 years or more, he has been denied the joys of victory over his favourite foes.

Nevertheless, he has not suffered alone, as I realized quite recently in Venice, when I enjoyed a quiet lunch with a New Zealand couple whom my wife and I met in a quiet backwater of that delightful city. Together, we explored many topics as we sat in the late autumn sun until, eventually, we reached the subject of sports, and I politely asked the New Zealanders if their rugby team, the All Blacks, was up to snuff.

Proudly, they answered that, as usual, their team was the best in the world and had beaten all comers. But then the man sighed and turning to his wife, he sadly said, 'Of course, it doesn't really count – being the best in the world – if you haven't beaten the Springboks.' Thoughtfully, I agreed as I realized, once again, how badly we all suffer when sports fall prey to politics.

However, there is now a glimmer of light at the end of the tunnel and, hopefully, the recent winds of change that have swept through South Africa will blow them back into the sports arenas, from which they have been so long excluded. If so, watch out Europe, America and the rest of the world, for these newly liberated Springboks, both black and white, will soar to heights of athletic achievement which only the Rhodesian impala could hope to surpass.

6. A Visitor From England

Perhaps I really expected too much, when I tried and tried, without success, to persuade my parents to visit this remote corner of England's far flung empire, and let me show them the full majesty of God's creation in Africa. It would have been so wonderful. They could have stayed with me in one of my splendid homes for a month or more and it wouldn't have cost them a penny. They could have sunned themselves under a tropical sky and been waited on hand and foot by a bevy of my faithful retainers. The good life was theirs, to be enjoyed as my guests – they never even paused to consider my offer.

Nothing would budge them from Chorley. To be fair, part of the reason they refused my invitations was because my mother's health was not good; but then maybe a trip to Africa would have been the tonic, without gin, that she needed. Certainly, I doubt if it could have hurt and, since Dad was now retired from the railways, they had all the time in the world to see the world. Plus, they were blessed with ample funds and the fares, by air or sea, were well within their means.

Yet, still they were adamant and steadfastly resisted my entreaties to venture so far from home, which was, I believe, the real reason they never came.

To them, after a lifetime in northern England, the idea of a trip to Africa, was not within the bounds of sanity. Their world, as they stubbornly saw it, quite simply did not include elephants and lions, and they harboured a deep resentment against anyone who suggested they put on shorts and go on a brief safari through the African bush. In short, they firmly believed that civilization ended just beyond the spot where the waters of the English Channel reached their knees, and they were determined to carry this prejudice to their graves – which is precisely what they did.

Still, I must also admit that Northern Rhodesia was definitely not a tourist mecca in the early 1960s and, with one notable exception, none of my other English friends had any greater success in enticing their families to test our waters. In general, we were outcasts on the edge of the known world and thus, I still treasure my memories of Mrs. Hawkins, Maurice's mother, who was the lone exception to the rule that only indentured servants and criminals travel. This intrepid lady spurned the advice of her peers and flew out to Lusaka to visit her son while Maurice was still in Lusaka and helping me, together with Peter and Michael, caretake a house.

Luckily she came just in the nick of time, since all of us had mountains of sewing that needed to be done. Since I think it pleased her to feel wanted, she happily spent her evenings repairing our tattered garments. But, lest I give the wrong impression, let me hasten to add that she was not allowed in the kitchen by our cook, and certainly never did a lick of housework, which would have driven our houseboy to distraction.

Fortunately, perhaps eagerly, she rapidly adjusted to a life of leisure, and this delightful lady soon became the fulcrum of our group, as she nightly regaled us with tales of our far-distant homeland. It was a most enjoyable few weeks and we all competed to be her chauffeur, as we tried to show her the wonders of our tropical land.

Soon Mrs. Hawkins and I became really good friends and she even told Maurice he should try to be more like me, which only caused him to grind his teeth in frustration while I, naturally, simpered with contentment. I was also deeply touched when, midway through her visit, she had Maurice take her to an Indian store, where she purchased knitting needles and some wool, and proceeded to knit me a gorgeous sweater as a thank you for letting her stay in my home.

Sadly, I watched from my doorway as Maurice left our house to drive his mother to the airport and wistfully I engaged in a few 'what ifs,' as I thought about the numerous times I had tried to entice my own parents to visit us. But, no one gets all their wishes granted, and at least my elephant had stopped when I really needed to have it apply its brakes. If it hadn't, I would not have been alive to complain today. That was a sobering thought, with a moral to teach, and so I quickly went back into the house, where I put on my sweater before mixing a stiff drink or two.

Chapter 10

The Final Days Of My Tour

1. Kafue National Park

My first tour of duty was almost over. Soon I would be on long leave. But not just yet. I still had time for a few more adventures and I particularly wanted to visit my first *bona fide* game reserve. If possible I did not want to go alone and I persuaded one of my friends, My Bike, to accompany me.

My Bike, obviously, was not his real name, but that was all we ever called him – due to his complete fascination with competitive cycling. He was, by birth, a Londoner, and his age was about the same as mine. His shoulders were broad, his height about 6 feet 3 inches and he had a good athletic figure, a testament to the endless hours he had spent riding his beloved bicycle.

Realistically I suppose that, in general, he was quite good looking but, regrettably, his face was somewhat marred by the absence of his two front teeth and the rather loosely fitting dental adornment which he wore in their stead. At times, this unique bridge would wobble when he spoke and, since he also had a loud husky voice, he was, to say the least, an interesting conversationalist. But he had a heart of gold and was an excellent companion, except for a tendency to dwell at length on the joys of riding his bike which, incidentally, was how he had forsaken his teeth – when two wheels proved too few during a fun-filled road race.

This sterling character was, like me, a servant of the Queen and did his bit in the Ministry of Local Government where he worked in the accounting department. He was also head over heels in love with an English girl who had the distinct disadvantage of being in England. Yet this was not a drawback to My Bike, who wrote her daily for almost three years before he saw the light and married a buxom keypunch operator who worked in the Ministry of Finance and loved his bike.

However, I am getting ahead of my tale. In October of 1961, he was still single, although he was beginning to show signs of weariness with the monastic life of a saddle-sore recluse. Thus, he was quite enthusiastic when I suggested we both take a spot of local leave from the daily grind and make a leisurely one-week tour of Kafue National Park in my four-wheeled automobile. Accordingly we set off bright and early one morning, with high expectations.

Kafue, which was neither well known nor oft visited in my day, is nevertheless one of the largest parks in Africa, being over 250 miles long from north to south and about 50 miles wide from east to west. It lies in the Kafue River basin southwest of Lusaka, and covers an area of approximately 8,500 square miles of the wide open nothingness which is so typical of Africa in general, and Northern Rhodesia in particular.

In late 1961, Kafue was still in its infancy as a game park, having opened its doors for the first time in 1958, and its main camp at Ngoma, in the south of the park, was still quite small. This oasis had, in the spirit of the times, strictly defined berths, with accommodation being provided for 24 Europeans, eight Asians, four Africans and, I suspect, a monkey in a pear tree. There was also, of course, a fully licensed bar at Ngoma, where My Bike and I had splurged by booking one of the European chalets for a week, at the outrageous sum of two pounds – four dollars – per day, inclusive of all meals but, sadly, exclusive of all drinks.

Still, one has to expect some uncivilized attitudes to prevail in the bush, especially in a fair-weather park which is only open to the public during the dry season, and sinks beneath the deluge when the rains begin to revitalize the African scene. Because it is then – from early December until the following July – that the annual rainy season turns most of the park into a lake, and its roads are no longer navigable without a canoe. But in October, when we went, it was the tail end of the dry season, and everything slumbered under a veil of oppressive heat, as life hung on by a thread. The view was bleak, the predominant colour was brown and the bush seemed lifeless.

In all truth, Africa just before the rains is not a pretty sight, and to make matters worse, the tinder dry undergrowth often explodes into flames as the landscape swelters in the sun. Heat and dust are pervasive and everything is dominated by the yearning for relief which only the rains can bring. Although, in our case, the fully licensed bar at the Ngoma game viewing camp would serve as a temporary salve.

Yet it was still a good time to see game, especially at dawn or dusk, and My Bike and I had decided we wanted a vacation, so we ignored the heat and thoroughly enjoyed our trip. The first day, we drove almost 400 miles from Lusaka to Ngoma, over almost non-existent dirt trails, and thankfully arrived at our destination without mishap. Tired but exhilarated, we quickly showered before happily savouring a few drinks and a wonderful four-course dinner in a lovely little dining room, fitfully lit by a couple of swinging kerosene lamps.

Ngoma was virtually deserted and, once again, I was blessed with the wisdom to appreciate how fortunate I was to be able to see the wilderness of Africa before it was either destroyed or overrun by tourists. Briefly, oh so briefly, I was privy to paradise before it vanished, or was tamed into a shopping mall. What I saw was irreplaceable and, I fear, like the vast herds of American buffalo, probably no longer exists. But, for a fleeting moment it was mine, and my eye will always carry its images, safe and secure.

One of these brief special moments occurred at breakfast on our first morning at Ngoma, when I watched a fish eagle fishing in the large lagoon which fronted the camp. This lagoon was one of the few permanent bodies of water in the park and, as such, was a centre of activity. Never before had I actually seen one of these birds, although the fish eagle was the national bird of Northern Rhodesia and was shown on our coat of arms in full flight, with a large fish in its claws.

That morning, as I ate my eggs and bacon, I watched one effortlessly soaring above our camp. Suddenly, without warning, it swooped down on the lagoon and, after dancing for a moment on top of the water, it skillfully snared a large fish in its claws before rising back into the sky with its prey. Just a moment, a fleeting moment of time, but another memory to be treasured in the cold winter of encroaching old age.

The rest of the day, we drove up and down the park's deserted roads, searching a near-deserted landscape for a view of its game. Occasionally, we saw a few buck, a zebra or two, and other lonely inhabitants of the sweltering veldt. But mostly we saw dust and flies because, apparently, many of the animals, unlike mad dogs and Englishmen, chose not to promenade in the midday sun. Luckily, and best of all, we never saw an elephant. Kafue National Park was famous for its lack of elephants which, to me, made it one of the world's most desirable parks to visit.

Next morning, we again went out for a tour of the local farmyard and, this time, we were rewarded with another magical moment. For suddenly, as we drove slowly down a trail, I spotted a large head peering down at me from above and behind a 12-foot high clump of bushes to my left. Startled, I ground to a halt, and then realized that I had just spotted my first giraffe. Slowly I eased the car down the trail, until the giraffe and its three or four companions came into full view. Silently My Bike and I sat and watched this small family group, as they delicately nibbled the topmost branches of some nearby small trees.

How lucky we were, I mused, as I soaked in Africa's diversity. At the same time, I truly began to appreciate how large, how tall a giraffe really is. Happily I gawked, perhaps subconsciously realizing that this was the only time I ever would see giraffe roaming free in the wild and, after they slowly ambled off out of our view, we returned to Ngoma for another four-course dinner in the wilderness. Once more, I had a mental snapshot to treasure, and a marvelous reward for the long hours we had spent scouring a virtually deserted landscape.

Or, so we thought. I am sure many pairs of eyes lazily watched from the sheltering bush as two neophyte voyeurs passed by, seen but unseeing.

Eventually our patience was rewarded when, late one morning several days later, we rounded a bend in the trail we were following and stumbled across our first ostrich, ambling along the same path with a hearty disregard for the rules of the road. At first, he treated us with disdain but, after a gentle toot from my horn, this giant bird took off across the bush at a reasonably good pace and once again, I was left to marvel at the vast diversity of African wildlife.

This is a creature which seems to have taken its own path down the evolutionary trail. Its body is too large for a bird, while its legs are too spindly for an animal. The combination is too striking to forget. In addition, since it can't fly, it doesn't seem fair to call it a bird but, since it has wings, you can't call it an animal. Perhaps it is neither, or both, which, come to think of it, may well be the best way to describe the strange creature we watched that day, as it strutted its way through the bush and into my memory bank of unforgettable sights.

Nevertheless, for me, the highlight of our vacation took place on the final day of our visit to Kafue National Park, just as the sun began to give way to the approach of night. Already the light was beginning to fade, as dusk began to dominate the African bush, and My Bike and I were slowly returning to Ngoma from our last review of the reserve. From force of habit, I continued to scan the veldt on either side of the road and suddenly I saw a dark shadow under some trees, at the far edge of a large meadow we were about to cross.

Once more, for the umpteenth time, I eased to a halt, grabbed my binoculars and focused on the dimly lit tree line about a hundred yards to my right. My intuition had been right, and I soon found a large cape buffalo standing at the edge of the meadow, just a few feet beyond the protecting trees. It was no big deal, I had seen many buffaloes before and I casually said to My Bike, 'It's only a buffalo,' as I idly panned the bush on each side of the one I had seen.

But then I froze, as my glasses revealed scores of other buffaloes, all standing just beyond the meadow at the fringe of the trees. As far as I scanned, from left to right, my glasses revealed a row of giant heads, with their enormous horns and tra   nquil cow-like expressions. It was not one buffalo I was seeing, but a whole herd of buffalo, probably at least 500 strong.

Quickly I gave the glasses to My Bike, so that he too could see this last remnant of Africa's once prolific wildlife and then, before the last light faded, I retrieved my binoculars for a final look at nature as once it had been. Too soon, it was dark and the show was over but, for a few magical moments, I had seen the largest concentration of game I had ever been privileged to see. Never again would I see so many animals at one time, and the memory of that dusk-shrouded herd will always burn bright in the African scrapbook of my mind.

It was the perfect way to end our odyssey and, since it was already pitch black, I reluctantly switched on my car's headlights. They somehow seemed to desecrate the surrounding darkness as I cautiously drove back to the safety and comfort of the Ngoma game camp. A final dinner, a final night of African mystery and then, early next morning, we left civilization and, without misadventure, rattled our way back over several hundred miles of rural torture to the comparative elegance of big city asphalt. As always, it was good to be home, but it had also been a privilege to visit one of Africa's finest game reserves before the tourists came in their droves, or the animals were swept away by the winds of change and progress.

2. The Perils Of Being A Best Man

Less than two weeks after I returned from Kafue, I was back on the road again. This time I was bound for Umtali, Eve's home town. The Big Day was almost upon us and next Saturday at noon my two dear friends, Michael and Eve, would tie the knot. I was to be the best man and Peter and Tom were to be groomsmen. All three of us had solemnly promised to behave, and not to pull any practical jokes. We also understood the importance of being in Umtali for the scheduled Friday rehearsal, and I had assured Eve we would not be late.

Bright and early on Thursday morning, the entire complement of the groom's wedding party climbed into my car, and we left Lusaka on the two-day drive to Umtali. The journey was uneventful for the first 300 miles, but then, just as darkness began to fall and we were within 25 miles of our overnight stop, I started to lose control of my car.

At first, as I veered slowly to the right, I assumed that I was getting tired and had suffered a lapse of concentration. Feeling a little foolish at my lack of attention, I quickly corrected the problem by turning the wheel sharply to the left. Nothing happened. I steered left and the car went right.

I don't know who was driving that car, but it sure wasn't me. But once again my luck held, for there was no oncoming traffic and no roadside ditch or embankment to impede my car as it serenely left the highway, at about 65 miles per hour, to follow its own drummer. With no further role to play in the selection of our route, I grimly hung on, as my independent-minded vehicle commenced a cross-country excursion through the African bush, despite my strenuous efforts to discourage it.

Thankfully, the brakes still obeyed me and after about 100 yards, we ground to a halt. My two friends wanted to know if I was sure that this shortcut was worth taking. I said that it wasn't. They reasonably inquired as to why we were parked in the bush. I said that the car did it, I didn't. They looked at me kind of strangely and then politely looked away.

After recovering our composure, we climbed out of the car, to try to find out what on earth was going on. To my amazement, I saw that the right-hand front wheel was turned as far to the right as it would go. I then discovered that when I turned the steering wheel, the left-hand front wheel obeyed me, but the right front was not intimidated and continued to point to the right, no matter how far I turned the wheel to the left.

The problem was obvious, once I crawled under the front of the car and examined the steering by the light of the flashlight I always carried. The right-front tie rod end had broken in two, and the right front wheel was now a separate entity and quite independent of the steering mechanism. The good news was that the car was quite drivable, except for the fact that we couldn't control one front wheel. We could, however, control the wheel by walking beside it and kicking it back into line whenever it started to stray, which is precisely what we did.

It took us about 30 minutes to back up and regain the highway, and then we formulated our battle plan. Peter and I would stay with my car, and we would try to drive and kick our way across the 25 miles, that still separated us from the next small town. Tom would hitch a ride with the next car that came along going towards Umtali, and try to make his way to our hoped-for destination, where he would book us into the local hostelry and explain the situation to the innkeeper.

Before Tom left, he was implored to please arrange for a dozen beers and a mountain of sandwiches to be sent to our rooms, for I had no idea when we could hope to arrive at the hotel. 'Please try to give us something to look forward to,' I pleaded. 'This may be a very long night.' Shortly thereafter a local car came down the road, heading in the right direction, and kindly gave Tom a ride into the Promised Land.

Lucky him, I gloomily reflected, as I watched the taillights disappear towards a shower and comfort. Sadly I realized that if only we had used his car instead of mine, that could have been me, hightailing it towards the bright lights of central Africa. I briefly indulged in a lovely wallow in the trough of self pity, soon realizing that a more positive attitude was needed, and so began one of the most unusual journeys of my life.

At first, I drove very slowly, while Peter walked at the side of the car. Whenever we started to veer from the straight and narrow path, so to speak, I would jam on the brakes and Peter would rectify the problem, by kicking on the wheel, until he had it pointing in the right direction again. It worked quite well all you needed was the patience of Job. Sometimes we could go for up to a hundred yards, without having to give the car a good kicking.

As the evening progressed, we grew more daring. Between kicks, Peter would now sit on the hood of the car, so he wouldn't need to walk and I could drive a little faster. Of course, with him sitting on the hood, I couldn't see where I was going, but in view of the other problems, we discarded this one as a minor inconvenience, and strange as it may seem, we made it to our destination without a hitch.

Indeed, towards the end of our journey, we became quite polished. My outrider now hopped off and on the hood with gay abandon, not even waiting for the car to come to a complete halt. With one judiciously aimed kick, he would straighten out our recalcitrant wheel.

As the miles slowly ticked away, I began to relax, once I became sure we were going to make it to town, and found time to wonder what the other traffic on the highway could possibly think when they passed our slowly moving vehicle with its frenetic crew. I even had time to ponder our chances of qualifying for an entry in the Guinness Book of World Records, possibly as a new category, created in honour of the most miles driven without a functioning steering wheel. I still regret that I never took the time to write them and find out whether or not we merited inclusion in their book.

Finally, just before midnight, after a five-hour journey, we kicked our way into the hotel parking lot and came to a halt beneath the veranda on which the faithful Tom anxiously awaited our arrival with the beer and sandwiches. We thankfully joined him in the cool darkness of that quiet porch, and had a leisurely supper before retiring to our rooms, too exhausted to think about the next step in our attempt to reach Umtali. But as I gratefully crawled into bed, I couldn't escape the thought that Michael's wedding would take place, with or without us, in the early afternoon of the day after tomorrow.

In central Africa, self reliance is the order of the day. If you get into a problem, then you get out of it, no buts, no ifs, no maybes. You can't call for a tow truck, because there are no roadside telephones and no tow trucks. Third World countries do not have all modern conveniences and this is particularly apparent in the almost total absence of any kind of emergency service.

Our breakdown that evening was our problem and we solved it our way. In reaching the decision to carry on immediately, we also, recognized the fact that, if we were going to make it to Umtali in time for the wedding, we had to continue to the next town that same evening. It was vital to locate a helpful garage by first light of the following day, so that we could immediately begin to repair my car and, hopefully, get back on the road before noon.

Next morning, after only a few hours sleep, we were all up at the break of day, in the fervent hope that this tiny town had a Ford dealership and an extensive selection of spare parts to fit my car. Frankly, my hopes were not high, when I saw how small the town really was, but our guardian angel continued to work overtime and the only garage in town happened to be a Ford dealership with a very extensive inventory of spare parts.

By 9 a.m., I had disappeared beneath my car and spent the next three hours replacing both tie rod ends, and most of the other moving parts of the steering system. I reasoned that if one tie rod end could get tired and break in two, then why not the other? Being loath to repeat yesterday's joy ride, I neurotically rebuilt the steering components for both front wheels.

As I worked, I wondered what would have happened if a car had been coming in the opposite direction when I unaccountably swerved across the road. If I had been killed in a head-on collision and my car had been badly damaged, would the police have assumed that I had fallen asleep at the wheel? If I was dead and my car was all torn up, then how could anyone possible realize that my steering had failed?

It was a sobering thought and since that day, I have never been able to read about an inexplicable head-on collision, in which one of the vehicles suddenly swerved into the path of the other, without harbouring a nagging doubt as to what may really have happened. As they say in the wrestling arena, 'It makes you think.'

In all fairness, I must point out that badly corrugated dirt roads will surely shake your car to pieces, and what happened to me on such a road is hopefully extremely rare on the more placid highways of the developed world.

Eventually, shortly after noon, I finished my repairs and, after a hasty shower, we set off once more for Umtali and our friend's wedding. It was a piece of cake, a beautiful drive through charming rolling hills at a sedate speed which brought us to the bride's house some four hours later, a full 15 minutes before the wedding rehearsal was due to start.

All's well that ends well, which would have been nice but, alas, was not to be. The rehearsal and its dinner were a huge success, and the wedding the following afternoon was as perfect as all weddings are supposed to be. Our run of good fortune continued well into the reception and for several hours after the bride and groom departed on their honeymoon. It lasted until about 11 p.m. when the not-so-happy newlyweds returned to the reception hall and rejoined their few remaining guests, in the waning moments of what had been, until they arrived, a thoroughly enjoyable wedding celebration. Michael was obviously unhappy and opened the proceedings by apologizing to me for doubting his wife earlier, when she had pointed out some obvious flaws in my character. He then expressed the hope that I could spare a few moments to step outside, so that he could kill me as painfully as possible.

But why blame me if his marriage was already on the rocks? So, while trying to keep a healthy distance between us, I politely asked why he had decided to forgo a honeymoon. 'Because I have no money,' he softly replied. I quietly allowed as to how that could be a stumbling block and prudishly reminded him that a bulging wallet is often a necessity for a successful honeymoon.

At the word bulging, a cold hard look settled across his face and he stiffly held out his right hand. At the same moment, an icy chill of understanding swept through my mind and meekly reaching into the inside pocket of my jacket I extracted his wallet and gently laid it in his outstretched hand. He left without saying goodbye. I didn't feel that it would be appropriate to say, 'Have a nice day,' so I also held my peace. Sad to say, I've never been really sure that he ever got around to believing that it was all just a big silly mistake. Indeed, if I was him, I would also have my doubts.

I had snookered Michael, quite by accident, without the slightest intention of causing him harm. It had all begun at about 7 p.m., when Eve and Michael were about to leave on their honeymoon. The happy couple had paused for one last photograph, outside the getaway car, to complete the wedding album. Always a fastidious dresser, I interrupted the proceedings by pointing out that his jacket didn't seem to fit right, due to the big bulge on the left hand side. 'It's my wallet. It's full of money,' he proudly boasted. 'Give it to me while they take the photo,' Judas said, and like a lamb led to the slaughter, he handed me his wallet, smiled sweetly for the photographer, climbed gaily into his car and departed in the usual cloud of dust. With a heart as pure as the driven snow and thoughts to match, I absentmindedly pocketed his wallet and happily rejoined the revelers.

That's the gist of my story and I'm sticking to it. Innocence or guilt is not for me to decide. Perhaps as so often happens, it mostly depends on whose ox is being gored. Back in Lusaka, when tempers had cooled, I asked Michael how far he had got before he missed his wallet. 'About 100 miles,' he said. 'What made you realize I still had it?' I queried. 'I stopped to buy petrol and was forced to begin my marriage by borrowing five pounds from my wife,' he sadly replied. 'What did you do next?' I probed. 'I cried,' he responded with dignity, 'and then I came all the way back to Umtali.'

I laid my hand on his shoulder, as a good friend would and silently gave him my sympathy. I also made a fervent vow to refuse if anyone ever again should ask me to be their best man.

One small window into a troubled future was briefly opened for me on the day following the wedding, when I went swimming in Umtali with the bridesmaid I had been privileged to escort to the previous evening's reception. We went to a beautiful, Olympic-sized open-air swimming pool, which had just been completed in downtown Umtali. It was a public pool and, to my surprise was almost deserted. We enjoyed ourselves immensely, but even though we spent the whole afternoon lazing in the sun and playing in the water, we still didn't see more than a handful of other swimmers.

As we drove away from the pool, I asked my companion why no

one seemed to be using it. 'It's the new law,' she told me. 'What law?' I asked. 'The one that says all swimming pools must be open to all races,' she explained. Now I understood: the whites would not swim with the blacks and the blacks couldn't afford the price of admission. So, the pool sat empty and everyone lost.

The next morning, our mission completed, three somewhat tarnished members of the wedding party returned without incident to their homes in Northern Rhodesia. However, as we drove across the veldt, I kept seeing that deserted swimming pool in my mind's eye, and I had a premonition that my country and my way of life could not last for many more years. It was sad and it made me want to cry.

3. Endemic Happiness

There were, in the British Colonial Service, two endemic diseases from which no officer was immune. The first of these was bush happiness. It afflicted young, single, male officers stationed in the bush for long, lonely periods. The second – leave happiness – was reserved for those whose long leave was imminent. Luckily, I had never been exposed to bush happiness, but soon after I returned from Umtali, I fell prey to the symptoms of the other dread disease.

Now, although I never had bush happiness, I was quite familiar with its symptoms, since I had heard many horror stories concerning those who had suffered its trials. On occasion, I had even witnessed its effects on close friends. Certainly it was one of our most dreaded scourges, and usually began to afflict its bachelor victims about one or two years after they had been posted to a lonely boma on the edge of nowhere. At first, when the disease was in its infancy, a sufferer merely began to drink more, and bathe less.

But then, as the malady intensified, our hero would develop, even for an Englishman, an extremely eccentric approach to life. He would cease to change his clothes which he now normally slept in – since he could no longer conceive of any practical reason for undressing before he went to bed. Finally, when the disease reached its zenith, the average sufferer would begin to head for the nearest African village at progressively more frequent intervals. To him, the black ladies had grown progressively whiter, and it now became crucial to remove him from the bush, before he went irretrievably native.

At this point the government always acted with commendable zeal and the diseased officer was returned to Lusaka, while another poor soul was sent out to the bush to suffer for the Queen, as the service rotated its youth through purgatory. Yet permanent scars were rare and usually an officer could be cured by spending a long weekend at Lusaka's open-air swimming pool but, on occasion, the damage to an officer's career could last much longer – if his previous conduct had been completely reprehensible.

Fortunately, leave happiness was not as socially unacceptable as its more destructive cousin. However, it was much more virulent and attacked all officers with less than 60 days left in a tour of duty. Normally, its onset began when one constructed an elaborate calendar in one's office, to precisely measure the exact number of days, hours and minutes which must pass before the blessed event became a reality.

Religiously, from that point forward, the stricken officer would update this oracle, so that he would instantly know the number of breaths remaining before departure day. Indeed, to most officers, this hallowed day often assumed a significance only slightly inferior to the day they were born, which, come to think of it, was how I also regarded my upcoming liberation.

For all of us, but especially for those officers stationed in the bush, long leave was a kind of rebirth and re-introduction to the miracles of modern civilization, including its greatest allure – TV.

Imagine, if you can, the impact of freedom upon the future of someone soon to be released from solitary confinement in a remote boma and ushered into Aladdin's cave. What treasure was theirs – especially since, for openers, they now had two Love Boat cruises at government expense to look forward to. They also had more than half a year of highly paid vacation in the western world. It was a kind of deluxe parole, and rural officers savoured its coming like rabid dogs as they began to glimpse the light at the end of their tunnel of isolation.

Thankfully, those last 60 days never passed slowly, since victims of leave happiness slipped gradually into a world in which time had no value. The end was discernible on their calendar and the interim was a temporary inconvenience. Accordingly, with each passing day, the smile on a sufferer's face would broaden in width and deepen in intensity. Soon he began to resemble a Cheshire cat, or an aspiring toothpaste promoter.

Nothing was too much for these officers to bear. All bad news was greeted with unrestrained joy, and any overtime they put in at work was considered to be a privilege they were eager to accept. For D-Day – departure day – was coming and, like the invasion troops in World War II, a leave-happy officer was unconcerned by life's little vagaries.

Indeed, during the last 10 or 15 days of a tour, it became impossible to engage these officers in any conversation that did not concern their upcoming leave. Women and booze were now of secondary importance; long leave was about to become a reality. They were about to be reborn. Luckily, by this stage of the disease, the stricken officer would have been replaced by a morose returnee from the real world, and would therefore have no duties to perform. Thus, he was free to enter the final stages of the malady whereby he would ceremoniously wish everyone a Merry Christmas in July, and float off into the outer space of the white man's world.

This then, was the world I began to move into in late October of 1961 when the first symptoms of leave happiness began to colour my life. Hence, when the Shaws returned from long leave, I enthusiastically gave them back their house, but not their dog and, together with Peter Ferrett, moved out of town to the Baymans' farm, for the last two months of my tour. Tom Baxter, our customs inspector, returned reluctantly to the government rest house. Mike Voysey, of course, had already left, since he and Eve had moved into a nice two-bedroom government house in the suburbs the day after they returned from their honeymoon.

It was over. A stage in my life was fast drawing to a close, and soon I would part company forever from many dear friends. My caretaker days were done, my country was getting ready to disappear. My world was beginning to end, but I didn't care about that kind of triviality, for I was leave happy, and I had more important things to consider.

4. A Close Encounter Of The Bovine Kind

Despite the thousands of miles I drove over dirt and the many narrow escapes I had, I never once was involved in a serious accident during my years in Africa. It must have been my guardian angel hard at work, because some of the stunts I got up to can hardly be excused by the exuberance of youth.

My luckiest escape, and the one that finally calmed me down, happened about two weeks after Peter and I went to live with the Baymans. Ken and Peter had decided to economize by car-pooling to work but I preferred the freedom of being alone in my own car. This meant that every morning at around 7:15, two cars would leave the farm and head off down the same dirt road. One car took my two friends to town and the other took me to Finance, and this was the crux of our problem.

Whoever left home first would have a very pleasant and most relaxing ride to work. But Tail-End Charlie would eat dirt all the way to town and arrive at the office looking like a great white hunter after a bad day with the elephants.

Each morning was a mad scramble to shower, dress, eat and leave before the other car could beat you to the highway. It was a constant re-enactment of 'Gentlemen, start your engines' as we battled for the laurel wreath of presentability. One fateful morning, we left the house neck and neck but, unfortunately, my friends got their car started first and reached the road to town about two car lengths ahead of me. This morning I was not prepared to accept their victory and a wild chase ensued for the next several miles as I fought desperately to overtake them. Finally, they inexplicably slowed down and, seizing the opportunity, I was able to accelerate past them in a wonderful moment of victory.

Triumphantly ahead of my friends, I burst through the dust cloud that had obscured my vision and was treated to one of those charming pastoral scenes that makes Africa such a picturesque place to live. Of course, the charm of this particular scene was largely wasted on me as I hurtled towards a large herd of native cattle which were ambling nonchalantly down the middle of the highway. It also seemed to me that something was amiss with the native herdsmen, since they were diving unceremoniously for cover. Only the cattle seemed unconcerned as they continued to amble happily down the centre of the road.

I still don't know what happened. One moment I was racing towards disaster; the next I was cruising down a deserted rural road with plenty of time in hand before I was due at the office. It was quite impossible but, in some miraculous manner, I had passed through that herd like a dose of salts and never bruised a single hoof. I quickly checked the rear view mirror, and from the little I could see through my trailing dust storm, it looked as if the herd was still blocking the highway. But neither the herdsmen nor my friend's car were anywhere to be seen. It was such a nice day to be alive, I reflected, as I continued sedately down the highway, vowing to learn my lesson and hoping to live long enough at least to get married.

About an hour after I got to work, the telephone rang and Peter Ferrett anxiously queried if I was all right. 'Of course, why do you ask?' I innocently replied. 'Because of the damn cows, I was sure you were dead,' he shouted down the phone. 'What cows?' I deadpanned back. He said something unprintable and hung up the phone.

That night at dinner, I had the story from their perspective. Apparently, they saw the cows in plenty of time to slow down and were horrified when I hurtled past them. Unable to prevent a tragedy, they pulled over to the side of the road and waited for the sounds of my collision with the herd. None came. Puzzled, they stayed where they were until the dust settled and then slowly drove up to inspect the carnage. There was none. The native cattle still blocked the road and none seemed the worse for wear.

The only fly in the ointment was the absence of the native herdsmen who, to my friends' surprise, seemed to have vanished without a trace. Somewhat relieved that I wasn't lying mangled in the middle of a decimated herd of cattle, Ken and Peter now assumed that I had swerved off the road to avoid a collision and plowed into the adjacent bush. They therefore spent an anxious 15 minutes searching the bush on both sides of the road, before they gave up in bewilderment and drove slowly to work.

I was deeply touched by my friends' obvious concern and could only smile the following morning, as each of us politely offered to let the other leave first. As I recall, they left first, and I had a leisurely second cup of coffee, while waiting for the dust to settle before carefully wending my way to town.

5. Signs Of The Changing Times

Shortly before my first tour of duty in Northern Rhodesia ended, another equally significant event occurred. The Evelyn Hone College of Further Education was dedicated and opened with all the appropriate pomp and circumstance.

It was the first college ever built in Northern Rhodesia. Prior to its opening, anyone seeking an education beyond high school had to go to Southern Rhodesia, South Africa or England, to name the three most popular educational destinations for our elite students. But with the approach of independence, local avenues for advanced education were sorely needed and, next to the post office in downtown Lusaka, the colonial administration built the Evelyn Hone College of Further Education. Evelyn Hone had, until recently, been our Governor and so, even as independence approached, we stuck to our guns and named the college after one of our own.

Together with many of my friends, I attended this grand event at which our army band played, our troops marched, and a long column of be-gowned dignitaries solemnly marched into the building, after our new Governor made a speech and declared the college open.

It was long overdue, but better late than never and some two years later I became one of its students. At that time, purely for interest sake, I enrolled in the college and took two A level General Certificate of Education courses: one in Economic History and one in Economic Geography. I passed both, not with distinction I'm afraid but with an enhanced confusion as to why some nations are rich and others remain poor.

Opening Day ceremonies for the Evelyn Hone College of Further Education in Lusaka in 1961.

6. Punched Out

Traditionally, in all societies, there are important social conventions that must be adhered to, such as weddings and christenings. In our society, the going-away party was a premier event, and one to which I now gave my full attention.

To begin with, I needed to select a site for my extravaganza, and although the Baymans were kind enough to offer me the use of their farm, I declined, because their home was so far from town. Instead, since my sins had been forgiven, I opted for Mike Voysey's new digs which were much more convenient for my guests. Everything was under control, and I scheduled my party for a Saturday evening in the middle of December, some three weeks before I was due to go on leave.

At first, my plans were simple (would that they had stayed that way) and I intended to serve beer and mixed drinks, in the time-honoured tradition of rational hosts. However, if that were so, my party would have no flair, so I determined to be different – and boy, did I succeed. I opted, in a moment of permanent insanity, to mix my own punch and serve it to my guests in lieu of the more boring traditional fare. I had never before mixed anything more complicated than a gin and tonic, yet I had no qualms, since I was immortal, leave happy and assured of the Almighty's infinite protection.

Ominously, my proposal was enthusiastically endorsed by the Voyseys, which should have been warning enough, and on the fateful afternoon we gathered in their kitchen to duplicate the performance of Macbeth's witches. We had at our disposal a very large enamel bucket, and we began the brew by pouring into it a large flagon of cheap Portuguese wine. This was to be our base, we confidently confided in each other. Next, we added a bottle of rum, a bottle of whiskey, a bottle of brandy, a bottle of vodka and two frog's legs. Finally, with a flourish, we dumped in a six pack of Fanta Orange, and our cocktail was complete.

It was a disaster. It tasted like a cheap brand of over-leaded gasoline. Tears came to my eyes as I inhaled the fumes from this vicious brew. No one, not even my friends, could stomach this concoction. But alas, there was more than 25 pounds of my money in that bucket and I had insufficient funds to go out and buy more booze. Desperate for a solution, I had a stroke of genius, or perhaps Neanderthal logic, when I remembered how my mother solved all her cooking failures. 'Add more sugar,' was her usual remedy and, like a faithful servant, I took my mother's advice. Four pounds of the best white sugar was immediately dumped into our bucket and for an hour, we all took turns stirring with ferocious zeal. At last, all the sugar had dissolved and I tasted the result.

How sweet it was. Victory had been snatched from the jaws of defeat. I had pulled off the culinary recovery of the century and had produced a slightly stronger version of strawberry Kool-Aid. My punch was a masterpiece. It was innocence personified and gave no indication of having any alcoholic content. Triumphantly, we filled two large punch bowls from our bucket and placed them on a large table at the end of the lounge. We then cut up several oranges, bananas, peaches and grapefruit and elegantly added them to the punch for scenic effect. Lastly, we placed two vases of flowers and 40 to 50 punch cups on the table, and we were ready for the party to begin.

Promptly, at 7:30 that evening, the first guests arrived and I proudly waved them to our charmingly displayed beverage, where Eve sweetly gave them a glass of our original home brew. One by one, the rest of my friends arrived and were, colloquially speaking, ceremoniously punched. Few, I subsequently realized, ever came back for a second glass and most of my guests seemed content to sit on their chairs, with a faraway glaze in their eyes.

In fact, it soon became obvious, even to my jaundiced eye, that my party was a total failure. It was, regrettably, the dullest party I ever saw. No one had a good time and, in all honesty, virtually no one was sober enough to have any kind of time, or even to stay awake. Most just slumbered happily in their seats, an empty punch cup dangling from their nerveless fingers while Mike, Eve and I innocently dispensed the culprit. To make matters worse, none of the three of us had found time to have a drink ourselves, since we were too busy welcoming guests and thus, by 9 p.m., we were the only sober people at my party.

Of course initially we did not know this. We demurely soldiered on, completely unaware of our punch's knockout punch until, shortly after 9, Janet Higgins lurched to my side and, with a loud belch, demanded in a slurred voice to know what the hell was in the punch. Shocked, I gazed in wonder at my good friend, whom I had never before seen under the weather and gently reproved her for bathing in our punch bowl. 'Bathing, be damned,' she muttered. 'I've only had two glasses.' This was indeed serious news, for if Janet couldn't hold our liquor, then no one could.

Sadly, I surveyed the room where most of my friends rested in peace and then I tried to talk to Sonja Henning, who resisted my advances and slumbered on. Even the Baymans seemed to have settled in for the long haul and Ken was melodiously humming a few bars, as he happily enjoyed the benefits of calling it a day so early in the evening. Clearly, or murkily, we had produced a Molotov cocktail, the perfect Mickey Finn, and my long anticipated party had speedily turned into a late night gathering at a geriatric convention.

Belatedly I realized I should have served beer and mixed drinks and then at least some of my guests would have been marginally functional until at least 10 p.m. But, hindsight is always twenty-twenty and morosely I asked Eve to make plenty of black coffee. Gradually, we helped our friends sober up and sheepishly they wished me *bon voyage*, before staggering off into the night with scant recollections of what had hit them.

In due course, everyone had gone home except for one friend, notorious for his freeloading ways at the parties he attended. He had clearly overindulged, having had at least three glasses, and refused to stay awake. Alarmed, we bundled him into the Voysey's car and Mike rushed him to the government hospital, where he was immediately admitted with acute alcohol poisoning.

Luckily, he was young and healthy and after they had pumped his stomach, he was taken off the danger list, although he remained in the hospital for several days before he was released. Subsequently, or so I was told, he enthusiastically took the pledge and became the guiding light of our local chapter of Alcoholics Anonymous.

Yet this silver lining to our 'X'-rated punch was understandably not in our thoughts as Eve and I sat on her stoop, with a glass of milk each, and solemnly reviewed the past as we anxiously waited for Mike to return from the hospital. Our time together had been fun, and if we could, we would do it all over again, which is the best sign of contentment when discussing the past. Plus, we ruefully agreed, tonight had certainly been a night to remember, in spite of my party being a complete fiasco. A little while later, Mike came back from the hospital and announced that, in all probability, we had avoided killing any of our guests. Soberly, I agreed that was nice and shortly before midnight, I left their home for the long drive back to the Bayman farm.

As I drove, I reflected on the past and the approaching future. I was a little scared at the thought of going back to Europe. It no longer seemed like home to me; Africa was now my home. I was now an African and was deeply in love with this exotic land. Granted, I had only been in Northern Rhodesia for three years, but in my soul, it felt like a lifetime. Europe was so distant and impersonal and I was afraid of how I would react to it. But the die was cast and soon I would know how much we both had changed.

At last, I reached the Bayman farm and saw with relief that Ken's undamaged car was parked in the garage. Solemnly, I eased in beside it and, after getting out of the car, went to look at the moon as it bathed the warm tropical night in its comforting glow. Silently, I bid it *adieu* and went to bed with the cheerful thought that perhaps I would soon fall in love with another Susan, whose path would romantically cross mine, somewhere on the long voyage back – to England.

Chapter 11

Going Home

1. Getting Ready

The final three weeks of my first tour of duty in Northern Rhodesia passed in a blur of activity as I feverishly prepared for my forthcoming departure from Lusaka. However, I think I finally realized how close I was to departure day when I picked up my tickets for my passage back to Europe. Somehow, there is something satisfying and reassuring about having the physical tickets confirming your dream vacation safely in your hands, all those magical place names you intend to visit spelled out in prosaic cold print. Now I knew it was not a fantasy; it was a timetable and reality.

I had, of course, planned my trip home with extreme care and using all the experience gained during my stint with Mr. McIntosh, in the Passages section of Finance. Thus, I spurned the mundane Capetown to Southampton route, since it was the path by which I came out to Africa, and opted instead for a lengthier way home. Accordingly, after much consultation with Mr. McIntosh, I had booked passage with the British India Steamship Company on board their cargo liner, Uganda. It was sailing from Beira, Portuguese East Africa in early January of 1962 and due in London, England in mid February.

This trip would last about six weeks and would take me up the east coast of Africa, through the Red Sea, the Suez Canal, the Mediterranean and the North Atlantic before London was reached. Fortunately, this very interesting way of seeing more of the world was possible because British India plied that route on their way to and from Bombay, India and, therefore, when I joined the Uganda in Bcira, it would already be part of the way back to England.

Incidentally, the term cargo liner perfectly describes the type of ship I would be traveling on and the type of voyage I could look forward to. The Uganda was not a freighter; it was much bigger than that and its main business was not cargo. Still, on the other hand, it was not a liner since it was much smaller than the average liner and also handled freight, as well as its 200–300 passengers.

It was, quite simply, a hybrid, a cargo-carrying passenger ship which, in all probability, would not be able to provide as much luxury for its passengers as its big sisters. Yet it also stopped at many more ports of call than the regular liners and provided the opportunity to visit out-of-the-way places. In essence, the Uganda was a medium-sized tour bus and, although I didn't quite know what to expect, I was ready to roll with its waves.

But first I had to get to Beira and, after Mr. McIntosh had handed me my ticket for the Uganda, he also offered me a first-class train ticket to Beira through Salisbury and Umtali. Naturally, I haughtily declined this unimaginative offer since my good friend, Ken Bayman, had come up with a much better idea (will I never learn?) and the two of us were going to drive to the coast in my car. Once there, we intended to spend a sun drenched week on the beach before I set sail for England and he took my car back to Lusaka. It was all planned out and I had done everything I could to ensure I received an adequate reward for my services to my Queen.

Finally, at long last, almost nothing else remained to be done, except to enjoy a few more days of consummate leave happiness. Christmas was celebrated with even more joy than normal as it also gave birth to my new freedom and, shortly thereafter, I skipped out of the front door of the Ministry of Finance with much more enthusiasm than the statue of Physical Energy could ever have inspired.

2. Conspicuous Consumption

There was, however, one last chore for me in Lusaka a few days before Ken and I left on the 800-mile drive to the Indian Ocean. To be on the safe side, I had two of my car's tyres retreaded to ensure that I would have no problems with blowouts on the long drive to the coast. I did this by the simple expedient of taking my car to the retreader in the morning and picking it up again in the late afternoon, with my two bald tyres miraculously restored to pristine condition. This was the norm and not once in all my years in Africa did I ever buy a new tyre. I did what everyone else did and drove on retreads over some of the worst roads in the world.

Yet I never had a problem with my tyres and I never found a friend whose retreaded tyres had failed. We seldom threw a tyre away, except when its wall had deteriorated too far to make retreading a safe option. When that happened, we always bought a retreaded tyre from the retreader. Indeed, to the best of my recollection there was no new tyre store in town nor did we have a mountain of old tyres littering the outskirts of our city.

Thus you can see why I could not believe my eyes or ears, when I first came to the United States and found out that no one except the airlines used retreads. I was quite shocked to discover that retreads were deemed unsafe, while, by coincidence of course, a vast array of discount new-tyre stores did a roaring trade in replacement tyres. Plus, as I subsequently learned, most towns had an ever-increasing supply of old tyres which naturally became an ever-increasing problem since no one had a plan for their disposal. To me, as it is to most non-Americans, this was a prime example of conspicuous consumption which made no sense.

Why, in America, do they seem to be in love with the dream of a throw-away society? Is it perhaps because if something is not 'new and improved,' it is patently inferior? Or is it simply because they have to consume more – in an endless, frenetic spiral – as they keep the wheels of industry turning and their economy growing with an almost total disregard for the utilitarian value of their endeavours? Whatever the answer may be, I, like most non-American natives, find a disposable society to be somehow unsettling – and slightly immoral.

I also remember how, when I first came to America, I tried diligently to buy a new bottle for my Thermos jug and a new element for my iron. But, unfortunately, neither of these parts was available so eventually, I became a good American and bought a new Thermos jug and a new iron which, in all probability, was the only option I had. Even today, after 35 years in America, I still am not an enthusiastic devotee of my garbage can.

Anyway, I will now return to my tale as Ken and I prepared to leave Lusaka on a new adventure. My last goodbyes had been said, I was ready for the unknown, and I even felt that I could cope with civilization, provided I only touched its fringes. Indeed, I had steeled myself for a renewed encounter with television and cold weather in a distant foreign land that had, for so many years, been the centre of my world. Now, at last, there was nothing more to do or say. It was time to put the show on the road and the pedal to the metal, as we headed once more towards Umtali.

3. Umtali, My Nemesis

It was, I believe, on or about the 27th of December, 1961, that Ken and I actually left Lusaka, just as the midsummer sun rose to greet the new day. We both kissed Olive and the girls goodbye before we drove off in the customary cloud of dust, leaving them in the safe hands of Peter Ferrett, who was still living on the Bayman farm. Surprisingly, Olive had been very supportive of Ken taking this vacation, since I don't think he had been on holiday for several years and she hoped the change would do him good. Certainly we all parted in high spirits, and by dusk of the first day, Ken and I had reached the outskirts of Salisbury where we checked into a small hotel for a good night's drinking.

The following morning we left for Umtali, which was understandably not my favourite spa but, as the fates decreed, we had no alternative, since the only road to Beira went through my nemesis. Thankfully, for the next several hours all went well and I quietly enjoyed the peaceful view of the rolling African bush as it gradually became more wooded when we neared the range of hills which separated us from Umtali. Confidently, for it was such a nice day, I began the long steep ascent towards Christmas Pass and, as I drove, I regaled Ken with the story of the night I had camped out at the head of this pass on my first visit to Umtali. Idly I wondered what Helen was doing now and shuddered at the memory of the numerous complications she had brought to that previous vacation.

But this time, I had Ken for a companion and all was right with my world as I headed towards the summit of the pass in grand style. Yet obviously my joy was premature as gradually, mile by mile, my speed dropped, until it could only be described as a brisk canter. Nothing I did made any difference and by the time my car reached the summit of the pass, I was doing a moribund five miles an hour. Fortunately, our speed picked up on the long, gradual descent into Umtali and at times, I was hurtling along at almost 20 miles per hour.

Something was undeniably wrong with my car which suddenly appeared ready to cash in its chips. Clearly, it was not practical to enter into Mozambique in this geriatric apology for transportation and so, with a heavy heart, I reluctantly headed for Eve Voysey's parents' house at a sedentary three miles an hour. In due course, I eased into their driveway, switched off my engine and cried the crocodile tears of someone to whom Umtali is never a friend. The Williams', God bless them, were glad to see me and willingly put Ken and me up for the night when I explained to them that my car had just died.

Next morning, my car started with ease and soon reached its top speed of about five miles an hour as it ambled down to the local Ford dealership. The chief mechanic at this garage did an autopsy on my engine and cheerfully recommended against the appropriate burial rites. Apparently my car was not stone dead but only half dead. Two of the engine's four cylinders had lost all compression. All I needed was a complete engine overhaul.

He really was a most helpful young man and was quite sure he could get all the necessary parts to rebuild it within two weeks for a mere 150 pounds. Quietly, I pointed out that I was sailing from Beira in seven days and, equally quietly, he pointed out that this car was not going to help me keep that appointment.

There was nothing to discuss, so I gave him the keys to the corpse and said that Ken would be back in 10 days to see if the resurrection was complete. 'No problem,' he said and assured me that my car would soon be restored to full health and vigor. Slowly, Ken and I walked back to the Williams' house, a scant two miles away, and held a council of war. Again, our options were simple and Mr. McIntosh's offer of first class rail tickets to Beira was beginning to haunt me.

Accordingly, we spent a leisurely day cursing Umtali and one more delightful night as guests of the Williams family.

Early the following morning, Mr. Williams drove us both to the railway station and we caught the 10 a.m. train to Beira. It was a nice train and a nice ride through the Mozambique countryside until, after six hours and 200 miles, we slowly steamed into Beira. By then, my spirits were beginning to rise and I enthusiastically hailed a taxi to take us to the same hotel where Helen and I had reluctantly shared a room. This time, Ken and I got a room with two twin beds and by 6 p.m., we were happily splashing in the Indian Ocean, our vacation back on track.

Lazily, for almost a week, we lay around on the pure white coral sand of the beach which fronted our hotel and swam in the warm tropical waters of this seaside paradise. It was all very nice; it was also very quiet. Beira was not crowded at this time of the year and we passed New Year's Eve with a restful dinner and a bottle of champagne on our hotel's verandah under a bright tropical moon. We didn't do much, because there wasn't much to do. We did go to the movies one night and saw Frank Sinatra in 'The Courtship of Eddie's Father.' That was a lot of fun and probably more convenient for us than it was for the Portuguese since the movie was in English with Portuguese subtitles.

Beira in January, 1962 was the perfect getaway place, just like the posters you see in travel agencies, which persuade everyone to go to the same secluded spot as everyone else – with predictably disastrous results. It was idyllic, the calm before the storm which civil war would soon bring to Mozambique, which no longer functions as a country.

But all that was still a few years away, and the real struggle for independence would not start until September 25th, 1964, when fighting broke out between the Portuguese colonial government and the Frelimo guerrilla movement.

During the next decade, Portugal dispatched as many as 70,000 troops to Mozambique to try to restore order, but eventually the struggle was lost by the Portuguese, and on June 25th, 1975, independence was granted to Mozambique. Unfortunately, the Frelimo government then adopted a Marxist-Leninist ideology and the country slipped into civil war and chaos, from which it has never emerged.

Sometimes it is almost better to postpone facing the inevitable and Ken and I almost managed to pretend that our way of life was secure forever and ever. However, the signs of the approaching storm were clearly visible and so, perhaps, we enjoyed ourselves so much because, in our heart of hearts, we knew there was no tomorrow.

Too soon our brief interlude was over and it was time to move on. Early one morning, we called a taxi and after booking out of the hotel, we headed for the docks. There she was, my new home, the motor vessel, Uganda. Quickly, I went through the embarkation formalities and then with Ken, who had been given a visitor's boarding pass, I excitedly followed several other passengers as we all trudged up the gangway which connected the ship to the shore.

For the next two hours, Ken and I explored the Uganda at will. First of all, a steward showed us to my cabin where we left my one medium-sized suitcase and then we explored the decks and lounges as the boat made ready for sea. Eventually, the loudspeakers requested that all visitors leave the ship and, with a last fond handshake, Ken hurried ashore while I found a vantage point on a dockside rail of the ship.

He looked so small standing on the jetty and as the ship cast off, we each gave the other a farewell salute. Slowly, we pulled away from the shore and, as the distance widened, I quickly lost sight of Ken's blonde hair and friendly figure. Suddenly I felt lonely and far from home and I somberly watched the African coast recede as we made our way out into the Mozambique Channel. I was on my way back to England. A new adventure had begun, so it had to be time for a drink. Pensively, I turned from my place at the rail and went off in search of my new beginning.

However, before I embark on a description of my voyage to Europe, let me first digress to complete the story of Ken's vacation. To begin with, after watching the Uganda until it slipped beneath the horizon, he took a taxi to the railway station and caught the afternoon train to Umtali. Once there, he took another taxi back to the Williams' house and once more imposed upon their hospitality. The following morning, he went to pick up my car, armed with the 150 pounds I had given him and, in accordance with the rules of the International Brotherhood of Mechanics, he was told that the car was not ready.

When he asked how long, he was told, 'Soon,' and for over a week, he enjoyed, he really did, a tranquil unplanned vacation in Umtali. The Williams' were happy to have him stay for Ken was quite charming. Each morning, he went down to the garage for the daily 'Soon,' before retiring to spend the rest of the day at the new Olympic-sized pool I previously mentioned. Eventually, probably to Ken's disgust, 'Soon' was replaced by 'Pay me' and after a wait of about 10 days, he was reunited with my car.

He then took the Williams family out to dinner as a thank you and early the next morning he left for Lusaka. Of course, since the engine was rebuilt, it had to be 'driven-in!' and Ken religiously went home at a steady 35 miles per hour. Fortunately, all went well, the car behaved beautifully and two days later, he was reunited with Olive and his four little girls. He then parked my car at the back of his garage where I came to collect it some seven months later. All in all, it had been a very nice trip and Ken was glad he had been for a drive in my car. I, meanwhile, was well on my way to Europe, although I did occasionally wonder if my car ever made it out of my nemesis and over Christmas Pass to freedom.

4. The Uganda

Memory is not ours to control and often we remember trivial things while we tend to forget more important matters. Perhaps our minds have a mind of their own and a different scale of values from those we deem valuable. In any event, I must confess that I do not remember much about the Uganda or my fellow passengers except for a few isolated episodes.

I do not recollect what kind of cabin I had, or who my cabin mates were, nor do I remember our dining room or the food we ate. In truth, I don't even remember if we had a swimming pool, a celebration when we crossed the Equator, a fancy dress ball, or even a dance. My mind is a blank on shipboard activities and I can't even remember the face or name of a single one of my fellow passengers.

My overall recollection of the trip home is basically of boredom at sea, interspersed with days of fascination and excitement when we put into some exotic port of call. Perhaps I expected too much of the Uganda, based on my memories of the Capetown Castle. But then again, in January of 1962, the Uganda was not a happy ship as it sailed through the troubled waters of an east and central Africa in political turmoil.

To begin with, many of the passengers who boarded the ship in Beira were Belgian refugees from the Katangese provinces of the old Belgium Congo. Most of the refugees spoke little English and most were family groups of a husband, wife and two or three children. All were leaving the Congo reluctantly and had no clear indication of what they would do in their foreign homeland.

These poor, homeless Belgians were the first visible sign I had seen that the winds of change were blowing many limbs from the trees. They were not a pretty sight and I was shocked. Their despair was obvious and their fate seemed unjust, especially when one realized that most of them were descendants of Belgians who had been in the Congo since the late 19th century when King Leopold II first encouraged European settlement in that part of Africa. But, by 1960, the end of Belgium colonialism was at hand, and on June 30th, the Democratic Republic of the Congo was born when Belgium granted independence to its former colony.

Patrice Lumumba, who was subsequently murdered, became the new country's first president and two weeks later, the Province of Katanga seceded under the leadership of Moise Tchombe. Within days, the whole country was plunged into civil war and, within months, the United Nations was embroiled as it sent peacekeeping troops to fight with everyone. Ultimately the United Nations stayed in the Congo until 1964. Then they left in triumph, just before a military coup democratically cooked the fragile Congo's goose. In 1967, Katangese resistance was finally crushed and in 1971, the whole sordid mess became Zaire as it gradually returned to virgin wilderness.

I knew that colonialism was wrong and had to end, but it was difficult to admire its replacement when I saw the results up close. Perhaps you can't make an omelet without breaking a few eggs but I did feel genuinely sorry for my Belgian shipmates as I stubbornly told myself it could never happen to me.

The rest of our passengers were mainly South Africans and Southern Rhodesians with a sprinkling of businessmen from India and, to my regret, nearly all were considerably older than me. I was also surprised to find that I was the only passenger from Northern Rhodesia, which was already beginning to seem like a far distant land.

The Uganda's crew was mainly Indian, with British officers and I remember the service as being quite excellent, although probably not up to Moses' exacting standards. Definitely the ambience reflected the traditions of a fast-fading empire, which had always trumpeted the good life. It sure was nice to sit in a deck chair sipping a gin and tonic in the warm tropical breeze. It was even nicer knowing that I was being paid to do this and didn't have to go back to work for another six months.

5. Zanzibar

From Beira, we steamed north through the placid waters of the Indian Ocean for almost a week until eventually we reached our first destination, the spice island of Zanzibar. This island lay about 1,500 miles north of Beira and was about twenty two miles from the coast of Tanganyika. It had a long and colourful history and was one of the ports I was most looking forward to visiting. In particular, Zanzibar is famous as the world's leading producer of cloves and is often referred to as the Spice Island, a term it richly deserves.

As our anticipated arrival time in Zanzibar drew near, but long before the island came into view, it began to register on my sense of smell. The air became heavy with the fragrance of cloves and it was just like being in an old-fashioned store where the spices were kept in open boxes. It was wonderful and mysterious, an unforgettable sensation which grew stronger as the island slowly rose above the horizon and we made our way into its ancient harbour.

It was a step back in time. On every side, the waters of the bay were full of Arab dhows. On a bluff in the distance, overseeing the whole scene, stood the most imposing structure on the island: the gleaming white palace of the Sultan of Zanzibar. It was definitely not a European scene and certainly not an African one either. Instead, it was straight out of the Arabian Nights and was, in many respects, more Arab than anything I have seen in the Middle East.

The Arabs were the first to venture down the east coast of Africa and had, for hundreds of years, traded with the coastal African tribes for slaves and ivory. Indeed, by the early 19th century, the Arabs had established Zanzibar as their main base and major slave market from where they traded with the African mainland. Even David Livingstone came to Zanzibar and it was from a house in its small town that he launched his expeditions to central Africa and the Victoria Falls.

Not surprisingly, for at least 100 years, or more, Zanzibar was the economic hub of East Africa and as such, was an irresistible plum to the British. Thus, with commendable zeal, the British invaded the island in the mid-19th century and in 1890, made it a British Protectorate which was their way of saying they now owned the whole enchilada. Therefore, when I disembarked on Zanzibar's dusty streets, I was happy to note the British flag briskly waving in the breeze of another far corner of our empire.

But this flag too was being challenged and on December 9th, 1963, Zanzibar gained its independence. Before long, following a well-established trend, further turmoil erupted and in early 1964, the Sultan was deposed and sent into exile. Shortly thereafter, on April 26th, 1964, Zanzibar was annexed by Tanganyika and lost its brief bout with freedom. In due course, Tanganyika and Zanzibar became Tanzania – Zanzibar had a new protector.

Yet when I landed in mid-January of 1962, all this was still in the future. The present was secure in the past and I contentedly mingled in the bazaars at will.

The island is quite small, being about 50 miles long and 15 miles wide with a total area of approximately 640 square miles. The population is part Arab, part African, part Indian but distinctly Arab in flavour. Mosques abounded and the call of the faithful to prayer was often to be heard. The streets were narrow and winding and the houses hidden behind excluding walls which often contained an elaborately carved door set in a very ornate door case.

For the most part, the people wore the traditional Arab headdress and long, flowing robes and I most definitely did not fit in as I wandered from street to street taking snapshots. Once again, I was lucky enough to visit an out-of-the-way place before the cruise ships began to arrive. In comparative solitude, I casually absorbed its unhurried charm.

The Uganda only stayed in Zanzibar for about eight hours, which, fortunately, was long enough to allow me and three of my fellow passengers to hire a taxi for a grand tour of the island. There wasn't a whole lot to see, mainly coconut groves and clove orchards, the two main exports of the island, now that slavery was frowned upon. But it was pleasant to get out in the countryside and enjoy its spice laden breezes. We also passed by the Sultan's residence where two old cannons flanked the ornate iron gates at the main entrance to the palace gardens which were otherwise completely surrounded by a high brick wall.

All too soon, it was time to return to the Uganda and in the late evening, we weighed anchor and set sail for Dar-Es Salaam. a scant 50 miles away on the mainland of Africa. It had been an exciting interlude, a glimpse into a little-known past and a brief introduction to a glittering piece in the cultural mosaic of East African life.

I had really enjoyed my visit to the Spice Island and as we sailed away in the setting sun, the strong scent of cloves wafted over the ship to remind us of the mysterious place fast fading from view.

Who knows what Zanzibar is like today? One never hears about it in the news. But at least I saw it in the twilight of its glory years and for that, I shall always be grateful. Perhaps it has somehow, despite the odds, been able to retain some of its old world charm as it adjusts to the realities of modern Africa and a new world order.

6. Dar-Es-Salaam

The following morning, I woke up to find us docked in Dar-Es-Salaam, the capital of Tanganyika and after breakfast, I cautiously ventured ashore in this, the first independent Black African state I had ever visited. I was not sure what I would find and even had doubts about the reliability of a black police force which no longer answered to a white government. Perhaps my fears sound foolish but freedom sometimes seemed to be out of control as it blew out the colonial light.

Anyway, faint heart seldom gets arrested and throwing caution to the wind, I joined my fellow shipmates on the jetty and headed for town. Once again, the Arab influence was obvious although this time, it was not as pervasive as it was in Zanzibar. Dar-Es-Salaam was predominantly an African town although, as its name suggests, it had been founded by Arabs. It was one of their main ports from which, for hundreds of years, they carried on a brisk trade with the inland blacks in ivory and slaves.

By the late 15th century, the Portuguese had begun to make their presence felt. The British, too, sniffed around and by the mid 19th century the Germans got into the act, although by then slavery had been abolished as colonialism tightened its grip. In 1846, German missionaries first saw Kilimanjaro – the snows of Africa – which, at 19,340 feet, is the tallest mountain in Africa although it is, in fact, an extinct volcano.

German influence continued to spread and in 1885, German colonists began to arrive as Tanganyika drifted under German control. Eventually, in 1907, the country became a German colony as the Europeans carved up Africa like a fruit pie.

When the Germans lost World War I, the British promptly picked up this plum with the blessing of the short-lived League of Nations. Henceforth, Tanganyika enjoyed all the benefits, and suffered under all the shortcomings, of a British Protectorate, until May 1st, 1961, when the country achieved its independence under the presidency of Julius Nyere.

Thus, the Tanganyika I visited that morning in January, 1962 was only about nine months old and was not well established as a tourist attraction. But I had paid my money and I determined to have a good look around this relatively small town with a very checkered past. As I approached the downtown area I came across a war memorial to the native troops who had fought for the British in World War II against the Germans (for whom they had fought against the British in World War I). Politics makes for strange bedfellows and I wonder if those loyal Africans ever really discovered whose side they were on.

A little further down the same street was a brand new memorial, a simple white column with a bronze eternal flame on top. Solemnly, I realized that this was the independence monument and, as I took its picture, I could but wonder how long it would be before Physical Energy would be replaced in Lusaka with a similar marker. The rest of the day was spent wandering the streets of this quiet little town which was surprisingly clean yet very unpretentious with few large buildings.

Naturally, I saw an occasional mosque but the bulk of the people were Africans with a sprinkling of Arabs, Indians and British holdovers from the colonial administration. Tanganyika has always been a poor country and there were few signs of industrial activity. The main export, once slavery was stopped, became sisal, or hemp, from which ropes are made. This is hardly a product on which a vigorous economy can be built. Yet sisal, along with some cotton and coffee, is about all that they have to export to an unsympathetic world.

Clearly, a country needs more than political borders to survive in an economic world and so many of Africa's newly independent states are fundamentally ill-equipped to trade in a product-oriented marketplace.

Freedom is more than a word and as I walked around Dar-Es-Salaam that day, I wondered how on earth Mr. Nyere was going to deliver the rewards which had been promised once independence had been achieved. Still, it was a nice day and I enjoyed myself immensely while the police, to my infinite relief, restricted their activities to controlling the traffic with commendable zeal.

In the early evening I returned to the docks and the Uganda. I was surprised to note that the ship next to ours was being unloaded under the watchful eyes of several soldiers in light blue berets. Curious, I wandered over for a closer look and discovered that these soldiers were members of the United Nations Peacekeeping Force, presently engaged in the suppression of freedom in Katanga. Apparently, they were supervising the unloading of supplies for their battlefront comrades and as I took their picture, I little realized that within two

United Nations Troops in Dar-Es-Salaam, January 1962

years, I, too, would be waiting to go to war with these same peace-keepers.

As I watched these soldiers doing their duty, I wondered what the average African in the Congo thought of his new world in which one foreign army had been speedily replaced by another. It's a very strange world we live in, Father Jack, and as I boarded the Uganda for dinner, I wondered if any of our Belgian passengers had noticed the U.N. troops. I hoped not since perhaps it would have spoiled their appetites and increased their level of discontent.

Next morning, the last of our two-day stay in Dar-Es-Salaam, I decided to look for a nice, quiet beach on the Indian Ocean to spend a restful day reading a book by the water's edge. Accordingly, I made inquiries at a couple of stores in town and was soon directed to what had previously been an exclusive club for Europeans on a beautiful white, sandy beach on the edge of town. A brief taxi ride quickly took me to this idyllic spot which was now more exclusive than it had been before. Because now, apart from the staff, it was totally deserted. The whites had either left town, or wouldn't come, and the non-whites apparently had neither the money nor the inclination to use its facilities.

This was an absolute repeat of the situation at the swimming pool in Umtali and once more, I was saddened by the practical results of progress. But I was just a tourist, so I paid for a day membership and spent a delightful day on that beautiful beach.

I spoke to no one – there was no one to speak to – I had my own beach. It was almost as if I was the last dinosaur, and definitely a little unsettling. The water was very blue and warm, and the beach was not too hot, since a soft coastal breeze kept the temperature in check.

At lunch time, a waiter from the club brought me sandwiches and lemonade, and a couple of hours later he reappeared with a cool Fanta, as I lazily enjoyed a perfect day from a vanished past. Too soon it was time to leave and I decided to make up for my idleness by walking the three miles back to the Uganda.

Almost immediately, I stumbled across Government House which had, for so many years, been the official home of the British Governor of Tanganyika. But now, there was a strange green, yellow, black and blue flag flying where the British flag had flown and His Excellency Julius Nyere was now in residence in this longtime symbol of British rule.

There were no guards at the main entrance to the grounds of his new home, just a simple little sign which said, 'Government House – Grounds Private.' The house itself was a large, white, two story, elegant home with spacious colonial style (what else?) verandahs on both floors. Its architecture seemed to me, to be reminiscent of the British in India and oddly suited for an emerging socialist African republic. I took a snapshot of change in progress and then strolled back to my floating hotel for dinner.

The following day, after breakfast in the Uganda's dining room, I stood by the rail of an upper deck and watched as more flotsam drifted towards our ship. But this time, our new passengers were British, although once more they were leaving under less than ideal conditions. Most of them (according to those I subsequently spoke to) were going back to an England they scarcely knew – yet preferred to an emerging Africa they did not want to know.

It was all rather depressing, especially since our new arrivals did not include any demure young ladies in need of solace from a gallant knight. Ironically, I also began to realize what it must have been like in England when the Roman Legions pulled out, and I was having much more difficulty in believing it could never happen to me.

Even so, I bravely determined to try and I saluted Tanganyika with a nice cold beer when, shortly after noon, we eased out of Dar-Es-Salaam before heading up the coast for Mombasa. As we cleared the harbour's mouth, I noted that yesterday's exclusive bathing beach was now totally deserted and seemed, by its emptiness, to speak eloquently about the future of the white man in the black man's Africa.

7. Mombasa

Our route now took us north for about 250 miles and by noon the next day, we were maneuvering alongside the jetty in Mombasa, the main port in East Africa and the second largest city in Kenya. Once more, I was back on British soil for although this coast had also been visited by Arab traders for hundreds of years, it had, by the mid-19th century, fallen into the British sphere of influence. By 1890, Kenya had become (what else) a British protectorate and in 1920, this euphemism was dispensed with when Kenya became a fully-fledged crown colony.

It soon became one of the most prized of the British possessions. The White Highlands, in particular, became a favourite destination for the younger sons of the British aristocracy. Coffee and tea were the major crops grown by these gentleman farmers who also enjoyed some of the best big-game hunting in Africa.

For 30 years the magic endured, until, in the early 1950s, the struggle for independence began. In Kenya, this conflict took the most violent form of any of the ex-British colonies as the infamous Mau Mau terrorists murdered more than 100 innocent settlers and thousands of peaceful villagers as they pursued a bloody road to freedom.

Thankfully, by the time I arrived, Mau Mau terrorism was beginning to wind down as the country edged towards home rule. In due course, on December 12th, 1963, Kenya gained its independence and in 1964, it became a republic under the leadership of Jomo Kenyatta, the reputed leader of the Mau Mau. Thus, I was once again about to disembark in a far-from-placid country and, before we left, we again picked up a goodly number of refugees from the demise of colonialism.

The Uganda was scheduled to make its longest layover in Mombasa and would remain there for at least a week, which created a golden opportunity to tour Kenya if one had a car and perhaps a heavy calibre machine gun. Having neither, I stood on the deck as we berthed and gazed in amazement at the long row of old cars that lined our pier and appeared to have something to do with our arrival. Each car was accompanied by a gesticulating driver and as soon as we docked, the more seasoned veterans among our passengers sprinted ashore with boundless enthusiasm.

Apparently, as I soon discovered, I was watching capitalism at its best – and the parable of the early bird's hunt for its worm – which was a fairly complimentary description of some of the rental cars on display. For that was what the pantomime below was all about. These cars were the cream of Mombasa's automobile junkyards and our veteran passengers eagerly endeavoured to obtain one whose afflictions were only slightly terminal.

If possible, it was also best to rent a small car, preferably the hallowed VW Beetle. Petrol was expensive and cars that did a minimum of miles to the gallon, cost a maximum of pounds to drive. Unfortunately, there were no small cars on offer and the selection was limited to a motley selection of Henry Ford's earlier models.

However, wheels are wheels and by the time I, with dignity intact, had ventured ashore, there were no Hertz Rent-a-Cars in sight. Reluctantly, I decided to walk to town and was just beginning the three mile hike when a black Mercedes hove into view. Curious, I stopped and watched as the car parked alongside our ship and a middle-aged Indian gentleman in a dark business suit got out of the driver's seat. Casually, he strolled over to my side and politely inquired if I would like to rent a nice car for a week.

'Yes,' I dubiously replied eying his Mercedes.
'Good,' he said and then quoted me a fairly reasonable rate, half of which he wanted in advance.
'That's fine,' I agreed, 'but what kind of a car will you give me?'
'You'll see when you get it,' was his astonishing reply. 'Just pay the deposit now to prove you trust me and I'll drive you downtown to my garage where I have the ideal car for your needs.'

Now I try to be a fair minded man but I have trouble with the concept of Mother Teresa in drag and masquerading as a car rental salesman. So I politely declined the opportunity to accept his unusual offer.

Yet he persisted and kept assuring me that if only I would trust him, I would not regret it. Eventually, since the sun was hot and I didn't want to walk to town, I decided to play the fool by agreeing to trust this persuasive stranger. Besides, my curiosity was piqued and I was intrigued by the earnestness of his plea. Therefore, I reluctantly gave him a sizable chunk of money and clambered into his Mercedes for the four-mile drive to his garage.

Once there, he proudly took me to the workshop behind his office where several mechanics were repairing cars and solemnly gave me the keys to my pig in a poke. Nervously I turned to where he was pointing and refused to believe my eyes. Truly this man was a saint, or at the very least a good friend of Mother Teresa, if not a close relative. For there, before my eyes, stood a 1962 VW Beetle convertible. This car was brand spanking new. A glance at the odometer showed a total mileage of 150 miles and the interior still had that wonderful new car smell.

'Well,' he said, 'are you satisfied?'
'Yes,' I replied, struggling to recover my composure, 'but why didn't you save the fuss and tell me?'
'Oh no,' he explained. 'If you were not prepared to trust me, then I was not prepared to trust you with a new car. Now please be careful and bring it back in a week.'

I assured him I would do both and then, before he could change his mind, I climbed into the first new car I had ever driven and set off to explore Mombasa. Was I lucky? I don't know. Common sense tells me I was and intuition told me to trust him. I could not believe that someone driving a Mercedes would come down to the docks to pull such a clumsy confidence trick.

If he was a crook, I felt he would have had a more plausible line. Certainly, I would have been more suspicious if he had said the car he was renting out was brand new. Then his tale would have been too good to be true. But, somehow, I felt I could trust him, so I did, and it worked. Certainly, on this day at least, my guardian angel had been on the ball, and for the rest of the day I contentedly toured Mombasa with the VW's top down, preening myself in my new found luxury.

Of course, the best was yet to be and shortly before sunset I returned to the Uganda's quay where I gleefully parked my thoroughbred next to a motley collection of candidates for the knacker's yard. In addition, just to emphasize the point, I lingered on the dock and, while several of my fellow passengers watched in amazement, I carefully wiped a few specks of dust from my car's pristine hood. It was a delightful moment and several times at dinner I was called upon to explain how I had achieved the impossible dream.

The consensus of opinion was that I deserved my success. No one else seemed to feel as if they would have taken the chance I took. They said I was lucky and deserved it. A few even said they would be willing to go for a drive tomorrow. I said I would post a roster and went on deck for a goodnight look at my prize before retiring to my cabin to sleep the sleep of supreme contentment.

The following morning, I continued my exploration of Mombasa which turned out to be a fairly typical industrial seaport. It was considerably larger than Dar-Es-Salaam and had the same cosmopolitan mix of peoples, although this time, the black Africans were, by far, the largest segment of the population. However, the Arabs and Indians were well represented and there was a notable sprinkling of British settlers who still faithfully administered this colony on behalf of their Queen.

From time to time, I parked my car and explored the interior of a Moslem mosque or a Hindu temple as I savoured the differences which unite us in the pursuit of salvation and truth. It has always disturbed me greatly to watch the devout at prayer in a religious setting which my Christian background rejects as false. Are these people wasting their time? Does their God really exist? How can he – if mine is the one true God?

In particular, I remember going into a large Hindu temple whose innermost sanctum was dominated by a life-sized statue of a Brahma bull which stood at the centre of its own courtyard. It was, to my untutored eyes, a most unusual statue to find in a religious setting, and not one with which I could feel comfortable. I was completely out of my depth as I stood unobtrusively in the shadows of that holy place and watched a steady stream of Indians pay their respect to the statue by scattering flower petals at its feet. The atmosphere was reverent, the effect charming, but what was I supposed to believe?

Could all these people be poor, misguided victims of a non-existent god? Or was there perhaps some great truth I was ignorant of and needed to learn. Either way, it was disturbing and proved once more that travel to a foreign land can be dangerous if it disturbs the insular beliefs of one's childhood.

For me, on that day, questions were raised which I have never been able to satisfactorily answer. I am still deeply troubled by the vision of that temple with its placid statue standing in a pool of colourful tribute. As I quietly withdrew from its presence, I could only believe I was leaving a holy place, although I could not quite comprehend its sacredness.

The rest of my stay in Mombasa was less provocative, as I cruised the city and surrounding countryside with all the aplomb of the local squire. One day, I even took a fairly lengthy drive up the coast and visited a special section of the beach where a coral reef was exposed at low tide. That was a unique experience and for several hours I tramped around the reef as I explored its wonders. Each pool was a miniature aquarium, vibrant with colour and full of small, exotic fish. It was quite beautiful and once again, the area was almost deserted, as the local tour buses seemed to be having an off day. This was nature as nature was meant to be seen and luckily, I saw it before it fell victim to progress.

Too soon, our week in Mombasa was over and I returned my almost-new car to its trusting owner. He was happy to have it returned in showroom condition and personally took me back to the Uganda in his Mercedes. As I thanked him for his courtesy, I could but wonder if he too scattered flowers in the temple, and religiously considered me to be an atheist. Surely not, since he had such good Christian virtues and two very nice cars. Thoughtfully, I watched him drive away and then slowly mounted the gangplank as our two civilizations went their separate ways.

Another hour passed and then, as the sun began to set, we resumed our northward voyage towards England and winter. It had been a fun week and I had thoroughly enjoyed our stay in Mombasa and Kenya. I stayed on deck until the coast faded from view and then I turned my sights towards Aden, our next port of call, some 1,500 miles over the horizon on the mysterious continent of Asia.

It was dinner time, and as I headed for the dining salon my appetite was piqued, by the charming thought that all my meals were still at taxpayer's expense. I was glad to be alive and serving under the flag of the world's last great colonial power, even though, as this voyage clearly showed, its heyday was fast drawing to a close. Yet, tomorrow was another day and tonight was enough for itself, so I had a few drinks before going to bed in the firm conviction that I was a very lucky man.

Chapter 12

The Final Leg

1. Aden

For the next several days, we slowly steamed north as we headed up the coast of Somalia across the equator and into the northern hemisphere. Our voyage was now half over and, as I suddenly realized with a jolt, was not going to last forever. Home, that distant dream, began to emerge as a disturbing reality, as we daily steamed closer to my past and away from my new colonial roots. To be sure, part of me was anxious to get home. Then again part of me was scared by this prospect which, I intuitively felt, may well reveal that I had already become a comparative stranger – in my old hometown

I don't recollect many details of this part of my trip, except that I vividly recall our rounding Cape Gardafui, the Horn of Africa. This is the most easterly point on the whole continent of Africa and our only glimpse of the Somalian coast. We all flocked to the rails to take pictures of the distant headland before it faded from view as the Uganda steamed out of the Indian Ocean and into the Gulf of Aden. A boundary had just been passed and black Africa was left behind as we closed in on the fabled shores of the Arabian Peninsula.

The following morning the shoreline of Asia slowly came into view as we neared the British Crown Colony of Aden. By noon, we were at anchor in the harbour of this vital British asset and shortly thereafter, we were ferried ashore for a brief six hour visit to the British Empire's number one, duty-free shopping centre.

Naturally I feared the worst but this time I was quite clearly wrong and soon joined my fellow passengers in a shopping frenzy. This was the Promised Land and the descendants of Aladdin were having a closeout sale. You name it, they had it, and their bazaars were a wonder to behold, especially if you wanted a camera, a radio or a record player. It was Hong Kong, decades before that city reached its present stature and a visit to Aden was a bargain hunter's passport to paradise.

Indeed, this had long been the case, since Aden was not a new city and because of its strategic location at the entrance to the Red Sea, it had, for centuries, been an important port in the Arab world. Its dhows had often controlled much of the trade with East Africa and many had also ventured to India and beyond.

Clearly this was an intolerable situation and in 1839 the British corrected the problem, by occupying Aden on behalf of civilization and progress.

From then, and for almost the next hundred years, Aden was administered by India, which is an interesting logistical problem but well within the bureaucratic competency of the British Colonial Service. Eventually, in 1937, this anomaly ended when Aden became a fully-fledged crown colony, and that was still its status when I landed there in late January of 1962. But not for much longer, the future was closing in fast, and the last British troops left Aden on November 29th, 1967, when the British granted independence to this prosperous colony.

The very next day, in a burst of Marxist zeal, Aden was taken over by the forces of the local National Liberation Front and together with several other local sultanates, it became a part of the newly created People's Democratic Republic of Yemen. Since then, Aden has been virtually ignored by the West and Hong Kong has replaced it as a bastion of capitalism in a turbulent world.

Of course, to be fair, Aden's glory years were closely tied to the fortunes of the British Empire and the vagaries of Middle Eastern politics. For almost the entire period of British occupation, Aden was the main refueling point on the shortest maritime route between Europe and India. Unfortunately, this trade route ceased in its entirety when the canal was closed thanks to an Arab-Israeli war, from June of 1967 until sometime in 1975. When the canal eventually re-opened, after having been closed for about eight years, Aden had become a forgotten backwater.

Nevertheless, for a while, it had its place in the sun and when I stepped ashore in 1962, it was still a bustling, vigorous symbol of British imperial power east of Suez. Even so, in stark contrast to its importance, this colony was really quite small, being no more than the town and its suburbs and was totally Arab in character. Everywhere one looked were bazaars stacked upon bazaars and everyone seemed to be bartering at the top of their lungs.

It was also hot, which was something I had not expected, since we had arrived in the middle of their winter and, judging from the terrain, I believe it usually rained about once every couple of hundred years. The dominant natural feature was sand, pure, unadulterated sand, with no trace of vegetation to disturb its pristine nothingness.

Anyway we were there and so, once we had shopped to exhaustion, I joined two other resolute travelers on a two-hour taxi crusade of the local highlights. There wasn't much to see outside of town. The villages were small, poor, parched and sun drenched. Yet I did get to see my first camels, which appeared to be as unfriendly as the local moonscape and didn't seem anxious to pose for a snapshot.

There was, however, just one exceptionally interesting sight to see and that was a series of giant cisterns which filled a ravine leading down from a small range of hills towards the coast at their foot. It was, quite obviously, an elaborate system to trap and store rain water and, equally obvious, was many hundreds of years old. Our taxi driver didn't seem to know much about these cisterns history, and was content to accept without curiosity, the existence of this prodigious engineering feat, which clearly pointed to a long-forgotten past.

Shortly thereafter, we returned to town and, with renewed vigor, I re-entered the fray clutching my Travelers cheques. Everyone had going-out-of-business sales, pre-Valentine's Day sales, British Empire Day sales and every other kind of absurdity that gladdens the heart of the average bargain hunter. Yet the price was right and the merchandise first class. Eventually, I bought two Japanese transistor radios, (my first exposure to the coming Japanese commercial onslaught) and a German slide projector and screen. In all, I must have spent the equivalent of at least 200 pounds. But in return I had a wide variety of first-class merchandise bought at bargain basement prices.

Finally, I joined a stream of other passengers, each accompanied by a native bearer, as we made our way back to the Uganda. Triumphantly our trophies were borne to our cabins and stashed wherever we could find room. The projector and one of the radios I still have and that is the very radio to which I subsequently sat glued as I heard the announcer proclaim Mohammed Ali as the new heavyweight champion of the world.

In retrospect, I would not say that Aden was a pretty place. It was too hot and desolate to be pretty but as shopping malls go, it had no equal in the world that I then knew. It was the ultimate trading bazaar. For a brief while, it filled a special niche in the capitalist world and then it opted for Marxist poverty. I wonder if Hong Kong will follow it into the shadows, as history gets ready to repeat itself, while we all grow older but seldom wiser.

Later that afternoon, we left Aden – and Asia – and steamed into the Red Sea on our way to Egypt. Little did I then realize as I watched that frenetic bazaar slip below the horizon, how soon, and how completely, it would fade into history. Today, the Yemen has a per capita income of about 500 pounds per year which is reputed to be among the lowest in the entire Arab world. It is strange, and a little disturbing, to reflect on the temporary nature of the permanent things in life.

Thankfully, such heavy matters did not concern me that night as I stood on deck and played with one of my new transistor radios while we headed towards Egypt, the oldest continuous civilization in the world. At first I heard nothing, but then I picked up an Ethiopian station. I stared into the darkness from where the strange chants were coming and then, satisfied that my radio really worked, I retired to my bunk to dream of tomorrow's adventures.

2. Egypt

The Red Sea is not red and I don't know why it has such a peculiar name but for the next few days, we slowly steamed up its 1,300 mile length as we headed for Suez and the entrance to the Suez Canal. About halfway up the Red Sea, we passed over the Tropic of Cancer and out of the tropics. Now, at last, after three long years, I was back in the temperate zone and would soon begin to experience the joys of a European winter. It was not a pleasant thought so I cast it from my mind as we cruised through still-balmy weather until, at the crack of dawn three days later, we berthed in Suez and most of us disembarked for a hectic day's visit to Egypt.

Our gracious host for this idyllic adventure was a company called 'Memphis Tours' (perhaps in tribute to Elvis). Two of their luxury coaches were waiting at the dockside for those who wished to take this optional excursion. The alternative was to stay on the ship while it traversed the Suez Canal. This I was anxious to do since I had never seen the canal which was about 105 miles long, 180 feet wide and 40 feet deep. Nevertheless, after much deliberation, I decided to forego this marvel of French engineering and opted instead for the marvels of ancient and modern Egypt.

Besides, as an Englishman, I felt it was my duty to visit this ex-British colony and see how it was doing now that it finally, after eons of foreign domination, had achieved home rule. Of course the British were not the only people to colonize this land; they merely had the distinction of being the last. The Assyrians may have been the first, in the 7th century B.C. while the Persians, in 552 B.C. and Alexander the Great, in 332 B.C. also tried their best to establish eternal kingdoms.

Then came the Romans, in 30 B.C. as anyone who saw Elizabeth Taylor in Cleopatra will confirm and they held the land until 395 A.D. At that time control passed to the eastern Roman Empire whose capitol was Constantinople. By now a firm precedent had been set and thus, in 642, the Arabs came in and stomped everyone with enthusiasm. From then on, Egypt became an Islamic, Arabic speaking state and its conquest by the Turks in 1517, did nothing to reverse this culture.

Next, in 1798, the French, under Napoleon, graciously attempted to bestow the benefits of French rule on this much-conquered land. However, their tenure was brief, due to Nelson and Wellington. Within a few years, old habits being hard to break, the country was taken over by Mohammed Ali. Now certainly, this sounds like a giant step forward but regrettably I must, in reverence to journalistic accuracy, point out that the Mohammed Ali in question was an Albanian and not his more famous American namesake.

This gentleman and his successors were imprudent and soon ran up a big tab with the British banks. In 1882 the current ruler Tewfik had his loans foreclosed by the British Army, in the best interests of the British banks, when his country's finances and internal stability began to spiral out of control. Egypt was now British, and in 1914 it was formally designated as a British Protectorate. In 1922 the British set up a constitutional monarchy and Egypt received nominal independence, while remaining staunchly British.

This delightful arrangement lasted until 1952, when Gamal Abdel Nasser staged a coup and overthrew the last Egyptian monarch, King Farouk, whom I clearly remember as being somewhat overweight. He then retired to the French Riviera and the British retired to England.

Peace now settled over the region for almost four years until Nasser nationalized the Suez Canal on July 26th, 1956. He then confidently predicted that the tolls collected from ships passing through the canal would pay for the Aswan Dam within five years and smugly settled back to await the Nobel Prize for Excellence in Economic Theory. Instead he found himself embroiled in a war, since the British, French and Israelis did not share his enthusiasm and, on October 29th, 1956, the Israelis invaded Egypt. The British and French soon followed and on November 5th, 1956, they also invaded Egypt.

The scene was now set for World War III as the United States immediately sided with Egypt and democracy and began to threaten its closest allies. Luckily, someone's sanity prevailed and on December 22nd, 1956, the British and French reluctantly pulled out of Egypt. The Israelis also accepted the inevitable and in March of 1957 they withdrew their forces, which meant that Nasser had achieved victory through defeat. Nasser became the greatest living Arab hero and the humiliated British and French lost most of their influence in the Middle East. Plus the French, in particular, ceased to regard the United States as an ally to be trusted.

Such was the checkered past of this ancient land and, as our luxurious tour bus pulled out of Suez, I anxiously scanned my surroundings for a glimpse of the next invader. Immediately, I spotted the new old enemy. It was sand, the relentless eternal foe which constantly threatens to engulf Egypt and is only restrained by the lifegiving waters of the Nile. Nowhere was this struggle more clearly evident than during our 100-mile drive to Cairo, for the road we were following was an absolute demarcation line between want and plenty.

To our right there was fertile land in abundance: Fields, farms, villages, palm trees, date groves and an endless web of irrigation canals. Often, we passed camels or donkeys walking in a monotonous circle, as they methodically turned a water wheel to raise water from a well or divert it from one channel to the next. Everywhere one looked, if one only looked right, there was prosperity, and it all depended on the availability of water.

By contrast, the view to our left was one of total desolation. Not a solitary living thing grew or stirred – all was barren. There in a landscape devoid of irrigation, civilization ceased, and the desolate sands of the Sahara Desert stretched away before our eyes in an unbroken sea of emptiness which reached across the continent until it met the Atlantic Ocean.

There was no middle ground: where the water ended, desolation began and our road marked the division between life and death. It also contained most of the traffic in the universe, and this astounding fact became more obvious as we neared the outskirts of Cairo. At first, I refused to believe my eyes but eventually I accepted the horrendous premise that our driver must be killing hundreds of people, horses, camels, goats, chickens and dogs as he cheerfully plowed through the impenetrable mass which jammed the road ahead.

Shocked, I rose from my seat at the back of the bus and hurried to the front for a closer look at the carnage of our passage. It was, without question, an absolutely unbelievable sight, since the way ahead was totally blocked by a seething mass of everything that Noah had on his ark. Miraculously, we passed through it as clean as a whistle because, in this Biblical land, the throng ahead parted instants before we plowed into it and, like Moses in the Red Sea, our driver never doubted that God would protect our passage.

Wisely, I returned to my seat and said a few prayers just in case the driver and I consulted different gods when we needed divine intervention. I then relaxed in the almost certain knowledge that the will of Allah would prevail and contentedly dozed until we reached the Pyramids at Giza.

It was a rude awakening. For instead of the grandeur and isolation I had expected, I was greeted by modern opulence as our two coaches pulled into the courtyard of a beautiful colonial-style hotel. Soon we were all enjoying morning tea and crumpets beneath slowly turning fans on a latticework shaded verandah. It was elegance personified – cool, quiet, restful and about two hundred yards from the Pyramids, which are not far out in the desert but right on the edge of town.

About half an hour later, after elevenses had refreshed us, we all trouped over to the pyramids and marveled at their towering strength. Luckily, the site was largely deserted and our tour was the only tour there during the two hours of our visit. Eagerly, we followed the guide as we clambered on the lower reaches of the main pyramid and filed down a long corridor to the main burial chamber at the centre of that colossal tomb. We then tramped over to the Sphinx and admired its inscrutable smile before bowing to tradition by taking a 15-minute camel ride back to the hotel.

That was a big mistake, as my rear end painfully attested, but otherwise it had been a wonderful experience to see these ancient monuments (although I did not find them to be as attractive as something like the cathedral at Chartres.) To me, it was their size and antiquity which was most impressive. I was also amazed to discover that I could stand at the Great Pyramid at Giza, and look one way over endless desolation, before turning on my heel to view the suburbs of Cairo.

Again, the demarcation line was absolute. Where the buildings ended, the sand began. To dramatically change your view, you merely changed your viewpoint. Look west and the empty Sahara stretched to an endless horizon. Look east and one of the largest cities in the world unfolded before your eyes. It was all very exciting and I was wise enough to know how lucky I was, especially since this journey was all still at taxpayer expense.

In due course, under our jailers' firm prodding, we reluctantly set frivolity aside and reboarded our coaches for the joust to downtown Cairo, where the Nile Hilton and lunch were next on our menu. Eagerly, I anticipated my first visit to an American hotel and when we got there, I had to admit that the Nile Hilton could not be confused with a pyramid. For this concrete-and-glass structure was a perfect piece of Americana, set down in the middle of an alien planet. It was opulent and garish in the best Hollywood style, and obviously made no attempt to blend into the city it seemed so anxious to reject. Nevertheless, I was glad to be there and, although I still felt slightly seasick from my uncomfortable excursion on the camel, I thoroughly enjoyed the wonderful buffet lunch it provided.

Afterwards, I wandered out onto the rear balcony of the hotel and gazed in awe at the world's most famous and longest river, as it flowed serenely past the hotel which bore its name and stood on its bank.

Now I could say I had seen Africa's greatest river which rose far to the south in Uganda and dominated its world for the whole of its 4,000-mile journey to the Mediterranean Sea. Yet how strange it was to stand there and acknowledge that it reached back almost as far as Northern Rhodesia – which meant it was almost a neighbour of mine.

A few lonely dhows plied the mile-wide river, which had only another 100 miles to flow before it reached the sea. Surely, I was becoming a seasoned traveler with many great sights in my memory bank, of wonders seen and dreams fulfilled. Reluctantly, I awoke from my reverie as our guide stridently called out, 'Memphis Tours this way,' as he prepared to lead us forth from the American oasis and back into Egypt.

Obediently, I rejoined our group and we soon headed off to explore the Egyptian Museum of Antiquities which is, I believe, one of the finest museums in the world. I regret to say that we went through this Aladdin's cave at a medium gallop as our shepherd herded his recalcitrant flock from room to room with repeated cries of his mustering call. Indeed 'Memphis Tours this way,' was already beginning to dent my enthusiasm for tour group travel. Yet to ignore it was unwise, since I had no intention of being stranded in Cairo.

Luckily, I did get to spend a few minutes gazing in awe at the splendours of Tutankhamen, which I found to be totally overwhelming. The amount of gold, the degree of preservation of the items on display, and the incredibly high standards of the workmanship and art were enough to virtually take one's breath away. Plus, when viewed as a whole, this treasure-trove presented a detailed and persuasive picture of a very advanced civilization which had blossomed in this desert. In particular, the golden death masks and headdresses of King Tut were almost like new and compellingly beautiful in their depiction of the young man at rest in all the finery of an Egyptian Pharaoh.

I kept telling myself that all this had been achieved long before Christ was born and yet I found it extremely difficult to believe that any such civilization could have existed before the British came on the scene. But these wonders were older than the dawn of British history; they even predated the Dark Ages by a few thousand years. It was almost too much to accept.

Could it be that civilization began in a foreign country, far from the majesty of England's green and pleasant land? Was it possible that my view of history was incomplete? Surely not! Yet all these statues, chariots, furnishings, utensils, ornaments and jewelry seemed to belie the idea that the Ascent Of Man was orchestrated by the British.

In addition, I was also troubled by the idea that although this civilization had lasted for almost 3,000 years, it had eventually ended. Is that what happens to everything? Does it all have a beginning, a middle and an end? If so, as this voyage had clearly shown, I was witnessing the end of the British Empire which had lasted a paltry 300 years. Kid's stuff compared to the ancient Egyptians who had lasted 10 times longer. That was probably a treasonable thought especially for a colonial officer entrusted with the preservation of the Empire.

Anyway, I dutifully hurried from room to room as we wound our way past an endless stream of sarcophagi and mummies until, about an hour later, we sprinted back into the modern world which now appeared, to my more sensitive eye, to be more primitive than the ancient. We then made a pilgrimage to Cairo's main bazaar, where there also seemed to be a very liberal amount of golden ornaments and jewelry, all of which was on sale to the highest bidder at what was guaranteed to be the lowest possible price.

Next, we toured the largest and most important mosque in Egypt, where I again fell to pondering how so many people could spend so much time worshipping a non-Christian god. Once again I felt the stirrings of uncomfortable thoughts and I wondered if the Moslems were equally perplexed by our inability to discern the one true light. Probably so. I suppose we shall just have to accept that man's search for salvation will always produce a wide variety of reverent answers. Would it were not so, but it is and, by now, I was getting used to the other side of the mountain as I became more familiar with the non-European outlook on life.

After visiting the mosque, we went by coach to a vantage point from which we could see most of Cairo spread out beneath us. It was a vast gray-brown city, not particularly attractive, and little different in its overall ambience from most other large cities. This was the London of Africa, and instead of Nelson's column, it had the Pyramids which I could dimly see on the distant horizon.

I had enjoyed Cairo and our remorseless guide had performed exceedingly well as he gave us an incredible tour under the most stringent of time constraints. But, as the setting sun confirmed, it was already late in the afternoon and it was time to start chasing the Uganda, unless we intended to swim the rest of the way to England. Consequently, when our leader issued his rallying cry of 'Memphis Tours this way,' we all flocked, with a chorus of contented 'baas,' to our coach and shortly thereafter, we left Cairo behind as we headed north towards Port Said and the Mediterranean Sea.

Our destination was about 100 miles ahead of us, and it was there at the northern end of the Suez Canal that we would rejoin the Uganda when it completed its passage through the canal. The drive soon lulled me to sleep, since I now accepted the joust as the normal *modus operandi* on Egyptian roads, and I felt no pain until I awoke with a start when someone shouted, 'My God, I can see the Uganda.' That was ridiculous, we were still at least a 50 mile drive from the coast. The Uganda couldn't be sailing on land, but I dutifully looked where everyone was pointing and, sure enough, there was the Uganda blissfully sailing through a wheat field about 200 yards to our right.

It really was the most amazing spectacle I had ever dreamt of seeing, especially when I was wide awake. From our vantage point, we couldn't see the canal but only our ship sailing upon it. Thus, for a few magical moments, we were privileged to see a large ocean-going liner making an impressive overland journey through a perfectly normal Arab countryside of farms, villages and fields. I will never forget the delight I felt, as I briefly watched the Uganda majestically defy reason, by elegantly cruising amidst the cabbage. Feverishly, we all waved our greetings, while the driver obligingly honked his horn, as we sped past our destination and continued up north.

This time, I noted with interest, the fields were irrigated on both sides of the road, which did not serve as any kind of a boundary, but seemed to be passing through a very prosperous region. In due course, after about two more hours, we reached Port Said and went to an opulent Egyptian restaurant for dinner and belly dancing. The food was exquisite and so were the dancers, who kept us entertained for at least two hours until finally, at about 11 p.m., it was time to head back to the Uganda.

True to his calling, our guide summoned the faithful with a last ringing rendition of 'Memphis Tours this way,' and we all obediently boarded our bus for the short drive down to the docks. A few minutes later, we arrived at the Uganda and after tipping my tormentor for his grueling day, I staggered up the gangway of my floating hotel. It had been an unforgettable experience, my first conducted tour, my first organized bout of pleasure.

Never before had I been packaged and delivered. I was appalled. However, I had seen Egypt, or at least a fair part of it, and there had been no conceivable alternative to the Memphis Tours excursion. It was do it that way or don't do it, and I was still young enough to survive the ordeal. Plus, as an added consolation, none of the sights had been crowded and even the Museum was almost empty until we arrived.

Our group may well have been the only package tour in Cairo that day. So even if I was one of a herd, which I abhor, at least the herd was only about 100 strong and not a teeming mass of 10,000 remorseless tourists. Besides, to be fair, without Memphis Tours, I would not have seen some of the wonders of Egypt and for that, I am ever in their debt.

It never occurred to me then that the package tour would soon become the staple of holiday fare and 500 tour buses would become the norm at the world's most secluded beauty spots. Nor did I realize that boats like the Uganda had almost run their course and soon would be replaced by fun-filled seven day cruises. How strange are the whims of progress, and I'm glad we are not cursed with the ability to foresee the future.

It was cold on the deck of the Uganda, yet I stayed there until we cast off our African moorings as we made ready to enter European waters. By then it was long after midnight, but I remained at my place on the rail until the last lights of Egypt slipped beneath the horizon. Home was now getting perceptibly closer, and so was winter, which seemed to be very near at hand as we ventured out into the Mediterranean Sea.

Another threshold had been crossed and I shivered with cold, or perhaps foreboding, as I began to wonder if either I or the folks back home had changed in the last three years. 'Oh well,' I told myself, 'you'll find out soon enough,' and then I went to bed as the Uganda headed towards the distant shores of France and Spain which still lay over two thousand miles away to our west.

I had seen so much and I was grateful. Hopefully, I had even matured a little and, as I fell asleep, I said a brief prayer of thanks for having been privileged to live in Africa during the colonial era. Whatever the future brought was OK, because the past was mine and could not be taken away.

3. The Mediterranean

My worst fears were confirmed the following morning when winter greeted me on deck with an icy blast that cut through my body like a knife. Quickly, I retreated to the library, the only room I remember on the Uganda, and spent the rest of the morning gloomily curled up on a settee, peering malevolently through a window at a foreign and hostile world.

The next day, we passed through the Straits of Messina, which separate the ball of Sicily from the boot of Italy, and sailed past the small volcanic island of Stromboli. Luckily for us, a minor eruption was taking place at the time and a thin plume of white smoke rose lazily from the crater of the volcano. However, there did not seem to be an accompanying lava flow, nor any immediate danger to the tiny cluster of modest white houses which clung stubbornly to the few acres of fairly level ground at the base of the mountain.

Graciously, our captain made a complete circle around Stromboli and we all obediently flocked to the ship's rail to take the obligatory snapshot, before wisely retiring to the comfort and warmth of the saloon. Rather them than me, was my uncharitable thought, as I once again marveled at man's almost infinite ability to wrest his living from the most inhospitable of spots. Sometimes, as in this particular case, we seem to be unwisely provoking the gods, and I certainly could not even begin to imagine why anyone would willingly choose to live at the foot of an active volcano, on a very small island.

But then, as a very good friend of mine, Bill Lowery, subsequently said: 'If we all lived in the same place, the world would tip over.' How true, and I'll bet those islanders couldn't understand why anyone in their right mind willingly volunteered to tour the Mediterranean, in the middle of winter. But then again, neither could I.

Early the following evening, just before dark, we arrived in Marseille, the large French seaport near the mouth of the Rhone River, and our ship tied up for a very brief stay of less than three hours. It was raining, of course, and we didn't have time to tour the town. Nevertheless I hurried ashore, just to say I had been to France, and did a quick tour of the local beauty spots adjacent to the docks. And boy, was there a bunch, since every single doorway I passed had a friendly prostitute smiling from its entrance, as she invited me to sample the joys of French cuisine.

It really was impressive. Indeed, I don't actually think I had seen so many white women in the whole of the last three years and certainly I had never been this popular before. However, I virtuously ignored their solicitations and within the hour I returned to the Uganda, cold, wet, but elated at the obvious passion I was capable of arousing in members of the gentler sex.

A short while later, still chaste, we fled from Marseille and headed down the coast towards Barcelona, a scant three hundred miles to the southwest. In the morning, we arrived at this major Spanish seaport, and I spent the next three days exploring its streets, since winter had relented by giving us a few mild days. Immediately, I stepped ashore I felt at home in this foreign city, which definitely was a European town.

The people were all white and the buildings and shops were quite ordinary, by the standards of my youth. Africa, the land of my dreams, was now several light years away and I was both comforted and disturbed, by the strange familiarity of this prosperous old port.

In Barcelona I did not stand out, but was merely another nameless face in a crowd of similar faces. I was not a curiosity and easily blended into the background of this elegant city with its many glorious churches and cathedrals, large squares, fountains and imposing statues.

One, in particular, caught my eye, a dramatic statue of Christopher Columbus, pointing the way west to the New World and beyond. This statue stood on the top of a large column and was perhaps a hundred or more feet above the large open square in whose centre it stood. Solemnly, from its vantage point, it surveyed the distant horizons, which Columbus had pushed back by several thousand miles and two continents.

The far side of this square was open to the sea and alongside its wharf, the city fathers had proudly moored a life-sized replica of Columbus's flagship, the Santa Maria. There it sat – a small, frail ship – and just a few hundred yards further away was the Uganda which had brought me here from Africa. I could but note the enormous contrast in size between the two vessels, and figuratively tipped my hat to the statue of the man who had sailed so far in such a small boat.

Spain and Portugal, not England, was the place where it all began. The place from which modern European influence first ventured forth to invade an unsuspecting world. I had come full circle, returning from the colonial lands, to those of their colonial masters. Thus, I would find no Moslem mosques or Hindu temples in this ancient city, but only the Roman Catholic churches of the one true faith, which had played so large a role in the development of Spain's New World. Naturally, my mind then turned to the Spanish Inquisition which in its zeal to save souls at the expense of bodies, was largely responsible for producing in South America, the most Christian continent on earth.

But did the ends justify the means? Or must we face the awful dichotomy of absolute certainty? Quite obviously, a colonial power which firmly believed that its God was the one true God would, by definition, have very little respect for the heathen, misguided savages it encountered. How can one honestly respect a man who worships a false god and is condemning himself to everlasting damnation? And how, with a closed mind, can one possibly admire a culture which is based on a false premise?

Without doubt the Spanish friars and the English missionaries, such as Livingstone, were all sincerely dedicated men, who fearlessly went out to spread their light in the midst of primitive darkness. Unfortunately for the natives, the light these just men brought seldom admired the darkness it had come to illuminate, even though, at times, it may have had some compassion for the night it encountered.

Consequently, I came to the somber conclusion that the deeper one held one's Christian beliefs, the less likely one was to respect and understand an alien culture. Love, compassion and friendship are all admirable, but they do not produce respect and understanding. There is much to be said for the argument that we in the late 20th century, with our more tepid views on religious matters, and our emphasis on the separation of church and state, may well be overlooking a major driving force of the colonial era.

Our fathers deeply believed in the sanctity of their faith and their beliefs ruled their thoughts and actions. Hence, when we factor in religious intolerance based upon absolute certainty, we can perhaps begin to better appreciate one often-overlooked facet of why colonial powers usually treated their conquered subjects as children in need of guidance. I am not, of course, trying to justify or condemn the actions of my forebears, I am merely trying to raise a seldom considered viewpoint, which may help to explain our heritage and past.

Certainly, at the very least, we have to admit that Columbus left his mark, for better or for worse, and as one colonial administrator to another, I waved him a cheery farewell when the Uganda left Barcelona at the end of our visit to Spain. Now, at last, there was just one more port of call before home, and eagerly I looked forward to our next destination – Gibraltar. It lay some 800 miles to the south of Barcelona at the western entrance to the Mediterranean Sea. Soon we would be in the Atlantic and soon I would be home. But first there was one more British colony to visit, surely the only civilized way to end my journey through some of the more remote bastions of British culture.

4. Gibraltar

Two days later, shortly before noon, I went on deck and braved the icy blast as we neared Gibraltar, the rock that had symbolized British imperial naval power for almost 300 years as it jealously guarded the narrow entrance to the Mediterranean Sea. Eagerly, I scanned the mist ahead until gradually I began to discern the familiar outlines of the fortress made famous as an emblem of confidence in the insurance industry. It was an apt choice, for it had long insured Britain's control of the shortest route to India and the Far East.

Slowly it grew more distinct until, with a flurry of activity, we finally dropped anchor just outside the breakwater of its modest harbour, and a flotilla of small launches came out to ferry us ashore for a four-hour visit. Hopefully that would be plenty of time to tour this tiny colony, which is barely three miles long and three-quarters of a mile wide, and encompasses only the rock which makes Gibraltar such a valuable fortress.

In fact, as I soon discovered, that is truly all it is, just a large lonely slab of granite surrounded by water on three sides, and connected to Spain on the fourth, by a low sandy isthmus that is about one mile in length. But yet, by the power of its brooding presence, this ancient citadel has long held the keys to the Mediterranean and, in times of war, the British have always been able to shut the door on their enemies.

Gibraltar, according to my history books, was reputed to have been one of the Pillars of Hercules and marked the limits of navigation in the classical Mediterranean world. Its name is derived from the Arabic 'Jabal Tariq,' which means Mount Tariq, and this was the name by which it became known after the Arabs captured it in 711 A.D. In 1462, it was taken from the Moors by the Spaniards and, in the best British tradition, it was taken from the Spaniards by the British July 24th 1704.

Since then, it has always been a British colony and is now self governing in all matters save defense. The local populace possess full British citizenship and, in 1967, they voted by a margin of 12,138 to 44, to remain British in preference to becoming Spanish. This disgraceful vote was a national humiliation, since it was hard to accept the fact that 44 people voted to learn Spanish. However, there is no accounting for taste and hopefully they soon recovered their sanity.

There are no natural resources or rivers on this barren rock nor does it have any farms, vineyards or manufacturing plants. It is therefore totally dependent on tourism and the extensive British naval base for its economic wellbeing. Ingeniously, some parts of the rock have been smoothed down and concreted over, and they now serve as a catchment area for rainwater, which is then stored in cisterns for later use.

Otherwise water has to be imported from England, since Gibraltar is seldom on speaking terms with Spain and, as a matter of fact, from June of 1969 until December of 1982, the border with Spain was totally closed. Consequently, Gibraltar has often had to muddle through as an island of British imperialism in an alien Hispanic world.

But, in February of 1962, when I was there, Gibraltar was tranquil. The only visible sign of dissent was 'Gibraltar es Español' painted on a wall, thus proving that one of those 44 radicals owned a paint brush. Yet I was not deterred, and soon after I had been ferried to shore, I set off on a brisk climb through the town's narrow, winding streets towards the summit of the rock some 1,400 feet above sea level. There was not much to enthuse about, as I slowly tramped up one hill after another. The shops I passed were mostly tacky tourist trade traps, while the bulk of the houses I saw were featureless drab and colourless. In short, this was not an attractive town although, to be fair, I have to admit that it was also cold and rainy, and so beauty may have been in the eye of the beholder who, in this case, was looking with a very jaundiced eye.

Nevertheless I persisted. In due course, arriving on top of the rock, where a lonely cannon menaced the straits below. In the distance I could see the Uganda and, if the cannon had been working, I could have sunk it with one shot. But I didn't, and anyway, I believe that nowadays all of the lethal armaments are hidden in caves hollowed out of the rock. Suddenly, to my horror, I noticed a puff of smoke from the Uganda's smokestack and I realized I had better head back at the gallop, if I wanted to stay on the tour.

Luckily my route was all downhill and soon I was back in town, where I bumped into some other passengers from our ship. Together, we made our way to the jetty and easily, with about five minutes to spare, caught the last ferry back to the Uganda and dinner. Too late, I realized I had never seen a Barbary ape, the small monkeys which roam the rock at will, and according to legend, guarantee by their presence that the British will always remain in Gibraltar. Oh well, I really had no doubt they were still there, since the British authorities had always taken great care, especially during the Second World War, to ensure that these guardian angels survived.

I stayed on deck until the rock slowly faded from view in the wake of our ship, as we headed out into the North Atlantic and turned for home. Gibraltar had been a surprise, an entirely different kind of colony from the others I had visited. Indeed, it was more like a transplanted part of England, since its people, culture and language were all basically English, and the pubs sold only the best British beer. Yet it was still a long way from England, and was just another small slice of the largest empire the world had ever known, or was ever likely to endure. Truly one had to see the British Empire to believe it, and now, during the last six weeks, I had personally seen enough out-of-the-way places to begin to realize for myself, just how vast and diverse our empire had actually been.

We had long been able to claim, that the sun never set on the British flag, and Britannia ruled the waves. But quite clearly all that was fast coming to an end, like this voyage, and, as the Uganda confidently steamed on into the night, I went below to escape the driving rain and biting cold of a wintry evening at sea. My odyssey was almost complete, as the weather so obviously confirmed, and soon, disturbingly soon, I would know if my England still felt like home to a wanderer, whose home had become the place where he lay down to sleep.

How strange, to think that only three short years ago, I had crossed this same stormy Atlantic Ocean on my way to Africa. Now, a hundred years older, I was retracing my steps with a thousand tales to tell. Three more days and we would be in London and then, would it really feel like home, or was my soul now rooted in Africa, the land which had already captured my heart?

5. Going Home

Chorley, my final destination, was no longer a distant dream, but was about to turn into reality. And yet, in spite of my growing excitement, I still found time to bemoan the harsh winter weather which constantly bedeviled us, on that 1,500 mile journey, from Gibraltar to London. It was far too cold to stay on deck. Thus I sat around the library and solemnly read the nautical charts, since all the pinup magazines had disappeared.

However, I did occasionally rebel and, on our second morning at sea, I spent a delightful hour watching a school of porpoises swimming beside the ship. They probably thought we were some giant playmate, as they flashed across our bow, and pranced atop the waves which marked our passage. Truly, they were poetry in motion, as they effortlessly matched our speed, and, until the cold soaked through to my bones, I thoroughly enjoyed watching their innocence at play.

But that was just one brief interlude and a temporary distraction. Now, with England so tantalisingly close, I was suddenly anxious to leave the cocoon of the Uganda and rejoin the real world. My scale of reference had dramatically changed and, as I impatiently chafed to get on with my life, I slowly entered a limbo which would only end when our long journey ended. Not surprisingly, my companions were also going through this same metamorphosis and, as we each prepared to go our separate ways, we once again became strangers, with nothing in common except our presence on a ship that had abruptly become both too small and too confining.

Time, like a watched clock, seemed almost to stand still, but eventually, in the late afternoon of the second day out of Gibraltar, we entered the English Channel and then, through the library window, I dimly saw the coast of England as it rose above the far horizon. At first, of course, it was only a barely discernible shadow. Yet, even so, it still brought a lump to my throat, which surprised me, and tears to my eyes, which embarrassed me. Gradually we drew ever closer until, with the shore no more than a mile away, the Uganda slowed down to a crawl, as a Coast Guard cutter eased to our side and a pilot scampered aboard.

Obviously this voyage would soon be over. It was time to pack my bags and make ready for disembarkation. So I adjourned to my cabin where, after several false starts, I triumphantly managed to find room in my original suitcase, plus a second one bought in Egypt, for all of my clothes, souvenirs and the treasures I had acquired in Aden. Happily I surveyed the result, confident that my mother would approve of my neatness which, if I was lucky, might even survive a trip through customs. Nothing else needed to be done, and so, after an early dinner, I went to an early bed, since tomorrow was sure to be a long day.

The following morning I awoke with the dawn which, in England, is when the rain grows lighter, and went on deck to discover that we were already approaching Tilbury Docks, in the heart of London. We were home. Fascinated, I stared at the hurry and bustle of the busy river until, within the hour, we had reached our berth. Wisely I next ate a leisurely breakfast and then, after thanking and tipping the stewards, it was, unavoidably, time to go.

For somehow, against all my expectations, I was now strangely reluctant to break my last ties with this ship, and venture into the unknown. Nevertheless, after briefly considering my non-existent options, I went to my cabin, had a last look around, picked up my two suitcases, and quietly joined the steady stream of strangers who were slowly making their way from the Uganda to England.

I was home, in a customs shed, and it didn't look too inviting. Warily, I scanned the suspicious faces before me and tried to pick a customs officer who looked non-threatening. Eventually, I chose a pleasant-looking young lady and humbly offered up my two suitcases for inspection. Bored and distracted, she airily waved me away and with no further formality, I was casually admitted to England.

Well, what more did I expect, a brass band? Probably, but then, since she didn't have a trombone, I solemnly picked up my two suitcases and staggered out into the cold, dark gloom of a London dockside street. Slowly, and equally timidly, my fellow passengers also trickled out of customs and morosely joined me in contemplation of winter's inhospitable face. One by one they hurried away, some with friends, some by cab, until soon I was left alone on the sidewalk. The rain showed no sign of abating and so, after failing to find a bus stop, I reluctantly hailed a cab. Swiftly, a traditional London taxi swept to my side and its driver gave me a cheery nod as he stowed my luggage before asking, 'where to, Guv?' 'Euston Station,' I replied as I awkwardly climbed into the first cab I had ever hired in England. 'Right ho,' he responded and off we sped.

How quickly things change, for it was only an hour since I had been at home on the Uganda. But now it was only a memory, with all of its passengers dispersed to a myriad of destinations in this big, lonely city. I looked through the windows of the cab at my country-men as they trudged to and from their daily chores. For three years they had been pounding these same streets in their monotonous daily routines, while I had gloriously been in Africa.

Yet today, when I passed through their midst, they ignored this unusual event and went on with their lives. Perhaps my homecoming was not an earth shattering event. Perhaps I was irrelevant to these dimly seen strangers, who seemed not to care who I was, or where I had been. Still, I cared, and when we reached Euston Station after a 30-minute drive, I tipped my first cabbie handsomely, as befits a colonial officer on leave.

Now I was once more back on familiar ground, since my father was a lifelong railroad man, and we had often ridden the trains to London for a weekend soccer match or a few days' sightseeing. Nothing had changed, the station was still as cavernous, busy and gloomy as it had always been, which was somewhat reassuring, and I confidently booked a third-class ticket on the next nonstop express to Manchester Victoria.

In due course, this train chugged into the station and I fought my way aboard, as my long-forgotten skills resurfaced in the primitive struggle to obtain a window seat. Obviously, being from a primitive land, I succeeded, and soon I was ensconced in one of the two most desirable seats in a crowded compartment, while my two romantically tagged suitcases balanced precariously in the rack above my head. Shortly thereafter, the guard blew his whistle, the train gave its well-remembered jerk, and gradually started to pick up speed, as we began the four-hour journey to Manchester, the capital of the north of England.

It really was strange sitting in that compartment, looking at my fellow passengers. They all looked so ordinary, and seemed to be doing such ordinary things, as they took an ordinary ride, on an ordinary train. Why didn't they know I was fresh out of Africa? Couldn't they tell I was different from them? Apparently not, because no one spoke to me. Perhaps they were waiting for me to leap to my feet and shout, 'Listen everyone, I'm just back from Africa, I've come half way round the world, I'm special, talk to me.'

But I didn't, of course. Instead, I just sat quietly in my window seat and gazed with wonder at the green fields and bare trees of the English countryside in winter. Yet no one else seemed to find the view unusual. They mostly ignored it, and slept. It was all rather disappointing and I could not, for the life of me, quite understand why these total strangers ignored me.

Anyway, about four hours later, my train steamed into Manchester and I quickly changed platforms, in order to catch the next local train to Chorley. Again, no one noticed me, nor seemed impressed by the exotic stickers on my two well traveled suitcases which soon proved their worth, as battering rams, in the ensuing struggle to obtain a beloved window seat. Once more the familiar jerk started us on our way, and within a few miles the little stations we passed through, began to bear names synonymous with my youth – Bolton, Horwich, Adlington and, finally, Chorley.

We were there, it was time to get off the train. Strange, I had always thought Manchester was light years away from Chorley. Yet now, as I climbed down to the windswept platform of my hometown, I suddenly realized that it had only taken this slow train half an hour to make the journey from one to the other. The platform was deserted and the light was beginning to fade, since it was now 4 p.m. on a very cold winter's day in late February. Reluctantly, as the English wind pierced my African soul, I slowly headed for the exit and gave my ticket to a disinterested ticket collector. I was truly beginning to feel invisible, but at least it wasn't raining.

Indeed it was not. It was snowing. A full blizzard by the looks of it, as the weather made a determined attempt to welcome me back to civilization. Bleakly, I strode off into the snow, a suitcase in each hand and a lump in my throat. Why didn't I take a taxi? Simple. In Chorley I had never in my life taken a taxi and old habits were already beginning to reclaim my mind.

Why didn't I call my parents? Simple. They had no telephone or car, and Dad was probably still at work in the locomotive factory in Horwich. And why, to complete the trilogy, had they not gone to London to meet me at the docks? Simple. My parents would never have contemplated such an outrageous idea, and also, to be fair, the arrival date of a cargo liner is always subject to change without notice.

I had left home alone, and now I was coming home alone, which somehow seemed appropriate. Besides, it was only about a mile to my parents' house – funny how small our town was and the snow was only about three inches deep. Slowly, (why hurry after three years?) I trudged the familiar sidewalks which led to my home, pausing occasionally to set my suitcases down in the snow and rest my aching arms. The streets were almost deserted, but what few people I passed ignored me. Why not? I obviously passed this way each day, like the Flying Dutchman, and they had better things to do than speak to me.

Twilight had given way to darkness, and the street lamps suddenly came on, as I turned into Mayfield Road. Our house, Number 22, was about halfway down the street and soon I had reached my parents' front garden gate. For a moment or two I stood there and stared, amazed at how small everything had become during my absence. Especially this house, and its tiny front yard. Had my home always been this small, and if so, why had I not remembered it that way?

Life was indeed a mystery, and finally, as the snow continued to fall, I solemnly unlatched the garden gate and walked the few feet to the front door, while the gate behind me swung to with a barely audible click. Hesitantly, I knocked on the door and, after a few moments, it gradually swung open to reveal my mother standing there in the hallway's dim light.

'Hello,' I said.
'Hello,' she answered, and I came in from the snow.
Gently, I gave her a swift peck on the cheek and for just a moment, she held me in her arms. Then she turned and said,
'Would you like a cup of tea?'
'That would be nice,' I replied as I walked into the smallest living room I had ever seen in my life.

Surely this was not the room I grew up in? Because that one had been so large and this one was so small. But yet it must be, since I clearly remembered my portrait, which stared back at me from its pride of place on my grandmother's dresser. Awkwardly I sat in the rocker, just to the right of the small coal fire which burned in the tiny grate in the tiny fireplace, of this once-gigantic room. I stared at the flames, which laboured in vain to dispel the winter's chill. A few minutes later, my mother came in with tea and scones on a tray and, after placing it on a buffet between us, she sat down in an easy chair on the other side of the fireplace.

We talked about unimportant things, until suddenly my mother said, 'What would you like for tea?'

'Fish and chips,' I replied with a big grin. My mother grinned back, before scurrying off into the kitchen to peel some potatoes. I knew, without being told, just how much she cared. I was home at last.

About half an hour later my Dad came home from work and, after giving me a brief hug, he opened his heart by casually asking, as if I had never been away, 'What's for tea?' 'Fish and chips,' I answered in the same vein, and the three of us started to bridge the enormous gulf that separates the wanderer from those he left behind.

My roots still clung to my heels, but my eyes had seen the wide horizon and henceforth, I would always be torn between the home of my fathers and the wide blue yonder. I was a tourist, a wanderer through life, and I firmly believed that I was born to see the grass on the other side of the hill.

But not tonight, nor tomorrow. Mother was cooking fish and chips, and it was going to be a long time before I asked for a change of menu.

Index of Names

Baxter, Tom – customs agent 170, 178, 190, 191, 192, 197
Bayman, Ken – Ministry of Native Affairs – accountant 31, 38, 39, 40, 41, 42, 44, 45, 46, 62, 63, 64, 65, 77, 103, 104, 172, 197, 198, 200, 201, 202, 204, 205, 206, 207, 208
Bayman, Olive – housewife 38, 39, 40, 45, 62, 63, 64, 65, 172, 197, 200, 201, 202, 205, 208
Bennett, Dorothy – author's sister 2
Bennett, Frank Senior – author's father 1, 2, 3, 6, 8, 40, 151, 179, 180, 183, 238, 239, 240
Bennett, Jack – author's cousin 179
Bennett, John – author's great uncle 180
Bennett, Lily – author's mother 2, 3, 4, 6, 8, 9, 22, 30, 34, 36, 112, 180, 181, 183, 200, 237, 239, 240
Bennett, Rose – author's grandmother 8, 240
Bennett, Samuel – author's grandfather 8, 179
Bokenham, Paul – Ministry of Finance – Internal Security – senior accountant 99, 100, 101
Burgess, Pat – Ministry of

Finance – Internal Security – finance officer 99, 100, 101, 113, 176

Clayton, John – Ministry of Finance – payroll clerk 81, 82, 83, 84
Crosby, Martin – Ministry of Native Affairs – accounts clerk 57, 58, 59, 60, 61, 62, 64, 65, 66, 67, 68, 69, 70, 107, 152, 159, 160, 161, 162
Curphy, Bill – Ministry of Native Affairs – accounts clerk 20, 21, 25, 26, 31, 32, 33, 34, 35, 36, 37, 38, 40, 41, 42, 44, 45, 46, 49, 50, 51, 57, 70, 107, 151

Dean, Dixie – radio engineer 46, 47, 48, 49, 55, 59, 60, 61, 62, 63, 64, 65, 66, 123, 124, 125, 126, 127, 128, 140, 141, 142, 143, 145, 147, 148, 173, 174, 175, 176
Dean, Sally – housewife 46, 47, 48, 49, 59, 60, 61, 62, 63, 64, 65, 66, 123, 124, 125, 127, 128, 140, 141, 142, 143, 145, 147, 148, 173, 174, 175
Dean's daughter 47, 48, 49, 63, 64, 140, 142

Ferrett, Peter – Internal Revenue Service – clerk 170, 171, 177,

Subject Index